THE ONE LIFE WE'RE GIVEN

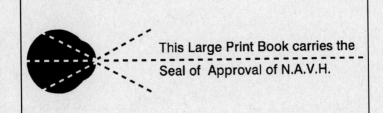

This Large Print Book carries the
Seal of Approval of N.A.V.H.

THE ONE LIFE WE'RE GIVEN

FINDING THE WISDOM THAT WAITS IN YOUR HEART

MARK NEPO

THORNDIKE PRESS

A part of Gale, Cengage Learning

GALE
CENGAGE Learning·

Farmington Hills, Mich • San Francisco • New York • Waterville, Maine
Meriden, Conn • Mason, Ohio • Chicago

GALE
CENGAGE Learning®

Copyright © 2016 by Mark Nepo.
Thorndike Press, a part of Gale, Cengage Learning.

LIBRARY OF CONGRESS CATALOGING-IN-PUBLICATION DATA

Names: Nepo, Mark, author.
Title: The one life we're given : finding the wisdom that waits in your heart / by
    Mark Nepo.
Description: Large Print edition. | Waterville : Thorndike Press, 2017. | Series:
    Thorndike Press Large Print lifestyles | Include bibliographical references
Identifiers: LCCN 2016042632| ISBN 9781410496638 (hardcover) | ISBN 1410496635
    (hardcover)
Subjects: LCSH: Spiritual life. | Conduct of life. | Large type books.
Classification: LCC BL624.N453 2017 | DDC 204/.4—dc23
LC record available at https://lccn.loc.gov/2016042632

Published in 2017 by arrangement with Atria Books, an imprint of
Simon & Schuster, Inc.

Printed in Mexico
1 2 3 4 5 6 7 21 20 19 18 17

*For Eleanor McHenry (1935–2015)
and Joel Elkes (1913–2015).*

*Both were heroic and humble spirits
who stayed loving and gentle,
no matter what life gave them.*

When all I wanted was to sing,
I was accorded the honor of living.
— RAINER MARIA RILKE

The highest reward for a person's toil is
not what they get for it, but what they
become by it.
— JOHN RUSKIN

Before practicing the art of immortality,
first practice the art of humanity.
— LU YEN

CONTENTS

10

SHAPED BY LIFE

My dear father, Morris Nepo, died three years ago at the age of ninety-three. He was at his strongest and happiest when working with wood, when building things. In his basement workshop, no one could suppress his love of life and his insatiable creativity. I learned a great deal from him, though I can see now that there were many times he didn't know he was teaching and I didn't know I was learning. Mostly, he taught me by example that we're called to make good use of the one life we're given. He taught me that giving our all can lead to moments of fulfillment and grace. And those moments of full living can sustain us.

When just a boy, I watched my father chisel boards with care and precision. He kept his chisels sharp. He'd always say, "Don't stop in mid-stroke or the board will splinter. Once you start, keep pushing all the way through." He'd lean over the board and his hands and the chisel would become one. A thin shaving of wood would peel away, as if he'd loved the board into giving it up. He'd pick up the light shaving from the floor and rub it between his fingers. Then he'd rub the grain his effort had revealed and smile. In that moment, he seemed content, at peace. When I read Plato years later, with all his squawk about absolute forms, I knew that's where my father went. For the moment, he seemed complete. He'd rub the smooth board one more time and drop the shaving. I loved to watch the feather of wood float to the basement floor. Looking back, I'm certain this was a moment in which he felt thoroughly immersed.

The wood shaving floating to the floor was an expression of effort turning into grace. Years later, I would feel a similar sense of completion when building things myself, and when arriving at intimacy in my relationships, after honest, loving work. Revealing the inner grain and watching the shaving float between us make us complete. Working the grain is how we love and labor, and no matter what we build or create, the shaving we chisel is the insight that lightens our load.

There were six vises stationed along my father's workbench. Each held a project in a different phase of development. The vises were never empty. One might hold a strip of pine that he was bending. Another might hold a layer of walnut that he was gluing to a layer of mahogany. A third might hold a table leg that he was sanding. He'd work on one, then move to another and circle back, one informing the other. I realized only recently that this is how I work on books. I explore several books at once, pursuing one, then moving to another, letting my interest and their vitality cross-pollinate. I gather images and stories and metaphors, keeping them in folders, as I weave and work on many levels at the same time.

My father also had a bin where he kept wood fragments that he might use in future projects. When he died, my brother and I looked for him in that bin. There must have been five hundred scraps of all sizes and shapes. Now I understand where my fragment folders come from. I see the underside of a cloud, or light shimmering off a broken piece of glass, or hear someone in a café say something profound. I save these rough gems to work with later, when I discover where they go.

With his immersion in what he loved, my father showed me that throwing ourselves wholeheartedly into what we're given brings us alive. Craftsman that he was, he left deep messages in all that he touched, some of which have only reached me now. I wish I could show him my workbench. I wish we could hammer the hot metal of our creations side by side, watching the forged shapes harden beneath their glow.

Yet work as we do to carve and shape, we are carved and shaped as we go. No one can escape the way experience forms us. Twenty-nine years ago, I was diagnosed with a rare form of lymphoma that shaped me forever. After a gauntlet of tests and biopsies, the tumor growing in my skull bone vanished. It was a miracle. Ten months later, a sister tumor began to show on a rib in my back. I fell into despair. I feared I had wasted the miracle, had not honored my second chance. Now I was afraid I would die. The rib and its adjacent muscles had to be removed. And within weeks of that surgery, I underwent four months of aggressive chemotherapy, which almost killed me.

Being thrust back into life turned everything inside out. Miracle was no longer an inexplicable event, but the very fabric of life showing the extraordinary in the ordinary. Life itself had become miraculous. I faced what everyone has to face: the prospect of dying without having truly lived and the

16

prospect of living without having truly loved. The rest are details.

I share my story and the stories of others as examples, not instructions. For everyone has to uncover the lessons of their own journey. The word *honor* means to keep what is true in view. And so, we live and honor the one life we're given by keeping what we learn in view — about ourselves, each other, and life.

We can begin by honoring the truth of our experience and learning from those who've loved us. Aware of it or not, we each have someone who's taught us something about how to live. Who is that teacher for you? And what are you learning in the slow blossom of time?

When I think of my father holding the thin shaving of wood that he chiseled before me, I can see the thin shaving I've become, now that I've been chiseled and shaped by life. It hurts to be carved by experience, though in time it reveals our strengths, if we can help each other through. And despite our dark worries, things are lighter on the other side of suffering, where we are asked to live wholeheartedly. This requires us to give our full attention, to feel, to love, to connect here and now, again and again. These ongoing devotions lead us into the craft of awakening.

The sections of this book point to how we might truly inhabit the one life we're given: by getting closer to life, loving what we do, finding what can last, and by being kind and useful. I present them in this order only because one page has to follow another. In life, these passages don't always appear in this sequence. One may lead to another. Being kind and useful may ultimately get us closer to life. And finding what can last may help us love what we do. In life, these passages appear more like spokes on a wheel. Each, if followed, can lead us to the common center of life-force. At any time, each of these passages can serve as a meaningful beginning.

Each chapter contains a story or metaphor or personal example that brings a question or quandary of living into view. From this, I try to surface and reflect on the life lesson or skill carried there. Finally, and this is the most important part, I offer a question for you to walk with, or a conversation for you to have with a friend or loved one, or a meditation through which you might discover where this question or quandary or lesson or skill lives in you. These invitations are seeds to water along the way. For insight is only abstract if we don't take the quietly courageous step to see where it lives in our very particular journey. To make all this real, I invite you to keep a journal as you read, as an intimate space where you might hear your own soul, as a sketchbook where your heart can personalize the themes we're exploring.

If something moves you or stirs you or troubles you along the way, take what works for you and challenges you, and leave the rest. If you recognize something essential in one of these chapters, but don't recognize the name I've given it, please find your own spiritual synonyms. During these conversations, I invite you to harvest your own insights and add to your own personal inner practice.

This book has evolved out of the rhythms of my own spiritual inquiry and the path of my teaching. Both keep merging and forming a new whole. Both keep forming me into a new whole. Working with you as readers and students is a path I am devoted to. This path is a continuous inquiry into what it means to be human, to be here, and to care for each other. And so I've structured this book in the shape of the one conversation with life that I've been entering with many of you through the years, which I welcome new readers to.

On this journey, we will affirm how precious this one life is and enter the chance we have to be fully alive and to be of use to each other and the world. We will uncover how, by loving what's before us and concentrating on what's particular and personal, we can begin to make sense of our experience. We will learn how, over time, the twin callings of enlivening our soul and enlivening the world become one, and how our sincerity and labor help us to survive and thrive.

We will explore how hard work and authenticity reveal meaning and ready us for grace. By grace, I mean the unseeable force of life that carries us, the way the wind carries a bird and the sea carries a fish. And so, we will unfold how a single life soars and dives in partnership with the unseeable force of life that carries it.

My hope is that, through the threshold this book opens, you will deepen your conversation with life. That through your own path of obstacle and surprise, you will be opened to your gifts and become somewhat freed of all you carry. My hope is that you will begin to discover and experience the particular expression of your own nature.

As a way to begin, I want to speak about another great teacher of mine who died last year, Joel Elkes. He was a friend and mentor. I was on my way to New York City when Joel passed away a few days shy of his 102nd birthday. Born in Lithuania, Joel was a child of the Holocaust. He became a groundbreaking doctor, one of the fathers of psychopharmacology, and was a painter in the lineage of Van Gogh and Pissarro. I learned so much from Joel. I miss him mightily.

Like others who knew him, I loved Joel dearly. His need to honor the truth, no matter how difficult, was only matched by his enormous love. Joel affirmed the best in us. He did this for everyone he met.

It's impossible to convey the sum of Joel's life. I can only point to the ways he touched so many. Joel was brilliant — in his gifts as a doctor, as a painter, and as a wise elder — but even more so in the brilliance and immensity of his heart. Though he painted, Joel himself was an exquisite work of art painted by life.

I first met Joel twenty-two years ago over tea, and I fell in love with him instantly. I wanted to record his stories and his wisdom. He said, "Never mind all that." He sipped his tea and we sat in silence for a while until we both grew tender and soft. He then leaned over and took my hand and said, "Now, tell me about you. Tell me what you care about." That was Joel, loving everyone he met into the open, where he could shine his light on the gifts we didn't know we had.

In our early conversations, Joel could see that I was troubled and confused. He took my hand firmly and said, "You steward a force of nature within you. Honor it and trust it." He was never out of reach. He walked the earth lending his strong hands and vast care to all who came his way.

A few days after his death, I wandered into Bryant Park in New York City, one of my favorite places. It was there that I thought I heard Joel's voice wrapped in the wind. Feeling him everywhere led to this poem:

Where Are You?
My teacher appeared to me
in the midst of my grief for him.
I was on a bench in a park in the
city. Buses were coughing by and
small shops were opening. And
since my teacher no longer has
hands, he swept a bird in my face
to break up my sadness. And since
he no longer has a mouth, the light
off the windows twenty stories up
drifted through the leaves. I said,

"I miss you." And I thought I heard him say, "Do everything while you're here." Then it began to mist, though the sun was shining. As if the Universe were crying at what it does to us in order to keep going. Just then, a child lost a ball. It bounced my way. Now my teacher was in the bounce and I thought I heard him say, "Enough of this. Pick up the ball and live."

When I think of those I've loved and lost, of all the kind pilgrims I've journeyed with, when I think of my wife, Susan, and my closest, oldest friends, I'm drawn to say that there is nothing as messy and magnificent as the incarnation of being human. And the one life we're given is more than enough, if we can help each other through the storms that time can bring. Though we shake our heads, admitting on bad days that it's all too hard, if some legendary film director were to offer you such a part, you'd think it the role of a lifetime — and it is.

■ ■ ■ ■

GETTING CLOSER
TO LIFE

■ ■ ■ ■

You shall no longer take things at second
or third hand, nor look through the eyes
of the dead, nor feed on the specters in
books;
You shall not look through my eyes either,
nor take things from me;
You shall listen to all sides, and filter them
from yourself.

— Walt Whitman

Each person is born with a gift. Our call is to find it and care for it. The ultimate purpose of the gift is to exercise the heart into inhabiting its aliveness. For the covenant of life is not just to stay alive, but to stay in our aliveness. And staying in aliveness depends on opening the heart and keeping it open.

Our dreams, goals, and ambitions are all kindling, fuel for the heart to exercise its aliveness, to bring our gift into the world, to discover what matters. Like a match, our light is revealed as our gift strikes against the needs of the world. When my sincerity strikes against yours, our gifts can give off their light.

We drift in and out of knowing our aliveness. Pain, worry, fear, and loss can muffle and confuse us. But finding our gift and working it will bring us back alive. It doesn't matter if we're skillful or clumsy, if we play our gift well or awkwardly, or if we make great strides or fail. Aliveness is not a judge in a talent show.

27

Aliveness shows itself in response to whole-heartedness, when we can say yes to life, work with what we're given, and stay in relationship — to everything.

The chapters in this section explore what it means to find our way. When we come out of hiding and bring up the lights, we begin to discover what it means to be awake. When we're knocked off our horse, we're brought closer to life. Then we're challenged to use our heart to break a path — this is the soul's work. Finding our way always depends on using the one life we're given to uncover the story behind the story, so we might find what can last.

So brave your way on. You are a blessing waiting to be discovered by yourself. The wisdom waits in your heart like a buried treasure which only loving your self can bring to the surface. And loving your self is like diving to the bottom of the ocean with nothing but who you are to find your way.

When We Set Out

My father has been with me since his death, speaking to me through the things he did, the things he built, the things he loved. So when someone recently asked, "Which should we listen to, our soul or our will," I suddenly remembered my father teaching me how to steer the thirty-foot sailboat he built when I was a boy. He would say, "It's the sail that follows the wind and the rudder that follows the sail." The sail by its nature will catch the wind and lean into it. The rudder is for steering once you've set sail.

In the relationship between our soul and our will, our soul is like a sail. Once hoisted in the open, our soul is filled by the wind of Spirit, and that wind establishes our course and direction. Our will is our rudder. Its job is to follow where the soul filled with Spirit leads us. Our soul shows us where to go, while our will helps to steer our way there. The times I grow stubborn or confused or lost are the times I lean on my will to make things happen. But forcing things to happen is not its job, though my will wants to take over. The times I feel at one with everything around me, the times I feel certain of my path, are when the sail of my soul is full and I'm being carried toward a vision greater than myself, feeling most alive along the way.

I sent this memory of our father to my brother Howard, who wrote back, "I remember him on the low side of the boat with his back against the stays looking for a break in the jib with his foot on the tiller. He loved watching the water and foam run up on deck through the scuppers. He'd smile, take a deep breath of that salt air, and say, 'We're really scudding along now.' It was the happiest of times for him, taking something he built and seeing it tuned to perfection, rushing down the bay. He loved the rocking of a heavy boat in a slight swell reaching to windward on a blue-sky day with a glint of sun on the water, the masts creaking, the wind slapping through the rigging. I wish I could take him back and have him live in that moment forever. And I would gladly go there with him."

In that moment on the sea, my father was

living once for all time, entering that moment so completely, he was feeling all of life rushing through him. The sensation of feeling all of time and all of life in any given moment is the sensation of joy. We all want to live in these moments forever. But we can't. Yet my father's love of the sea affirms that if we lift our heads, life will touch us. Even a taste of aliveness can fill, sustain, and refresh us as we make it through the daily grind of doubt and confusion.

Sooner or later, we're all faced with moments beyond our control, when our will can't make life follow our wishes. These are the times we're asked to work with life and not fight it or curse it or hide from it. When we're out of reach of the wind for the moment, out of reach of what matters, we begin to doubt if there *is* a wind, if there's anything like Spirit at all. In that vacuum, the will can flutter out of fear, out of lack of a direction to steer toward. During such painful times, we can flap about at everything we encounter. During those times — when we fear that nothing has meaning, when it seems there's nothing to hold us up — our will can puff and snap in a desperate attempt to fill what looms as an empty life.

My father talked about the difference between sailing across the sea to arrive somewhere and sailing for the experience of sailing. He said, "It's always harder to sail toward a fixed point, because you will inevitably have to cross the wind several times to get there." In contrast, a boat moves its fastest and cleanest when it simply follows the wind wherever it goes. When devoted to experience, we discover our way.

We usually think about where we're going instead of listening for where life is taking us. This is the tension between our soul and our will. For sure, there are times we have to sail for a particular spot on land, times we have to cross the wind. But it helps to remember that these journeys always involve a smaller destination, as we often seek refuge in a temporary port. My father would say, "It's always the experience of sailing that one remembers." And it's always the experience of Spirit filling us that lets us find our way, by inhabiting our true nature.

When we set out, it's important to get far enough into the sea, so the sails can catch the wind at all. For each life must be out in the open before the wind will show its face. We can't know what direction awaits us if we hover too close to the shore of our past, the shore of our family, the shore of some-one else's dream for us, or the shore of an old identity. If we are to feel the wind in our face, we must leave the shallows and harbors and make our way into the open, where we can drift in the deep. Only then will the larger, timeless destination show itself. Only then will our soul be filled enough with Spirit that our smaller self will have no choice but to be engaged in steering us toward all that matters.

Seeds to Water

🐦 In your journal, tell the story of a time when you followed what you wanted rather than following the truth of the path before you. What happened to you and those around you? What did you learn from this experience?

🐦 In conversation with a friend or loved one, describe a moment in which you briefly felt the presence of all of life. Where were you? What opened this moment? What closed this moment? How did such a moment affect you?

THE SOUL'S WORK

I was such an awkward teenager. I didn't fit in anywhere, not in school or at home. During this time, I discovered basketball. It began as an experiment in solitude. I'd walk to the concrete courts outside McKenna Junior High School and spend hours by myself dribbling, stopping, and shooting. Then chase the ball and do it again.

I don't remember why I picked up a basketball in the first place. But I do remember the first time the ball went cleanly through the metal net. I'd been shooting for thirty minutes or so and had only managed to bounce in one or two shots. I was lost in the jump, clang, and chase of the ball. And finally, the ball left my hands without my thinking and floated through the net without touching the rim. I stood still and all the awkwardness was gone. For the moment, I felt complete. I didn't know it at the time, but this was my first conscious experience of effort leading into grace.

Gravity returned and I ran after the ball. I wanted to feel that moment of completeness again. And so, I was excited to keep practicing, to keep jumping, to chase down the ball and keep aiming past the clang of the misses. Slowly, over weeks, I was able to net the ball cleanly a few times in an afternoon.

Eventually, I began to play with others, first in the schoolyard and then on the school team. There I learned the next phase of effort that leads into grace. Alone, I experienced the practice that brings us to the edge of unifying what we try to do with what we actually do. But all the practice, all the effort, was preparation for the live moment in the game when I couldn't see the basket. Then, somehow, my body and hands knew what to do.

In my junior year while playing for our high school team, I found myself in such a moment. The game was in overtime and the clock was winding down. I was in the corner, twenty-five feet away. With a hand in my face, I jumped to my left and flicked the ball, which slipped cleanly through the net as the buzzer sounded.

There was a loud roar and people flooded the court, but honestly, I hardly heard them.

I was feeling complete in that moment, which all my effort had readied me for. I felt very little difference between the buzzer beater in the crowded gym and the first time the ball went through the metal net when I was alone in the schoolyard. Both were hoped-for but unexpected moments of grace.

A central theme of this book is that effort readies us for grace, as grace can never be planned for or willed to appear, only entered.

Through the years, I've worked just as hard and awkwardly at love. I've practiced care in the same way: jumping, missing, and chasing after my mistakes. Eventually, as when the basketball went through the net, there came a day when care came through me cleanly. This thoroughness of care was my first experience of feeling complete with another, a moment of shared grace. In time, I came to understand that all my awkward attempts to love were preparing me for the unrehearsed moments of heartbreak when I was very near what matters.

When sitting with Grandma Minnie in the courtyard of the hospital where she spent her last days; when realizing while eating sandwiches with my oldest friend, Robert, that he and I had saved each other's lives;

when falling into Susan's eyes for the first time, long before I knew she would be my wife — in each of those life-changing moments, all my misguided efforts to care somehow let my soul show itself. My heart knew what to do and I was suddenly in the right place at the right time. In each of those moments, the very pulse of life jolted through us like electricity and we came away bonded. In truth, I've been humbled by all my failed efforts to love, and I see that they have readied me for the grace of being loved.

I have also accepted that in my efforts to know and tell the truth, I must do so not simply by conveying facts accurately, but in bearing witness to the invisible streams we move through every day. Along the way, I climbed a rough mountain, not knowing I would find and gently stroke a worn stone at the top. I found my way to a distant coast, not knowing I would kneel and feel where the sand had worn an ancient shell smooth. I walked hours in the snow, not knowing I would stop where I began to watch the tall pines sway and hear them creak. I made these efforts so that during my father's last months, I could run my fingers through his hair as he slept and feel how time had worn his shell smooth. So that when a storm broke the back of our cherry tree, which we'd planted so many years ago, I could honor its fall in the middle of that heavy rain. So that, when the time came, I could gently stroke our dog's face as she was dying.

All our efforts to get close to the world only ready us for the intimate kinships that are always near. This is a form of shared grace.

In essence, the journey of this book is to understand and personalize how effort is the teacher and friend who leads us into grace. Effort at its most fundamental level is just that: the commitment to try, to work hard, to give our all, not knowing what the outcome will be. Trying hard and giving our all without knowing where that will lead is also a working definition of faith. Life has taught me that, regardless of what we face, effort and faith will lead us into the larger stream of life that holds us. And being held by the larger stream of life is another way to describe grace.

Psychologist Mihaly Csikszentmihalyi named the experience of being carried along in the stream of life as the flow state. He described the experience of flow as the complete sense of feeling alive and content, regardless of the activity that leads us there.

We can immerse ourselves wholeheartedly in anything. We can shoot a basketball cleanly through a net. We can sit with a loved one in the sun. We can climb so long that we are nothing but the climb. We can stroke our dog's face or kiss our father's cheek. We can plant flowers. We can plane a board of walnut till we are completely in the stroke of the plane. Whatever the activity, once we love it, the task opens us to all that is holy and our effort leads us into the flow of aliveness that is within us and around us.

Throughout the centuries, one inherent notion about life has been that what is essential to being alive precedes us, comes into us at birth, and returns to the unseeable stream of life when we die. In nature, the soul of the fish returns to the river. The soul of the bird returns to the wind. The soft brilliance of the flower returns to the sun. Our experience while here as human beings is that all our heart and effort and thought, when filled with authenticity and sincerity, lead us into a state of flow, into a state of active grace in which we briefly feel the aliveness that precedes us, fills us, and which will outlive us. Then, after so much living, the soul of a person returns to that unseeable stream of life, which Lao Tzu called the Tao, or the Way.

In our humanness, effort is pointed and singular, while grace is all-encompassing. Effort is the snail inching along, while grace is the current that lifts it from the suction of its path. Effort is keeping the break in our heart open, while grace is the light of everything not broken washing the break clean.

Half of the soul's work is to be. The other half is to be of use. It's in our nature to try with all our heart, at everything and anything, until we chance to inhabit grace and come alive. And being so alive, we become a conduit for life and a resource for others. The way cells regenerate to heal a wound, we regenerate the Universal body each time we come alive. The soul's work is ever-present, if we can put down everything that gets in the way.

In the Sufi tradition, *muhasiba* is a practice of self-examination by which we're encouraged "to make an inventory of our actions, moods, behavior, and thoughts at the end of every day." This is not done to be self-praising or self-critical, but to develop an inner habit of course correction. And so, along the way, I encourage you to engage in your own practice of self-examination, so you might understand the nature of your own soul and the nature of what gets in your way. So you might understand in detail the nature of your own effort and your personal relationship to grace. So you might deepen your chances to be and be of use.

Seeds to Water

&❧ In your journal, describe two efforts you've made in learning how to be and two efforts you've made in learning how to be of use. What do these central tasks mean to you? In the Sufi tradition of *muhasiba,* examine your efforts in order to develop an inner habit of course correction, not to be self-critical or to praise yourself. Without judging yourself, write the next step in each path for you.

&❧ In conversation with a friend or loved one, describe in detail a moment of flow you've experienced, which some sort of practice led you to. Where were you? Were you surprised into this moment or did you sense it was coming? What does such an experience say to you about the nature of hard work?

LEGACY

Sitting beside my father during his last months, I became aware that I'm part of a lineage that goes back four generations.

My great-grandfather was a leatherworker. He made saddles for a feudal baron in Russia. He endured his uncertain livelihood by pouring himself into his craft. During a pogrom, he was chased by Cossacks into the Dnieper River but wasn't killed, because they didn't want their horses to get cold. After this, it took him fourteen years and three trips across the Atlantic to bring our family to America. Toward the end of his life, on summer nights in Williamsburg, Brooklyn, he would say, "When in trouble, wait till you see a way out."

His son, my grandfather, was a gentle soul who became a letterpress printer in New York City, only to lose his job during the Great Depression. Even with little to eat, he'd bring strangers home for dinner. When

Grandma would pull him aside with "We don't have enough," he'd kiss her cheek and say, "Break whatever we have in half. It will be enough."

When his son, my ninety-three-year-old father, was in the hospital, bobbing inside his stroke-laden body, I sat with my mother at the foot of his bed. As we watched him sink away from us, she shook her head and said, "I don't know how he did it." She stared into the trail of their lives. "No matter what we faced, he'd always say, 'Give me a minute, and I'll figure out what to do.'"

They're all gone and I braid their lessons into a rope I can use: to see a way out, to know there will be enough, to figure out what to do. In the midst of trouble, we're always challenged to stand still in the river, till we're shown how to stay alive and give.

Seeds to Water

    ⭕ In your journal, describe at least one story or saying that comes from your birth family or your chosen family that has shaped your sense of effort and grace. It might be a positive or negative example. How have these lessons helped you to stay alive and give?

In conversation with a friend or loved one, share this story or saying and discuss its meaning. In the days to come, share this story or saying with a third person and ask them for a story or saying that has shaped who they are.

Personal Mythology

Even before recorded history, myths and stories have been a way to carry forward the quandaries of living, to help keep in view what's hard to keep in view, to return us to what matters when we forget. Under all our troubles, we each have a constellation of personal, foundational stories that we can rely on to remind us of what matters, a personal set of myths that have shaped us and which, when retrieved and honored, help us come alive.

Remembering the stories that have shaped me doesn't cause me to retreat into the past, but opens a storehouse of resilience that I can enter and access. This is the purpose of myth — to carry timeless tools that we can use *Now*!

To discover your own personal myths, simply give your heart the quiet space it needs to surface these stories. If you still your overactive mind, these stories will show themselves: the time someone helped you see something for the first time, the time a grandparent let his or her belief in you shine like the sun, the time you got up — after being knocked down by life — stronger than before. These stories help us see the truth of what it means to be alive. These stories carry deep guides who often appear through the surprise of kindness and the crack of suffering.

Writing about landmark stories from my own life has strengthened and deepened my soul. The great Chinese poet Tu Fu helped me through cancer by coming to me in dreams to teach me about fear and to ask me to enter my own life. The mountains outside of Albuquerque, New Mexico, taught me how to be steadfast below all the names we're given. Reading about Nietzsche, when he protected a horse from being whipped in Turin, Italy, taught me that, in the end, how we live is the poem. My mother's father, Pop, leaving the door open on Passover for the angel Elijah, taught me to stay open no matter how dark it seems. My dear friend Robert, holding my hands in the sun, both of us numb from neuropathy, affirmed that we can absorb each other's pain. And when Grandma Minnie placed my small hands as a boy on my grandfather's Talmud, saying, "These are the oldest things you own," she taught me what it means to be someone else's flower. Each of these moments is part of my personal mythology. Together they reveal a constellation by which I find my way.

I imagine the large myths we know from earlier cultures began as very personal stories. Because they had such lasting meaning, these stories outgrew their particulars. I imagine the Greek myth of Achilles began as the story of a warrior tired of war. I imagine the Buddhist myth of Kuan-yin began as the story of a person of great kindness who had the capacity to hear other people's pain. I imagine the myth of Moses began as the story of a sage of great presence who couldn't easily speak.

As I travel, I hear modern myths everywhere I go. Consider Carla, who couldn't bring herself to sell her parents' things after they died. After four years, she began to empty their dresser, only to find a handwritten letter from her father to her mother just before he died. She sat on their bed, in the silhouette of their love, and read the last note her father wrote. For Carla, her myth unearthed a lineage of tenderness.

Consider Kirsten. Forty years after being left by her first love, she discovered that her mother had told the boy never to call again, that he wasn't good enough for her daughter. Long after her mother had died, long after Kirsten and her first love had gone through decades of living their own lives, always wondering what happened to each other, her life story unraveled. In her sixties, Kirsten understood that who we are exists beneath all the ways we're deceived. Her myth confirmed that the heart can hold what it loves for a lifetime.

Then there's Thomas, a doctor left powerless when his oldest friend was dying from leukemia, and all his experience and practice seemed small and out of place. Only his broken-hearted presence seemed to soothe his friend. For Thomas, his myth showed him that the medicine of presence covers all our knowledge like honey.

And Megan came home to find her unhinged grandmother Mimi sleeping in the middle of a smoke-filled house. She'd left the soup boiling on the stove and went to take a nap. Knowing that she could no longer keep her grandmother safe, Megan felt like a failure, and it pained her deeply to move Mimi to assisted living. When she asked her friend Elesa, "What can I do?" Elesa kissed her hands and said, "Accept that what you've done is enough." For

Megan, her myth taught her that love will hold us all, if we can let go and ask for help.

Through stories like these we discover the tribe we belong to. Through our landmark stories, life leads us to the lineage we're a part of. The difficulties of living can often make us put this lineage aside to deal with trouble first. I've done this and found myself diminished for putting these kinships last, when it's precisely these kinships that help me move through trouble. Telling our stories helps us re-establish our bond with kindred spirits across time.

Once lived, our stories become seminal. Once told, they serve as candles in the dark. The myths we live and tell reveal the most enduring truth of all: that who we are is more than enough.

Seeds to Water

- In conversation with a friend or loved one, tell one story that seems foundational to your life. Tell this story as you would a myth. Discuss the lesson this myth carries and how it applies to your life now.

- Go to an elder in your life and ask them what they see from where they are in life.

Journal what transpires and, at another time, share their story with a loved one.

Getting Closer to Life

In the 1960s, my family would sit around a small black-and-white TV and watch the NASA space rockets launch from Cape Canaveral. It seemed the stuff of science fiction, to be sending human beings into the galaxy. As a boy, I was amazed at all the years of work by so many to design and build a space rocket. I thought of all the years of training that an astronaut undergoes in order to enter into the vast emptiness that holds our world. I thought of the effort put into all the encasements, the booster rockets and scaffolding, the structure of which would fall away in order for the capsule to break through gravity. Only the capsule with the crew would enter the quiet weightlessness waiting beyond our experience.

All these years later, I view the journey of life as the hard work to design and build an identity and career and a story that will carry us through the weight of the world, until these encasements and propulsions are jettisoned. Until dropping all that was necessary, which is no longer necessary, only our soul is left to enter the vast regions of being.

After my journey with cancer, I had jettisoned any particular sense of ambition. The urge to get somewhere began to leave me. I thought I'd done something wrong by being so devoted to ambition. I thought I'd failed by living in the rocket I'd made of my dreams. But like all souls who mature against their will, who are allowed to survive, I was only growing large so I could inevitably grow small again, the way a storm builds only to dissipate.

It was watching a heron step softly in the marsh that made me realize, in my late forties, that this is how the soul grows: by dreaming of something to build, only to build it and inhabit it, until we fill it so completely that it starts to confine us, until that confinement presses us to be born anew, the way a cocoon births a butterfly. Having served its purpose, my ambition tore open like a cocoon so I could breathe freely and be delicate. It's made me wonder: if allowed its full course, will ambition exhaust itself and force us into the open? I think when undressed of all we strive for, the soul remembers itself and sets us free.

This doesn't mean it's bad to strive or to have ambition or to accomplish things. But enshrining these things will leave us disconnected as we bear the weight of the world. Like those space rockets in the sixties, we need the engines to launch, but we need to jettison all the machinery of our will, if we are to experience the depth and breadth of life.

Twelve hundred years ago, the Chinese poet Po Chü-I recounted in a poem how he became lost while traveling on horseback. With a sudden urgency, he began prodding the horse to push on, to go here, then there. After a time, he exhausted himself and fell asleep in the saddle. While dozing, his reins slackened. It seemed like an instant, but he'd gone a hundred lengths. When he woke, the horse had found a better way. Only while asleep would he loosen his grip and give up control, and the horse, which seemed to wait for this chance, carried him easily.

This is the tension between will and surrender. We push and push, insisting we know the way, even when we're lost. If we can outlast our will, we exhaust ourselves and let go of the reins, long enough for the horse we're riding to quicken its pace and carry us on.

Watching space rockets launch, watching herons step softly in the marsh, and falling asleep in the saddle while our horse finds the way — these stories point up our struggle in knowing when to bend what comes our way and when to go with it.

As human beings, we're asked to choose, more than once, between inhabiting life or consuming life, between finding our kinship with others or trying to manage and dominate the things around us. Every day, we're given the chance to lean into life or turn away. These basic covenants make all the difference.

Consider the butterfly effect, where the slight movement of a butterfly's wing in South America can become a mammoth wind after building for a thousand miles. Or how a small wave can become tidal after traveling across the ocean. Likewise, our slightest turning away from life can create tides of separation after crossing the ocean of time. But our slightest leaning toward life can begin a golden age of cooperation, waiting to happen a thousand years after we're gone. What we do matters, when it arises from the essence of our being. Our deepest leanings join with the tides of life to set great confluences in motion. When we show up with who we are, we join with other life, the way atoms form molecules. This joining of aliveness is at the heart of all creation.

On the other side of ambition, I've learned that being who we are is how the heart learns, while arriving at understanding is how the mind learns. We need a working harmony between the two. Letting go of the reins has humbled me into bettering myself by inhabiting the simple motions of my life and immersing myself in work that is real.

Carrying only what is necessary, I can see that the things that matter are everywhere, like secrets hidden in the open. Who would have imagined — the world is only hidden because we believe it needs to be. Often, we get in our own way, layering assumptions and conclusions like blinders over the fresh experience of simply being here. All the while, we're asked to participate in life and not control events. In very real ways, suffering and beauty return us to direct living.

Recently, my doctor explained why, at my age, it takes longer for the discoloration of a bruise to heal. Our skin thins the longer we're here, and therefore holds its markings. In the same way, we're more permanently touched by the world the longer we're here. The longer we live, the more we hold the world's markings. As it should be, the reward for getting closer to life.

Seeds to Water

❧ In your journal, describe the face you show no one and the face you show the world. Without judging either, begin a conversation between the two.

❧ In conversation with a friend or loved one, discuss one habit that keeps you from the truth of life and one habit that brings you closer to all that matters. How do these habits differ? What leads you to each of them?

MAKING OUR WAY

Eighteen years ago, I encountered a teaching moment while driving the coast of California. And yesterday, I encountered a twin teaching moment, less directly, through the news, all the way from Australia. Today, I see how they go together. One was waiting like a seed in my consciousness for the other to arrive, once I'd tumbled through years of slow living.

The first teaching startled me while I was driving north of Monterey on US 1 in late October of 1998. I was aching and vulnerable, feeling far from home, when, through the harsh shore wind, I saw a large rock surrounded by the rough, churned-up sea. The rock was covered with all kinds of animals: willet, gull, cormorant, sea lion, seal, pelican, otter. All had found refuge from the hammering of the sea: climbing, winging, hauling themselves onto the rock; leaning into each other, lying on each other; finding this rock-oasis of wind and sun; too tired once on the rock to fight or be territorial, each having been wrung out by the pounding of the wet hours.

I realized this is how we make our way, how we find each other. Every survivor, regardless of what they survive, knows the hammering of the sea, and the rock we find refuge on is an exposed place where we finally accept each other, too tired from swimming to think any longer about territories, too tired to talk except through simple touch.

The wellness group I attended weekly during my cancer journey was such a rock. The meeting rooms of recovery are such a rock. The thousand quiet rooms of therapy are such a rock. For those who have suffered, tolerance is not a political position, or even a principle. For those of us who have been tossed out of the storm, who have hauled ourselves into the sun, anything exhausted beside us is family.

The hard gift of any storm is that when too exhausted to uphold our differences, there's room enough for everyone. When I can accept what we have in common over what sets us apart, somehow my deepest self is mysteriously affirmed and I begin to heal. There is some inexplicable braid of all our troubles and all our dreams that will not snap, no matter the storm. Yet we resist folding into each other until the disturbance exhausts us. We fear the worst we have to offer, when the best is close at hand.

The second teaching stopped me, just yesterday, while drinking coffee in the morning and watching the news. Every year pilot whales swim in pods through the Bass Strait, which separates Tasmania and southern Australia. They migrate to and from the polar waters. But yesterday, sixty-four long-finned pilots stranded themselves on a stretch of Anthony's Beach.

The sight of these mountainous creatures — the ocean pooling along their slick and heavy sides — stopped everyone. Within an hour, fifty volunteers were pulling slings beneath their soft whale bellies, trying to drag them back into the sea. Some spent the night pouring water on their ancient faces. They saved eleven.

What made these whales strand themselves? What made strangers rub water on their mammoth backs? It is as much our destiny to swim with no end as it is to get stuck, as it is to return each other to the deep.

The whole struggle of making our way, together and alone, is carried in this poignant, unstoppable migration, year after year. While we all have a path we must follow, we will all be beached at one time or another. And when we find each other stranded, the exercise of compassion demands that we interrupt our lives to return each other to our own true nature — to our God-given element.

I have not been able to quiet these twin lessons from the sea: *When we're too exhausted to uphold our differences, there's room enough for everyone. And when we find each other stranded, we must interrupt our lives to return each other to the deep.*

We are all en route. We are all exhausted. We are all beached. We are all making our way in this unstoppable migration in which the destination is no one place, but rather, the quality of heart we finally reveal in each other's presence.

Seeds to Water

&❧ In your journal, describe a time when you were exhausted enough to relate more fully to others. What did you learn from this experience?

&❧ In conversation with a friend or loved one, tell the story of a time when you interrupted your life to help someone back into their own. How did getting involved this way affect you?

LOVE YOUR WINDOW

There is nothing more profound, more mysterious, more pregnant . . . more dazzling than a window lighted by a single candle.

— Baudelaire

The word *window* comes from the Old Norse *vindauga,* which means "wind-eye." The Old English word for window is *eagpyrl,* which means "eye-hole." From birth, our eye is the inborn window through which we know the world. In *A Midsummer Night's Dream,* Shakespeare uttered the now famous line "The eyes are the window to the soul." The great Chilean poet Pablo Neruda had his desk against a window that looked out on the sea, so he could be advised by the ancient swell of all those waves. In Amsterdam in 1942, Anne Frank wrote her remarkable diary while hiding with her family in small, concealed rooms behind a bookcase in the building where her father had worked. Her diary was a dazzling window through the dark cloud of her time.

The earliest windows were holes in a wall. And the human journey between opening and closing has always been about the relationship between our walls and our windows. In a cob house, an ancient type of dwelling built of mud and clay, there's always a wall that has a truth window. This isn't a window to the outside, but an opening that shows what the wall is made of. We would do well if our walls had truth windows, so we could be honest about what they're made of.

When shut in or closed off, we need windows we can rely on. Our health and ability to dream depend on having life-giving windows. Like a window through the dark clouds when they come, or a truth window to show what our walls are made of, or a window to the soul so we can access what is eternal. It helps to remember that windows go both ways: letting things in and out, and letting us see and be seen.

I'm writing this upstairs in my study near my favorite corner window through which I have the company of some very old maples. They seem to stir when I'm confused and nod when I'm relaxed enough to learn. The morning light creeps through them onto my desk, encouraging me to begin.

I remember Grandma Minnie's kitchen window on the Brooklyn alley of my youth. It was spacious compared to the porthole she looked out of in the bottom of the steamship she came to America in. Grandma talked to me about windows. I was staring past her stove into the alley when she said, "Good friends are like good windows. They save us from ourselves."

Windows have been carved forever. A great example is the Puye Cliffs in the Santa Clara Canyon in New Mexico, which contain over seven hundred dwellings carved into the face of the mountain. They date back as far as 900 AD. Windows must have been important for these Native Americans to carve an entire village into the face of a mountain. It must have been important for them to live in the open, to wake and stand on the edge of the vastness. It was a long and arduous carving, all to live in the mountain and not on it.

There's a story of a Pueblo family living in the cliffs. While the men were hunting, the women cared for the young children. In one family, a mother found her young son standing on the edge of their dwelling, looking out across the canyon. She asked what he was looking at. The little boy said, "I'm seeing all of time." She moved closer to her son and asked, "And what does all of time look like, my son?" The little boy spread his arms toward the canyon, "I'm flying with my eyes, Mama." She kissed him on the top of his little head and replied, "Remember this. For there will come a time when you will be surrounded by other ways, and you will need to remember what you're seeing now."

Windows worth opening fill us with truth for another time. What I saw through the window of my death as I was being wheeled into surgery all those years ago filled me with a sense of truth that I have returned to countless times.

Each moment that touches us is a window to the vastness of life. Somewhere along the way, probably from exhaustion, I stopped trying to make these moments last. I stopped trying to keep the wonder from vanishing. I began to see that trying so hard to keep our moments of love, mystery, and wonder from going back into the unseen depth of life is like trying to keep a whale from re-entering the sea once it's breached the surface. Better to have windows that face the sea.

We're each left to live our days with the

window of our heart open, so that grace has a way in. Whenever the majesty of life presents itself, it's our humble, simple work to open our window and receive it, fully, with gratitude.

Ultimately, each of us is a window through which the great forces of life enter, the way light fills a home. Through us, the Source of Life can revive those who are bruised and those who are waiting to find their way. So, hard as it is at times, love your window open, and become the opening itself until your walls come down. When the walls come down, the opening is everywhere.

Seeds to Water

❧ In your journal, describe someone whose eyes are open windows to their soul. What have you seen while looking into their eyes?

❧ In conversation with a friend or loved one, describe your favorite window and why it speaks to you. Where is it? What do you see through it? What can you learn from this window that will help you understand more about the window of your heart?

THE SECRET KINGDOM
IS EVERYWHERE

As a boy, the poet and teacher Jack Ridl was lost in wonder in a grassy field, when his mother said, "It's time to go." And he said, "I can't." And she asked, "Why?" And he replied, "Because there are still blades I haven't paid attention to." Something in this little story holds a very large wisdom about where the attention of love can lead us.

I identify with this story because, even when rejected or ignored or misunderstood, I have found my way back to what matters by giving my heart's attention to whatever is before me. When so completely present, some other depth has always answered me in a way that helps me grow. To be honest, I have never experienced an act of caring that did not flower in its return.

Still, you might ask, how do we access all this? The great poet Rilke shows us one way in, when he says:

In order for a Thing to speak to you, you must regard it for a certain time as *the only one that exists,* and through your laborious and exclusive love, the one and only phenomenon is now placed at the center of the Universe, and in that incomparable place, on that day, it is attended by angels.

Seeing all of life in the one thing before you is the devotion with which the child-poet wanted to be with every blade in the grassy field. This devotion of attention is the medicine that waits every time we feel bereft and cut off from the rest of the world. It's the awakening of attention that leads us back to the safety of love.

The threshold to the secret kingdom that is everywhere, hiding in the open, is that no matter the pain or weight we carry, we're challenged to regard whatever is before us as the only thing that exists. Until our labor of love coaxes the one thing open, letting the light of the Universe flood all around us. And in that presence we come alive again.

In the recovered fullness of life's presence, we can see directly and hear directly. In those moments of direct seeing, there is no seer — only the merging of who is seeing with what is seen. In those moments of direct hearing, there is no hearer — only the merging of who is listening with what is heard. In those moments of direct loving, there is no lover — only love. This is how feeling thoroughly present can lead us into brief but life-transforming pulsations of Oneness.

As the Zen sage Shidō Munan says:

The experience of Oneness is beyond a single self. Once you enter through a doorway, you're beyond the door. Once you see directly, you are no longer separate from what you see. Once you hear directly, you are no longer separate from what you hear.

In my own life, I'm coming to see that the less there is between who I am and what I experience — between in here and out there — the less I need to process, filter, or cipher from my head to my heart. When feeling thorough and present, my heart beats in direct rhythm with the pulse of the Universe.

Ever since my cancer journey, I've known that Eternity is in each moment. I'm no longer looking ahead. I'm no longer looking for something better to happen in the future. Instead, I try to give my all to every blade of grass, so I can stop being separate from what I see and hear. We're constantly drawn in the surface world to move through time, but experience, when met with authentic innocence, asks us to *enter* time. When no longer separate from those around us, we experience a complete moment of compassion. And those moments of complete compassion remove all our excuses, leaving the heart with a sensitivity that never leaves us. When one with what we see, hear, and feel, we enter the secret kingdom of aliveness that is only secret when we remain separate.

Seeds to Water

❧ This is a meditation that leads to a journal question. Choose one small object — a feather, a stone, a small statue, a spoon — and, as Rilke suggests, regard it for a certain time as the only thing that exists. Give this object your love and full attention. Center yourself and breathe slowly. Reflect on this object until it begins to show its presence. Now breathe deeply and give your love to that presence. Welcome it in. Be with it. See where it leads.

འ Later, in your journal, describe your experience of regarding this object as the only thing in the Universe and what this meditation revealed to you about the nature of your own love and attention.

KNOCKED OFF OUR HORSE

Remember that everyone you meet is afraid of something, loves something, and has lost something.
— H. Jackson Brown Jr.

Saul of Tarsus was an intransigent Roman citizen, zealous in his persecution of early Christians in the first century. At the height of his fervor, Saul was blinded and knocked from his horse by a visitation from Jesus, who appeared in a bright light. After three days, he regained his sight and rose to find his deeper self revealed as Paul, the apostle, who spread the gospel of Jesus. He became the very thing he had persecuted.

Falling tends to break us open, often against our will. Once fallen off our horse, we have the chance to accept the humanity of others, which we're suddenly not so far from. It opens us to the fragile acceptance that "there but for the grace of God go I."

So be careful what you so sharply condemn, for you just might become it.

Saul fell into an opposite, though equally zealous, calling. More often, our tripping into what we condemn isn't that exalted or extreme. A friend of mine who was highly principled, absolute in his code of ethics, once cut off a mutual friend completely, because he learned that friend had lied. It wasn't even to him. But he couldn't tolerate any falsehood in his relationships. Almost a decade later, my principled friend fell into hard times. His wife had died, he'd lost his job, and, desperate for work, he lied on his résumé, saying he'd resigned. I learned all this because he wanted me to be a reference for him, which I was happy to do. But in the process, he confessed to me that he had become what he had condemned. It humbled him.

It made us both suspend our judgment about such things, because in real life, good people suffer and find themselves being less than their best selves. But how do we respond to this? Do we turn our backs on everyone who is less than their best? Do we stone them? Or do we love them by holding a mirror to their vulnerability, showing them who they truly are until they can heal? Just because someone lies when in pain doesn't make him incapable of truth, and when someone says something hurtful, it doesn't mean she's now incapable of love. Although, living in the lie and hiding in being hurtful can keep us from our true nature.

Another friend of mine vowed never to cheat on her husband. She had great disdain for infidelity. But after fifteen years, she fell in love with someone else. She couldn't explain it or deny it. And she couldn't bear to tell her husband, unless she was sure. So she found herself in a clandestine relationship for a while. She didn't do this well. Her husband found out and was, of course, deeply wounded. The marriage ended and she pursued her new life. Though their lives went in different directions, they somehow managed to stay connected. One day, almost eight years after she'd left, her former husband told her that he was falling in love again. With great humility, he uttered that it was with a married woman, and in a brief and rare moment of honesty, the two talked openly. In the strange center of their storm, her former husband confessed, with an odd tenderness, that he now understood her leaving years before.

The more we separate ourselves from the heart of the living — whether by judgment or condemnation or self-isolation — the more likely we are to be thrown, with sudden impact, back to the ground of our common humanity. In time, life will break us of our differences. It is a law of inner motion. At the same time, we are accountable for the mistakes we make. But when broken of our self-centeredness, our tenderness leads us to understand each other more than condemn each other. And beautifully, the breaking of self-centeredness doesn't send us into insignificance but into being an irreplaceable part in a magnificent whole.

Seeds to Water

&❧ In your journal, describe a time when you felt judged without compassion and how it felt to be reduced to the one mistake you made. How did this affect the relationship? Then describe a time when you were held accountable for your actions within the whole context of who you are. How did this affect the relationship?

&❧ In conversation with a friend or loved one, tell the story of a time when you violated a principle or belief that you feel strongly about. What led you to veer from your own sense of ethics? Do you judge yourself or forgive yourself for this unexpected act? How has this experience affected your sense of self and your understanding of principle and the unpredictability of life?

THE THREE FEARS

My fifty-ninth year was a period of great suffering for me, a time of heart and path, a time of being blind and sighted. During this time, I was knocked off my horse while being carried by the inexhaustible Resource of Being that informs everything. Through this painful journey, my soul eventually remembered itself.

I'm still learning from the alchemy of events that unfolded that summer. In June, I made a pilgrimage to see my ninety-year-old father for the first time in fifteen years. Upon my return, my stomach stopped emptying properly, damaged from a nasty flu that had settled in me in winter. I couldn't eat very much and was losing weight. Severe attacks made me afraid to eat. And in mid-July, my job was eliminated without notice after sixteen years.

One by one, important parts of my life were being stripped away. I feared nothing would be left. I felt plucked by fear and anxiety, and punctuated by moments of calm and release. In those brief moments of release, I felt liberated, though less and less sure from what. At times, I still trusted that my experience was pressing my soul into a diamond, if I could only withstand the pressure.

At this time, I had a sequence of three dreams over three nights. The third one woke me at 4:30 a.m. I couldn't go back to sleep. Didn't want to go back to sleep. So I went to my study and grabbed my journal, the one I'd started in 1996 and tucked away on a lower shelf. I was drawn after years to take it with me when I finally saw my father. It felt familiar but incomplete, like our relationship. I've been carrying it with me ever since.

That night, I opened it and quickly looked for the next blank page to jot down details of the dream I just had before it would evaporate. But the journal opened itself to the one blank page I didn't mean to leave empty at the end of my visit with my father. I haven't been able to fill it. But that night I realized what goes on the missing page.

What I wrote then and share with you now in the next two chapters are the three fears I experienced during this difficult time, and the three dreams that appeared across those three nights. Initially, I feared that these intense experiences would burn me, but, once lived through, they actually illuminated the strength I needed and had been carrying within.

The first fear was of seeing my father after fifteen years. This was my fear of the past, my fear of having my sense of self thwarted by returning to the crucible that was home. I'd struggled for too long like a weed growing through a crack in my parents' sidewalk. The second was the fear of my stomach twisting and burning because of the condition I had, the fear of a pain that would come suddenly and bring me to my knees. This carried my fear of the present. This is the fear in all pain, that it can grip us unexpectedly at any time. One of the roles of pain is to remind us how little we're in control. And the third fear came from losing my job. It was the fear of what would happen if I couldn't pay the mortgage, if I couldn't buy new health insurance. This carried my fear of the future.

I didn't realize till later how perfect the three fears were, how I was being forced to submit to fear completely or drop fear altogether. Not forever. No one can do that. No one can escape fear. But I can, in time, drop fear as a master and a guide. This will not happen all at once. Or be easy to maintain. But even now, I'm in a process of letting fear drop from the status of a god whose thunder makes me stop everything life-giving every time it speaks. I don't know how to do this or what effort to make; nonetheless, since the three fears appeared, this quieting of fear is happening to me.

For most of my life, I've been able to endure and outlast fear and pain; meeting each with an inner presence that eventually restores my sense of being part of a larger Whole. Somehow to embody that larger perspective has helped me align with the stream of Mystery that carries all things. It never eliminates fear and pain but always seems to right-size them in a way that gets me through.

But during that difficult year, I realized that the fear and pain of seeing my father was barely opened when the fear and pain of my damaged stomach took over. And both these fears were overwhelming me when the fear and pain of losing my job and my world of friends wedged the first two fears deeper. During that time, I didn't have the chance to close the fear or right-size the pain. Instead, I was stuck — ripped open to a penetrating anxiety I'd never known.

Harshly and in unison, the three fears captivated all my attention. All at once, I was drowning in a fear of the past, a fear of the present, and a fear of the future. I had run out of tenses. And to my surprise, the only thing left to stand on was the touchstone of being that exists beneath everything. I recognized it as the ground I stood on when facing death during my struggle with cancer. That foundation was still there, though I hadn't been so rawly forced to it in all the years between. If I looked out in any direction, there was the turbulence of my fear and pain. So I stood where I was, letting life infuse me from this touchstone of being. There was nowhere else to go. And so, life began to show itself, yet again, renewing me, infusing my soul with inches of light, as long as I stood where I was.

It was a time where, on the surface, all the tools had failed. And under that was the chance to rely on no tools at all but on the substance of my personhood, trusting it would eventually meet the wind like a wing.

Seeds to Water

> ❧ In your journal, assess to what degree fear runs your life. Is it a punitive god you avoid? Is it a guide you always listen

to? Try to describe its proper role in your life.

🙿 In your journal, describe something you feared that turned out to be strengthening and helpful. What did you learn from this experience?

🙿 In conversation with a friend or loved one, discuss the times you feel afraid and the times you feel safe, describing the conditions that surround your fear and your safety.

THE THREE DREAMS

Dreams give us a glimpse of our lives from the view of Eternity. Imagine you're driving along a crowded highway and, for the moment, you're able to lift out of your body and glimpse yourself, your car, and the highway from above, as if from a plane. In this way, dreams give us an aerial snapshot of our lives. As for what these glimpses mean, it was Carl Jung who said, "Only the dreamer knows the dream." So while we can enlist help from others, no one can tell us what our dreams mean. We can only tease out our own sense of truth in them.

After seeing my father, being gripped by my stomach ailment, and losing my job, I had three dreams on successive nights in the midst of all my fear. In the first, I'm going through an old warehouse that has burned to the ground. It's where all my artistic tools have been stored: charcoal, pencils, brushes, chisels, notebooks, my used piano, and uncarved stone. I'm happy to find them spared by the fire, surprised they are still intact. I'm eager to clean them up and devote myself to them again, to immerse myself in the space they point to. As I'm holding a brush, my former wife Ann appears and wants me to bring her out again, too, to bring her along. I tell her, "I'm sorry for all that's happened between us, but I can't. That time has passed." It saddens me to hurt her, but I'm certain that this part of my past will keep me from where I need to go. I'm stunned to dream of someone I dismissed, while in the pain of being dismissed myself. Am I being asked to see that, beyond the particulars, we all take turns leaving and being left? How am I to hold all this?

The next night's dream was so vivid it seemed not a dream at all. Friends and colleagues are surprising me with a going-away party, a ceremony to acknowledge all our years of work together. It's slow and touching, filled with soft moments with each of them. I tell them how much they mean to me. There's time at the end to read some of my poems, and we discuss them — not as things I've written, but as totems found along the way that we must decipher together. After that, we all go swimming in a very warm pool. As I enter the water, I wake coldly to realize this is a dream. I sit in the dark, feeling how being dismissed without notice robbed us of this chance to say good-bye. In our fear of conflict, we often do more harm by not allowing the space for honest closure. Now I search for ways to close this part of my life, by myself.

And then, the most important dream. The one the fears and the other dreams had been leading to. I'm in a room at night. I can't tell if it's my bedroom as a boy or my office at the job I lost. I'm sitting on a bed going through an old notebook of mine that has young, handwritten poems. I'm going over the marked pages to see if I missed anything worthwhile, even though the pages are checked off. I'm interrupted by the presence of a professional woman who enters the room. She looks like an attorney from an old episode of *Law & Order.* She starts complaining how hard it's going to be to stay in hiding, as if she's a noble spy. She complains how hard it's going to be to keep pleasing all the others. She seems to be talking to me. I try to answer her, when I realize she's talking to someone behind me. He looks like Tom Selleck, playing a detective pretending to be a CEO. He answers her and assures her they can pull this off.

They don't seem to see me. I wonder where I am.

For some reason, I realize I must remain still and not give myself away. Now the man and woman see me. And the man whispers to the woman that he'll take care of me and meet up with her tomorrow. She leaves and he points a gun at me that shoots needles. I know somehow that he wants to inject me with the cancer I had so many years ago. I grab his arm and as we struggle, he says, "Be quiet. Haven't I always been good to you?" I'm shocked. He thinks he knows me. Then I realize that he and the professional woman are old masks I've relied on. I hold him off and say, "Oh, you think this is then, but it is now. Now it's my turn." With each realization, I get stronger. Suddenly I hold him in place by the shoulders and say, "Don't worry, I'll be good to you." I won't let him go, and face-to-face, I inhale all his will. He stops resisting, and I somehow begin to reintegrate both the detective and the spy I have created. I bring them back home, into my heart, where they flutter as insecurities but no longer act on my behalf in the world. I inhale them back to their beginning. Then I wake breathing deeply.

Have I been burned up by crisis these long months so the fire can eat my past, my present, and my future? Is this all to quiet the noble detective who's been guarding my soul, leaving him nothing to detect? All to bring the hidden me who wants to please others out into the open? Am I being torn from all the schemes I've laid and inlaid, no matter how beautifully put in place, to be a simple and unadorned voice?

I resisted my father, who hurt me, and though it took years, I found a way to love him. And loving beyond the hurt has let me grow to my full stature. Then I surrendered to the unexpected stomach pain that gripped me just below my breastbone and all at once it made me softer. Now I've been broken of my diligence and loyalty to a community of work that forgot who I am. This difficult time is returning me to a truth I knew all along, that the covenant is work for the sake of work, and beauty for the sake of beauty, and kindness for the sake of kindness.

I know I will keep wrestling with my diligent detective and my noble spy, to keep them in the open. I know I will keep struggling to be more present when I'm poked by pain and anxiety. I know I have fallen on the other side of this trance, awake now with a new face and a new heart full of understandings. I know I am softer and truer and fuller, though at times I'm still afraid.

Sometimes what we carry is devoured by the storm to free our hearts. Sometimes what we hold too tightly is broken from our grip to free our hands. Sometimes we're broken of the words we know so well, that we might learn a more immediate language.

When faced with the appearance of the Infinite at the bottom of our fear, there is nothing to be done other than to accept its grace. There can be no preparation, only a readiness the likes of an orchid awaiting light or rain. But scouring our patina of mind is quite another issue. In this, the human will can find a purpose worthy of its effort, more demanding than any external ambition and more rewarding than any crown of recognition.

Seeds to Water

    ❧ In your journal, describe your history of experiencing the strength of the Universe beyond your own. Where did you first experience this? How did you first connect with or benefit from strength beyond your own?

    ❧ In conversation with a friend or loved one, tell the story of a time when one dream you were working toward came apart, which in time revealed another. What did you learn from this difficult unfolding?

STRIVING JUST TO BE

My wife, Susan, is a potter. When she was first learning to center clay on the potter's wheel, it was very difficult. This is a threshold all potters have to cross. Centering clay looks fluid and easy, but you have to allow your center of gravity to move into your hands. The pace of your whole being has to align — through your hands — with the movement of the wet clay on the spinning wheel.

Like all beginning potters, Susan had to stay committed and repeat her attempts at centering, over and over. For weeks, the clay would fall over or spin off the wheel or simply collapse. Until Susan's sustained effort moved her beyond her willful attempts to manipulate the clay and control the wheel. Finally, when at one with the clay and the wheel, the clay seemed to center itself and rise into its form.

As a potter centers clay on the wheel, we

center our being in the midst of our striving and effort. The great potter and poet M. C. Richards wrote an entire book exploring this lesson, a classic called *Centering: In Pottery, Poetry, and the Person.* She shows how the act of centering makes all the outer tasks easier. She affirms that attention must be given to building a solid foundation, if we are to create anything that will endure: a vessel to drink from, an expression to help us live, or a substantial sense of self that will enable us to make our way in the world.

The challenge as we strive is not to attach our identity to what we're striving for, but to give our all with faith in how such complete giving of who we are — through what we do — will reveal our deeper nature. Just as a blossom can't be seen until its flower fully opens, our true identity forms out of our deeper nature, once we're exhausted of our plans.

As a young man, I was driven to pour everything into my art. My identity was completely tied to what I would create, and more, to how my work would be received or not. It was an agonizing time, for my self-worth hinged on whether what I created was seen and valued by others. I worked so hard to be liked and wanted so badly to be loved, only to have each attempt pruned back by the insensitivities of a world that wouldn't slow down. Once I could drop down below the pain of my loneliness, I came to accept my solitude. And in that solitude, I found Eternity — and everyone else. I came back out into the world, offering my love and simply bearing witness to what is. It was only when I could give my love freely that I felt loved, only when I let myself see the beauty in everyone without judgment that others approached me with a smile and an open hand.

This is a personal example of a paradox everyone encounters. We have to become until we can be. In time, all our striving finally dissolves so we can blossom right where we are, in the peace of our being. Just as a peony grows its roots and shoots until it blossoms where it is — simply, beautifully, and completely.

Over time and through life's journey, through cancer and two marriages and the death of my beloved grandmother, I found that I kept growing until my identity as a poet and an artist felt too small for the being and Spirit that were evolving in me. Now the identity I so longed for was containing me. It was confusing to have to break it open and walk out of it, so I could keep growing. Of course, I'm still a poet and an artist. But these innate callings no longer define my being. Rather, they are sacred forces that flow through me when I am most myself.

What we accomplish and create matters. But we're not defined by what we create. We're defined by how the engagement of our being shapes and creates us. When we can honor this mystical fact, then we will continue to grow, regardless of what happens to what we create. While what we do might be praised or criticized, our worth continues to form within, independent of how what we do is received. While I put my heart and soul into this book, I am not this book. Our aim is not to strive at all cost or to be at all cost. Being human, our journey is to strive in order to be.

Seeds to Water

🐦 In your journal, describe something you've worked very hard at that in time has become fluid and easy. What happened that moved you from striving to being?

🐦 In conversation with a friend or loved one, tell the story of a time when you over-identified with a dream you were working toward. Discuss something you're working toward right now and how your worth is tied to this work. How might you stay committed to this work while not attaching your self-worth to it?

WANTING TO GO BACK

> You may have expected that enlighten-
> ment would come like *zap!* Instantaneous
> and permanent. This is unlikely. After the
> first "aha," it can be thought of as the thin-
> ning of a layer of clouds.
>
> — Ram Dass

Every pilgrim on a journey feels the exhilaration and glow of being liberated. Then, as
the work of the new world becomes real and
trying, there arises a want to go back to
where we lived before awakening. Because
in the challenge of growing, we can feel,
"Oh, God, this is too hard. I just want to go
back to before I was aware."

Even when we give ourselves completely
to life's journey, there's always a dweller on
the threshold, trying to distract us from
what matters, just as we arrive. Like those
among the Jews who, after leaving Egypt
and experiencing freedom, went to Moses

to say, "We really hate the desert. What do you say we go back? Sure, we were slaves but it was clean and we were fed. It wasn't so bad, was it?" There is always someone among us or some aspect of ourselves that wants things to return to how they were.

This undertow of consciousness is understandable and inevitable. Life always seems to progress by the expansion of revelation and the contraction of hard work. We feel refreshed and then enervated. Being diagnosed with cancer a second time, I awoke after my rib surgery to a kind, gruff nurse who said, "Get out of bed. It's time to walk down the hall." Immediately, I felt excited to walk again and overwhelmed that it would be now. My healing showed itself quickly as two steps forward and one step back: two days of getting stronger and one day of feeling weak. I think it's the same spiritually. We can't just follow the glide-line of a hawk. We're in a body that's bound to the Earth. We're wedded to gravity. We're climbing hills and stepping through valleys. Every day has its release and bind. Every revelation opens us to a new form of work.

As we awaken more deeply into the pilgrimage of the heart, there are always new things to lift and new things to build. It's not just "Oh, we're awake! Isn't everything wonderful?" The path of wakefulness is rugged and slippery every step of the way. And there's always a part of us just waiting to turn back. When feeling weak or in a weighty place, it's easy to think, "OK, so I wasn't awake and maybe I struggled with some form of addiction. Maybe I was in an abusive relationship. Maybe I was in a job where I wasn't valued and I was humiliated. Or maybe I never valued myself. But today it seems like that was easier, even though I know I shouldn't go back."

Addicts know this voice of return well. After years of life unraveling, after hitting bottom and beginning again, all it takes is a gray, stormy day in which life seems to be hiding. It might be while waiting in the rain for the crosswalk to flash its green command to go. And we see someone in the window of a corner bar laughing and it seems that the secret joy of things is on the other side of that window.

Sad lovers know this voice of return too. In the ordinary days of living with a loved one, long after the intoxication of falling in love has faded, a small voice of longing might whisper, "I need to find that spark again." Suddenly, there's an ever-present choice: to move more honestly into the relationship we're in or to feed a secret fantasy, imbuing strangers with a far-off glow we believe we can't live without. But here, the want to return is disguised as a yearning for what we think will be new.

Since there will always be voices calling us back, a central part of the work of awakening is the need to stand firm in our new-found wakefulness. The beauty and challenge of staying close to what matters resides in the truth that once we're awake, we can't un-know what we know. The gift and work of wakefulness is to believe that life is always where we are, no matter what it holds.

Living where we are requires that we bring a tender heart to the brutalities of life. Part of our spiritual work is to sustain the gift of our sensitivity, and to exercise the faith that our sensitivity will reveal itself as the source of our strength. As we negotiate the real work of staying awake, we need to be vigilant with the pilgrim in us who wants to move forward and kind with the fearful one in us who wants to go back. For all I've learned, for all my wakefulness and sensitivity, for all the turns in my journey, there's always a small voice in me ready to say, "Let's go back. It's easier to hide."

I feel this want to turn back because I'm human, even though I'm certain that inhabiting a former self is not really an option. It's just familiar. The only way is forward, a step at a time, becoming ever more sensitive and resilient. Our enlivened sensitivity is our true enduring strength, by which we keep meeting and appreciating the world.

Once out of our particular bondage, self-made or otherwise, the long pilgrimage of spiritual work demands a commitment to wander into a life of authenticity and truth. Once awake, the journey of our promise is always near and challenging. At the same time, the journey of our bondage is still near and disheartening. This is our crooked path to enlightenment: two steps forward, one step back; two days of being heartened, one day of being disheartened. This is the dynamic of being alive. This is what we work with and for.

Seeds to Water

&. In your journal, describe a time in your life that you've outgrown and your temporary longing to live there again. How do you make sense of this conversation in yourself?

&. In conversation with a friend or loved one, describe a period of healing in

99

which you experienced alternating epi-
sodes of being heartened and disheartened, stretches of feeling strong, then
weak. How did you understand these
rhythms of healing? What guidance
would you offer others in the midst of
such healing?

CREATING SAFETY

A friend betrayed me and was complicit in my losing a job. I thought our friendship was deeper than it was. Her betrayal confused me. Had I misread our closeness? It shook my confidence in recognizing friendship. We've had no contact since. She hasn't reached out at all, and it's too painful for me to make contact, nor do I want to. I feel that she's forfeited the right to be close.

When I'm hurt I do two things. First, I immediately remove myself from danger. The second effort, though more subtle, is just as important and involves how I understand the hurt. Where I place the hurt within my map of experience, whether conscious of it or not, will darken or lighten my worldview, and weaken or strengthen my ability to meet new experience. Though I may re-establish safety fairly quickly, understanding the hurt and where to place it may take some time.

I had a dream about my friend the other night. I woke and wrote this: *I'm afraid I'll run into you while shopping for butter. You broke my heart. You convinced yourself it was necessary. I have nothing to say to you, but here I am, writing to you anyway. It took a long time to pick out the pieces of glass from the broken story that's become of us. That I'm still afraid, that I'm writing this, means I missed one. I can feel it cut when I think of you. Last night, we met in a dream at a conference. You came over as if nothing happened. I took you aside and pulled my chest open. You were horrified but you didn't cry. You never cry. It's not that you had to move on, but that you didn't honor the continent we crossed and the times I lifted you when you fell. It's being erased that hurts the most. I'm trying to remove the one imbedded piece of you before it starts growing in the back of my heart.*

Upon waking, it's clear that I still love her, though the dream confirms a more accurate truth about our relationship. While justice is the flooding of light into dark places in the world, healing is the flooding of light into dark places in the heart. Throughout history, far worse violations than my broken friendship have required those disfigured with loss to heal and move on with no acknowledgment from their violators. So just as there will be debris from storms, there will be scars, visible and not, that fall to each of us. We're left with the confusion and pain of making sense of our hurt and those who hurt us, with or without their admission or amends.

I was at a party recently where the conversation meandered to friendship and equity and the setting of boundaries. I heard someone admit to not being there for a friend. I thought his admission brave. Then he complained that his friend was too sensitive. He admitted he'd made a mistake but bemoaned that it was time to move on. I asked if he'd said all this to his friend. He said it was impossible. His friend was too emotional. Going to sleep that night, I thought *my* friend could be having the same conversation about me at a party a thousand miles away. That was the night I dreamt of her.

After trying on everyone's position, I have to say that those who cause grief don't get to say when the grieving is over. Those who cause hurt don't get to say what's too emotional. Those who place intelligence over kindness don't get to be held when suddenly lonely. And those who break their word have to live with a broken tongue. As those who deceive have to live with double

103

vision. Yes, those who take when no one is looking can never trust that the things they hold dear are where they left them. This is the fate of those in between: not whole or free.

I know this because I've lied and been lied to and have in turn lied to myself. I've done the betraying and been betrayed and have in turn left the hurt place inside of me for dead. But I'm here to say that while accepting my failings has humbled and clarified me, it has not hardened my heart. It *is* possible to own our mistakes and still be kind. Standing firm means being honest about who we are, mistakes and all, *without* retreating from the world.

It's hard to see someone you love, someone you've been there for, turn indifferent and cruel. Hard to know what to do with this. Difficult not to drown in our versions of what happened. Challenging to hold all things as true. Yes, my old friend betrayed me. Does it make her completely evil? No. Is she suddenly bankrupt of all the gentle wisdom that made me so admire her when we met? No. Do I need to demonize her to justify my hurt? No. Do I need to accept that she is not trustworthy? Yes. Do I need to assess if we gave to each other equally? Yes. Do I need to accept that our friendship wasn't essential to her? Yes. And what to do with all this? Where to put the tension of these knowings?

Last week, I saw a pitcher plant for the first time, a tropical masterpiece you could just curl up in forever. But in its soft and beautiful bell are digestive juices that will leave only bones. What is nature telling us? While the Oneness of the Universe is to be trusted, it seems we need to discern which parts of the Universe to trust along the way. The practice of seeing things as they are is more complicated than any of the sages have said.

And though I fear this friendship has ended, it's clear that to love is not as simple as stay or go. I only know that when I stop bypassing things and enter them, the truth — like a vaccine — builds my immunity. This seems to be the lesson that waits inside the messenger. We're challenged not to run from the hurt and not to succumb to it. But to keep our heart open and take in just enough of the hurt and betrayal so we can build an immunity to the infections of experience when they come our way.

Seeds to Water

❧ In your journal, explore whether you think the world is inherently a safe or dangerous place. Based on your position, how would you advise a child to enter and meet the world?

❧ In conversation with a friend or loved one, describe a relationship in which you were hurt. Tell the two stories this relationship contains. First, tell the story of how you were hurt and how you responded. Then, tell the longer, slower story of what you did with that hurt and what it has taught you.

Taking Off the Armor

Love takes off the masks that we fear we cannot live without and know we cannot live within. I use the word *love* here not merely in a personal sense but as a state of being, or a state of grace — not in the infantile American sense of being made happy but in the tough and universal sense of quest and daring and growth.

— James Baldwin

We all have to protect ourselves but the question is how. We all construct walls that we believe are castles, though they slowly turn into prisons, because we can't wall out pain and sorrow and loss.

I protect myself from the intensity of life by retreating into the inner dimension. There I wait in the world of being for the storm to disperse. In this way, my castle has clear walls. We often take our walls with us and think we're free, even though we're clunking around in a suit of armor that makes life burdensome. Armor, no matter how thin or clear, keeps the air from touching the skin. It keeps aliveness from touching the heart. Withdrawal and accommodation, turning away and aiming to please, become plates of armor that can prevent us from living our lives.

For years, I told myself that withdrawing was staying calm and balanced, while accommodating was meeting others with no preferences. But there's a crucial difference between acquiescing to the demands of others and cooperating with life. Moving through my fears doesn't mean I have to absorb or placate the demands of others. Facing my pain doesn't mean I have to withdraw from what comes my way. On the contrary, I need to open the ancient door of my own making and let life kiss me on the forehead.

Ironically, our reflex to keep out what we fear is often too late. When we realize we're afraid, the fear is already inside us. Mysteriously, feelings move more quickly than the mind's want to stop them. By the time we try to wall out these feelings, the pain is already poking at us. The worry is already breaking down our clarity. The anger is already stirring up our bottom. And the sadness is already staining our heart.

Putting up walls only walls in what's ready to pass through us, if we would only let it out. The truth is, the only way out is through. When we resist what's already moved inside us, we intensify all the difficult feelings by trapping what we resist in our tension.

The only way we can mitigate these feelings is to let the experience of being human move on through. For the most part, walls are useless. It's meeting the sensations of being alive that cleanses us and shapes us, the way fast currents scour the bottom of a river, making the river stronger.

We need to be porous, so that other life can reach us and fill us. This means we have to learn to neither shut ourselves down nor give ourselves away. Whether we live behind walls of our own making or put down our armor depends on how we close and open. We close when we're hurt or afraid. And open when pain goes away or we're held and loved back into life. Closing and opening are both necessary, like inhaling and exhaling. Day by day, we're called to stay open to the life of feeling, while not letting pain, fear, and worry shut down our heart. When we stop opening our soul to the world, we become burdened.

When closing makes us insular, we tighten and miss the depth in everything. We start to become wall-builders. When fearful, we harden and impose our fear on everything we meet. We start to hammer our armor into place. This is the cost of closing without opening. But when we can open into what feels real and true, especially after great fear or pain, our heart widens like an inlet and we ready ourselves for grace, however it might appear. These rhythms of closing and opening are constant. And staying in relationship to both is a constant struggle in which we're asked to trust our own experience, while listening to the truth of others.

One day last fall I was working at my desk, deeply immersed and yet aware that I was staying there too long, slipping behind another kind of wall that praises life while removing me from it. Our sweet Lab, Mira, was wagging her tail and pushing a toy in my lap. My wife, Susan, had just come home. I could hear her unpacking some groceries. I thought, *It's time to put down what I'm learning and live it.* Always, learn and live. Susan was chopping onions and jazz was drifting upstairs. I'm grateful for those moments in which life pulls me out of my chair. This is why we love.

Seeds to Water

❧ In your journal, tell the story of a wall you built and why. If it has come down, describe what led to its fall. If it's still standing, describe your life behind it and what it would take for you to take it down.

❧ In conversation with a friend or loved one, describe which you are better at: closing or opening. How does each serve you? How would you like to better the way you close and open?

FINDING SOLID GROUND

John's father had built their home when John was a boy. It was perched on the side of a mountain overlooking the sea and John wanted to stay there as long as possible. But over the years, the ocean had worn away the shore and compromised the integrity of the foundation. No amount of repair could hide the fact that John would have to live elsewhere. He faced a heartbreaking but essential turning point in his life. He had to find more solid ground.

In the geography of a life, there are times when what once was solid starts to shift, because life as we know it has evolved and changed in some deep way that no longer supports us. There are times when the integrity of our foundation is compromised and we have to find new footing.

A shift of foundation can appear in many ways: the banks of a river can crumble as the river gets stronger, the shore of a marriage can be carved out by the tide of time, the trunk of self-identity can be wormed of its strength, and our secret ambition can open like a dandelion that in time will drop its petals and turn to mulch. It doesn't mean that the banks of the river, or the shore of the marriage, or the ground of identity, or the goal we worked toward, was faulty or false. Each simply evolved, as rivers and mountains and dunes change over time.

During this last year, I had to accept that the ground of a long-term friendship was no longer solid. Like John who didn't want to leave his father's house, I kept trying repair after repair, not wanting to accept that the integrity of our foundation had been compromised. Too many storms and not enough trust. It was heartbreaking, but I had to find more solid ground. The house of our friendship was magnificent when she and I had built it. I still remember the view. But we're constantly asked to stay current with what is solid and authentic, to stay close to what will sustain us and help us live. Listening for when relationships and dreams begin to shift — for when they're no longer foundational — requires an honesty that can take years to understand and accept.

Developing such a personal skill is two-fold. When the ground under us shifts, we need to recognize that a change has happened. We need to act on this truth first, before focusing on the need to know what went wrong. Both are worthy inquiries, but removing ourselves from what is no longer life-giving is immediate and imperative. There will be time enough to enter the slower, introspective work of understanding why and how this shift in ground occurred.

We must stop the flooding before designing a better dam. We must set the broken bone before finding a regimen that will strengthen our arm. Facing that where you are is no longer safe or enlivening is crucial to making it through today, while understanding how things changed is crucial to making it through tomorrow.

It's the same with the journey of our soul, our love, our relationships and dreams. We're challenged to accept the truth that something significant has changed in our lives and make our way to safety. From the new safe place, it's possible to learn from these changes and to integrate their lessons. The honesty to look at our foundations and to accept what we find, and the courage to find solid ground and build anew — these are braveries that help us stay real.

Recently, I ran into my former friend in the grocery store. It was bound to happen. She was coming out of the juice aisle and we paused, surprised to see each other. It was awkward and I felt a rush of alarm — what to say, what to do? We said hello, no more, and briefly, I sensed a moment of love between us with no way to touch, as if seeing each other from the windows of two apartment buildings. I could also tell that while she missed me, she hadn't changed. Though my heart went out to her and back, there was no footing between us. And so, I stood on the solid ground I had found and continued with my life.

Seeds to Water

❧ In your journal, describe a situation you knew was unhealthy, but which you stayed in because you were focused on figuring out what went wrong before making a change. How did this approach serve you? What would you do differently, if you could?

❧ In conversation with a friend or loved one, describe something dear you had to let go of — a home, a friendship, a way of thinking or being — because it had ceased to be life-giving. How did you become aware of the change? How did you accept the truth of the situation? How did you let this dear thing go?

The Path Is Wider Than We Think

While visiting a wildlife refuge south of Charleston, South Carolina, I was walking with friends through a protected swamp. In the water, off the path, was an enormous alligator, its primordial eye coldly watching us. It was clear by the cold stare of the alligator that it had no knowledge that it should stay off the path. The safety of the path was an illusion.

That moment has stayed with me. It's a reminder that life is real, that we're part of everything we go through and everything we watch. It's all one dynamic, living world. We're always in it and touched by it. Because we watch — from the car, from the couch, from the front row, from the last row, from the perch of our beliefs, from the wall of our fears — we grow entranced by the illusion that life is some colorful entertainment that we are outside of. But nothing is off-limits. Life is closer than we think. The path is not separate from the swamp. This is only dangerous when we're not aware of it. And so, we need to always remember that life is real and touchable, that *we* are touchable. We're never outside of life, but always in it.

We work very hard sometimes to convince ourselves that we're safe from the unpredictable nature of things. But we're always reachable and shapable. It's why we're here. Love makes us enter life and stop watching. Then the conversation with life truly begins.

In her profound book *Heart* Gail Godwin tells us that the medieval Sufi philosopher Ibn al-Arabi thought of a loving heart as a heart of wax, because caring makes the heart pliable and receptive. Just as wax can be imprinted with a seal, our softened heart is capable of taking whatever shape life imprints on it.

This makes great sense to me, as I can feel the many imprints within me. We think we choose what we love but love chooses us and shapes us. And no amount of hiding or distraction can keep us from being touched by the wild and vital territory that lies between our birth and our death.

Seeds to Water

❧ In your journal, describe a time when you realized that there was nothing between you and life. How did you become aware of this? How did this sudden experience of unpredictable reality affect you? How has this experience changed your view of life?

What Talent Do I Have?

Now in her seventies, Ruth remembers being a girl, the daughter of a sharecropper in South Carolina, one of ten kids. They lived in an old wooden cabin. One day in spring, her fourth-grade teacher said there would be a talent show. Ruth went home troubled, thinking, *What talent do I have?*

She couldn't sleep that night and paced the back porch before the field. It was then the clouds parted and the moon, almost full, filled her face and turned the boards in the porch blue. Her little mouth dropped and she knew she was part of something larger. When asked the next day, she said her talent was seeing the moon.

Ruth hadn't thought of this in decades but now she told me about it. I could see the moonlight in her eyes. We both fell silent. Later that night, I stepped out onto the porch where I was staying and looked to the sky, vast and accepting as it was almost seventy years ago.

We often miss the gift of being that leads us to ourselves. We forget that knowing we are part of something larger *is* a talent all by itself. We're so focused on our talents of doing that we often ignore our talents of being.

There's nothing wrong with doing or being. They're innate capacities we need to be intimate with. While we may be naturally inclined toward doing or being, we need to work hard at both so the two can complete each other and bring us more deeply into life. Grace reveals itself in those moments when doing and being are one: when the effort to inhale meets the air ready to fill our lungs, when the effort to care meets the love waiting like air to fill our hearts, when we put aside our personal history in order to hold someone in pain so completely we're not sure whose pain it is. We can't plan or will these moments of grace. But we can practice by bringing our ultimate concern to any given moment.

Under all the pressure to create, build, repair, and achieve, there are tendencies we're born with, the way a fish is born to swim and a tree is born to grow toward light. As human beings, we're taught to imagine a purpose, or goal, and to dream and work toward making it come true. But nature works the other way. The purpose of a fish is to swim and the purpose of a flower is to bloom. It doesn't really matter where the fish swims or how big the flower's blossom.

We are part of nature too, and so, our quest for purpose begins with knowing our natural gifts. Then our life's work becomes the inevitable journey of becoming what we already are. The Islamic philosopher and pioneering physician Avicenna believed that the immortality of the soul is a consequence of its nature, not a purpose we set out to fulfill.

My dear friends George and Pam are getting to know their newborn granddaughter, Evie, and every first seems a small miracle. At three and a half months, Evie has begun to reach for things and bring them close. This is one purpose of the soul: to reach and bring things close. As Evie grows, what she reaches for and what she brings close will change, but this lifelong gesture is a talent of being, as important as Ruth's talent in knowing she is part of something larger.

Often in our pain and confusion, we ask, "Where is God?" I would offer that God is alive and well in the bareness of being that lives beneath all that doesn't matter. And our talents of being lead us there. Our ability to know that we're part of something larger and our capacity to reach and bring things close help us feel how everything is connected. I've discovered that God is in the glow and muscle of every connection. Perhaps this is at the heart of every teaching: that nothing compares to the sensation of being alive in the company of another. That being completely who we are while in the company of other life is noble work that connects us to God.

When Ruth reaches for the moon, when Evie reaches for her rattle, when I reach for the silence under all that confuses me, when you reach beyond your pride for the person you can't live without, when any of us reach for what seems real in the center of the storm, we're reaching for God.

Under all the good we do, under all the things we build, we're asked to treat everyone we meet as a seed that needs the water of our love to open. To have any chance of knowing joy, we must love everything in the way. Simple and hard as this seems, pouring our love on all we meet is another talent of being that brings us alive.

Pouring our love on each other lets us grow our talents of being, which in turn help us find our place. Einstein said, "If you judge a fish by its ability to climb a tree, it will live its whole life believing it's stupid." While we can force ourselves to become something we're not, it never ends well. But our talents of being never leave us. Finding them depends on our belief that teachers are everywhere and that what we love brings us closer to who we truly are.

This brings us to the effort to learn, which is the mind's way of reaching and bringing things close. I confess and celebrate that the only thing I've done longer than teach is to learn. Early on, it became clear that teaching is learning with others by living into the questions that experience opens.

In my second year of teaching high school, I began to ask questions that had no answers. Opening questions like windows, I saw how my students began to perk up. We could wander in these open questions together. To my surprise, we began to grow together. Ever since, I've been devoted to asking over telling, and to learning from one rather than teaching many. When we enter life as a question to be lived rather than a problem to be solved, we can find our way in the world.

In my journey, I've been worn like a stone shaped by an unending river — from young poet to young teacher, to my tumble through cancer, to my life as a listener and a witness of the mystery that lives below all names.

The seed of truth that waits in our un-knowing continues to be my teacher. It speaks profoundly about the deepest kind of learning and reminds me that life is a journey from no to yes. The classroom appears wherever we dare to imagine life as a transformative question that we somehow awaken into together.

Asking over telling, listening to the one thing before you, and learning *how to* rather than teaching *how not to* — these are essential ways of reaching and bringing things close that will return us to our talents of being.

So if you find yourself wondering, *What talent do I have?,* feel your lungs breathing and feel your heart loving. Try to remember that we're each born knowing how to breathe, but it is we who have to do the breathing. No one can breathe for us. And we're each born knowing how to love, but it is we who have to do the loving. No one can love for us. We all know: if you stop breathing, you will die. It's equally true: if you stop loving, you will not be alive.

Our ability to know that we're part of something larger, our capacity to reach and bring things close, and our heart's yearning to pour love on everything we meet — these are talents of being that serve the soul and the world.

Seeds to Water

🍃 In your journal, explore this question: If you were alone on a clear night, what would you say to the moon? On a clear night, go out and be still under the stars until you feel the company of the Universe. Then go ahead and say it.

🍃 In conversation with a friend or loved one, explore this question: If your life is a flag, what wind are you here to make visible and what is your flagpole?

I Awake

I discovered the poetry of the medieval Zen Buddhist monk Dōgen by following voices through time. I was reading a heartfelt poem by Ryōkan, an eighteenth-century poet, in which he recounts discovering a six hundred-year-old manuscript, written in the hand of Dōgen, the founder of the Sōtō school of Zen in Japan. Ryōkan admits to being so moved that his tears fell on the worn page. Ashamed that he'd marred the manuscript, he put it back where he found it and told the others it was caught in the rain.

Before this, I hadn't heard of Dōgen, but Ryōkan's poem compelled me to "meet" him. Likewise, it was hearing the Miles Davis version of John Lewis's song "Django" that moved me to want to "meet" Django Reinhardt and his music.

Like Miles Davis, Django Reinhardt was an astounding innovator. He redefined jazz guitar in the 1930s with complex, fiery solos that were unprecedented. Born in 1910 in France, Jean Reinhardt, whose gypsy name Django means *I awake,* lived in a caravan. By the time he was five, his father had abandoned the family. Django spent most of his youth in gypsy encampments close to Paris, playing the violin by ear. He became fascinated with the banjo and by twelve was a precocious professional. By fourteen, he was a star. But at the age of eighteen, he was maimed and almost killed in a caravan fire. His left leg and hand were horribly burned. The third and fourth fingers of his left hand had to be burned again with silver nitrate, so they could heal and be usable. The burns on his leg were so bad that doctors wanted to amputate it. Reinhardt refused the surgery. He left the hospital a short time later and within a year was able to walk with the aid of a cane.

During a painful rehabilitation, he found it almost impossible to play the banjo. His brother Joseph bought him a guitar. Forced to try different things in order to go on, Django relearned his craft in a completely new way. He played all his guitar solos with only two fingers, forming new chords. As Reinhardt biographer Michael Dregni says:

Instead of playing scales and arpeggios horizontally across the fretboard, as was the norm, he searched out fingerings that ran vertically up and down the frets, as they were easier to play with just two fingers. He created new chord forms. . . . He pushed his paralyzed fingers to grip the guitar as well. . . . Employing these chord forms, he began to craft [an unprecedented and] fluent vocabulary [on the guitar].

Would Django Reinhardt have discovered a new way to play jazz guitar, if he hadn't been transformed in that fire? Would Claude Monet have discovered his masterful *Water Lilies,* if his vision hadn't been undone by the onset of cataracts? Would Beethoven have discovered the Ninth Symphony, if his deafness hadn't opened him to the deepest music of all, blossoming out of silence? Perhaps all this would have happened anyway, in a different manner, at a different pace.

The point is not to deify the events that break us down or open. But to lift up the mysterious fact that what we think we want, what we think we strive for, is often not the goal at all — just what we hold on to in order to discover what is truly calling us.

Often, when we think we're building one thing, we're building another, or we're the ones being built. When we think we're giving one thing, we're often giving another, or we're the ones being given to. When we think we're enduring one thing, we're often being undone by life into the birth of a gift we've been carrying for just this opening. The point is, we're challenged to follow our heart beyond our intentions in order to find our quiet destiny, the way a tulip or peony follows its urge to break ground, hardly imagining its life in blossom.

Seeds to Water

❧ In your journal, describe a time when you thought you were giving one thing but discovered you were giving another or were, in fact, the one being given something.

❧ In conversation with a friend or loved one, tell the story of someone you admire who made more out of less, the way Django Reinhardt made more music with limited use of his fingers. How do you understand this sort of resilience? Where does it live in you?

DRAWN TO WHAT WE NEED TO LEARN

One should accept the truth from whatever source it proceeds.

— Maimonides

As bees are drawn to nectar, as animals are compelled to their migrations, as plants are drawn to grow toward any inch of light, we are drawn to what we need to learn.

Nor is it by accident that authors and artists are drawn to the subject matter they need in order to grow. Over the years, I've written about awakening, risk, courage, listening, and now I'm exploring effort and grace. I do so because I'm sorely in need of being awake and staying awake, in need of knowing how to take more genuine risks, and in need of more courage.

Having almost died from cancer, having landed back in life, having been humbled to accept my fragility as a simple being in an infinite world of simple beings, I confess that I'm investigating the risks of being here simply because my experience has led me to believe that entering this life fully and deeply is the surest way to feel the presence of all that is eternal. And I want that. I pray for that. I work toward it. I need that presence to keep coming.

More than thirteen years ago, Susan and I brought a yellow Lab puppy into our life. And as I tried to inquire into what it means to be here, our dog would tug at me like a wordless sage, demanding that I stop writing and *just be*! No accident that her name was Mira and that, within weeks of naming her, we learned that *mira* in Spanish means "to look." Almost daily, she would knock the pen from my hand, dog-asking me *to look,* coaxing me to get on the floor and hold her and stare into her animal eyes, which would say everything and nothing in the most innocent of ways.

Though our dear Mira is gone, her fresh dogness reminds me of Rumi when he urges us to

Weep and then, smile.
Don't pretend
to know something
you haven't experienced.

Like you, I'm on a journey to deepen my own experience. With each day, I try to lean into what I'm drawn to in order to keep learning, to keep growing. Along the way, I wonder about your story and the stories of others. For we're all on the same journey, richly different yet beautifully the same. The way birds go through the same process to fly, though no two birds ever wing the same path.

Seeds to Water

   🐦 I invite you to explore in your journal one person, place, or activity you were drawn to in the last year and what lesson it held for you.

REGRET

Everything that slows us down and forces
patience, everything that sets us back into
the slow cycles of nature, is a help.
— May Sarton

We all struggle with regret and making
amends. It can be hard to climb out of the
canyon of lament at how our lives have
unfolded, and to discern what can and can't
be done as we move forward. The word
regret comes from the Old French word *re-
greter,* "one who bewails the dead," and this
goes further back to the German root meaning, "to greet." We always face these two
phases of regret: to bewail what is dead and
gone, and, if we can move through that
grief, to greet the chance to do things differently as we move on.

I regret the years my father and I wasted
while we were estranged. I regret having
fallen backward on my dear dog's right paw

when she was five, which broke a bone under a tendon. I can still hear her yelp. I regret that fifteen hundred copies of my second book, my epic poem *Fire Without Witness,* were destroyed without my knowledge. I can hear the characters trying to run off the pages as they burned.

I've learned that regret is like striking a large bell in an empty field and then running through the wild grass trying to gather the sound of the strike back into the bell. It's impossible. All that's possible is to strike the bell again, to have the new sound layer itself over the old. The grip of the first phase of regret is that the pain of grief can make us think if we only did this or that, our pain of loss might be somewhat lessened. In our grief, we can become fixated on wanting to undo what can't be undone, when the precious urge born of grief, in time, is the want to do something new differently.

I've also found that making amends can help loosen the weight of the past. Making amends means that I finally remade my bond with my father when he was ninety. And that I loved my dog even more, that I told her I was sorry as I rubbed her lame foot and kissed her head, that I was patient with her slow, arthritic gait when she was older, because I had contributed to it. And making peace with the burning of my books means that I had to move beyond the injustice to the deeper conversation I was being asked to have with impermanence.

When tangled in regret, we can fall into a storm of urgency, as if our future depends on whether we can unravel some knot in our past. And the grip of regret keeps us from the immediacy of life around us. All the while, we continue to suffer through our fears: that we're not good enough, that we'll never find love, that we won't be able to face our suffering or endure the loss of those we love. All the while, our heart only needs the open air and the life-force waiting in the next moment to revive itself.

Think of the pipes that bring water to your home. When segments of a pipe are aligned, the water flows freely. If any part of the pipe is askew, the flow is interrupted. Likewise, when our thought, heart, speech, and actions are aligned, the resources of the Universe flow through us easily. This alignment, which some call integrity and others call authenticity, is necessary to access the resources of everything larger than us. When feeling bereft and out of touch, check your pipes. The storms of pain and grief and the ice that comes from hiding will knock us out of alignment. Inner alignment is the unending practice of staying in clear, flowing relationship with the Whole.

Still, on any given day, the attempt to undo what can't be undone and our preoccupation with the knots of our past can plague us with a dark thirst that can't be quenched. When packed to the brim with memories, wounds, worries, dreams, opinions, and schemes, we become limited in what we can hear or receive. With no room in our cup of being, less and less can touch us. So if you have trouble hearing or taking things in, give of yourself — anywhere and everywhere. Sometimes, the only remedy is to empty ourselves and begin again.

This is the work of love: to give, to empty, and to make room for life. Why? So we can listen to all that is abundant, to all that is needed, to all that is not us. Our small fate is to be a constant carrier of abundance to wherever we find need. The more we are emptied of our personal echoes, the more we can be present to what is alive before us.

When I regret something now, I try to let the sound of my heart play itself out like the strike of the bell in that field. I try to be with the emptiness I'm left with. Until my pain over the friendship that failed miserably twenty years ago makes me want to be a better friend to the person I just met.

Until the cup I broke that my wife, Susan, made, that couldn't be put back together, has me hold everything I pick up as if it were a baby bird. Until the love I've spilled throughout my life has me pour what's in my heart slowly on whatever I meet that needs watering.

Seeds to Water

❧ In your journal, describe in detail one thing you regret having done or not done. How much space is this regret taking up in your heart? How might you begin to stop lamenting your loss and do things differently as you move on?

❧ In conversation with a friend or loved one, tell the story of someone you love with whom your feelings are entangled. Separate what feelings are yours and what feelings are theirs; make a list. Let a week go by and revisit the list. Describe your entangled love for this person and your love for yourself if you were not entangled.

BURNING THE MAP

Expectation is premeditated disappoint-
ment.

— Sogyal Rinpoche

Everyone's life journey eventually arrives at
a precipice or fork in the road. At some
point we will come to the end of a path and
no longer know our way. Hard as this is,
this is where the inner journey begins, when
all we've carried has served its purpose and
now we must burn our expectations to light
our way. This is when we assume our full
stature in order to see what's ahead. This is
when the soul shows itself, if we listen.

My group and I were discussing this when
I asked them to describe a time when their
hard work led to an unexpected outcome
and what that experience taught them.
Mark told us that, from an early age, he had
an uncanny ability to hit the center of a
target with a gun. His father was an avid

139

hunter and competitive marksman. Delighted to discover his son's gift of accuracy, he steered him and trained him to excel at target shooting. Mark was a prodigy. His young life revolved around marksman competitions and the lift of his father's approval. For more than ten years, Mark set records in competitions. His father was pleased and had him train harder. Mark was even invited to join the Olympic team.

When twenty-eight, Mark was at a competition, waiting his turn. He was videotaping the others, when a missed shot ricocheted into his right wrist, his trigger hand. As Mark was telling this, he began to well up. I was surprised by what he shared next.

Mark said that the injury prevented him from competing anymore. And while his father was devastated and everyone felt the whole thing a tragedy, he secretly felt relieved to be free of his father's dream. He felt liberated to have an unknown path freshly before him, and grateful that he could walk away from his life of shooting without having to disappoint his father. Quite unexpectedly, beyond all his years of work to find the center of the target, it was an errant shot that let him fly like a tiny bird through the hole in the target into the rest of his life.

Patty spoke next. An executive working in a man's world, she had earned a black belt in karate and became obsessed with the art of breaking boards. Once breaking two boards, she immediately began training to break three. She kept training harder and harder, out of a fear of failing. She felt a momentary satisfaction in breaking the boards, but her fear of failing made her keep going. Finally, she reached the board that couldn't be broken, no matter how she tried. In fact, that final board broke her hand.

The pain of the final board also broke her trance of ignoring limits. It was as if she were running in a tunnel and couldn't stop, though it wasn't clear what she was running from or running to. She'd come to know she was alive by the sound of her steps in the tunnel, but the pain of the final board shattered the tunnel. She realized that, while she needed to inhabit her strength to be treated fairly in an unfair world, she'd become a prisoner of her own strength training. Like Mark, all her effort had led her, unexpectedly, to an unknown path that was the rest of her life.

Effort itself is a blessing, but when effort races ahead of our love for what we're doing it becomes destructive. Each of us is called by others to work our way to the center of the target. Each of us is challenged by circumstance to break the next board. But sometimes it's the gift of limitations that returns us to the pace of what we love. It's the gift of limitations that frees us to find our own dream. It's the pain of the final board that breaks the trance of protecting ourselves from life with the armor of accomplishment.

There's nothing wrong with mastering any skill or accomplishing any task, as long as that mastery or accomplishment is born of our love, as long as we can remember it is *we* who are being created and shaped by our immense effort. What we often perceive as failure is an unexpected opening in our lives. Nothing is wasted. Sometimes the map we work so hard to chart and follow needs to be burned in order for us to live our own life.

Seeds to Water

&❧ In your journal, describe an inheritance of values or goals that no longer works for you. Describe your history with this inheritance: how it came to you, how it worked for you, and when it stopped being relevant. Describe how you're find-

ing your way beyond what others dreamt
for you.

• In conversation with a friend or loved
one, describe an expectation you had for
yourself that didn't come true. What
happened when you reached the end of
your expectation? What did you discover
at the end of your pre-imagined path?
How do you hold this unfolding?

THE JOURNEY BEFORE YOU

It was a summer day. Bees were sticking their heads in flowers. Birds were bringing worms back to their nests. And the master was walking another apprentice through the garden. The young man was confused, "You tell us to work hard, and you also tell us that what matters just happens." The master said, "Yes, both are true." The young man felt toyed with, "Why should we work hard if it doesn't matter?"

As the apprentice kept talking, the master led him into a flowerbed of bee balm, zinnia, and salvia. The apprentice was lost in his want to have an answer, "I don't know when to try and when to let go." The master put a finger to his lips, urging the young man to be quiet and watch. A hummingbird hovered, its wings moving so fast they didn't seem to be moving at all. It was hovering above the bee balm, drawing nectar into its thin bill.

The master whispered, "Look at the effort it takes to hover there. What a teacher. Just like this, we have to work so hard to ready ourselves for a drop of grace." The young man fell silent and they both watched the hummingbird sucking nectar while working so hard to stay aloft. And yet, its motions appeared effortless. After a time, the master said, "You see, effort and grace are two sides of the same moment, and this is not to be feared."

Each of us struggles to learn when to give our all and when to surrender and simply receive. But often, we're asked to try like the hummingbird until we're in a place to receive. Often, it's our effort that leads us to a drop of grace.

From an early age, we're taught to try hard and do our best, which is necessary to accomplish things in the world. We try to get from here to there, from inexperience to experience, from apprenticeship to mastery. But just as we're clearing a path, we experience heartbreak and loss. Things don't go as planned. We are betrayed. Our trust is broken. We lose our way. And without warning, we're thrust into a life of transformation, which no one can escape. Now we're introduced to a different sense of effort that asks us to put down what we accumulate in order to discover beauty and wonder. As our inner life unfolds, we grow from ignorance to truth and from loneliness to love. This kind of work is necessary to join with the world.

We clearly need both to accomplish things and to join with other life. While trying so hard to get from here to there leads to achievement and even excellence, giving our all lets us grow like a root and blossom in the world wherever we are. Ultimately, the effort to grow inwardly is more life-giving than the effort to get. How we grow inwardly leads in time to meaning and grace, a journey we can't control, but only enter.

To make the most of being here, we're required to learn when to try and when to let go. This is our initiation into grace. The practice of being human centers on our effort to connect to all life and, when in trouble, to make good use of our heart. No one quite knows how to do this, but we must learn how. Our life depends on this journey through the heart. There is no other way. By fully living the one life we're given, we're led to the wisdom that waits in our heart.

Like the hummingbird that works so hard to receive a drop of nectar, I'm learning how to be and to be of use. I'm learning from birds that to be is to have wings but to be useful is to fly. I'm learning from fish that to be is to have gills but to be useful is to keep swimming with our mouths open. I'm learning that it's necessary to open the wings of our heart in order to be fully here, but to be useful we have to love, which is how humans fly. And no matter how much we learn, none of it will prevent us from the precarious and tender experience of being human.

In ancient times, seekers consulted oracles in order to translate the winds and whispers of the gods into wise counsel. They deciphered the Universal into the personal. For us today, our soul translates the larger, timeless truths — the mysterious winds and whispers of life — into what's integral and personal. Reaching the edge and depth of our experience is the province of effort. How the soul translates what we discover in our experience is the province of grace. The journey before each of us is to know our own soul and to become our own oracle.

As a master carver whittles aged and weathered wood into a sturdy tool, effort and grace shape us in time into a beautifully wrought instrument ready for use. In truth, our first step toward understanding grace is to summon the fortitude and openness *not* to resist being turned into an instrument by life.

Seeds to Water

❦ In your journal, describe an experience of effort that moved you from ignorance to truth or from loneliness to love.

THE ONE LIFE WE'RE GIVEN

No matter where we think we're going, the journey of every life is to find its home in the moment where everything touches everything else.

When we can feel what is ours to feel, and inhabit our own particular moment — of love or suffering, of beauty or pain, of peace or agitation — that depth of feeling allows us to live once for all time. To live once for all time means that the depth of our one life, once opened, is filled with the stream of life from every direction. To live once for all time means that try as we do to *add* to the one life we're given in our attempt to run from death, the incarnation of being human forces us to *open* the one life we're given, so we might be immersed in the well of all life for the brief time we're here. One life lived wholeheartedly and without disguise is more than enough. Nothing could be more precious or out of our control.

Though we can try.

As a jazz musician spends years learning the intricacies of his instrument, never knowing when the goddess of music will sweep his practiced hands along, we master many paths, never knowing when we will be swept into the presence of beauty. As a shortstop fields thousands of grounders until his hands are blistered, all to be ready for the unpredictable bounce that will happen under the lights, we meditate, study, and field thousands of questions until our mind is blistered, all to be ready for the unpredictable bounce of circumstance that will bring us closer to life. In just this way, the heart learns the scales of love, never knowing when the work will be turned into song.

This journey to inhabit the one life we're given is archetypal. Everyone who's ever lived has had to go through it, though no two souls ever go through it exactly the same way. Yet we all experience common passages. As we start out, we're preoccupied with finding our way, with discovering who we are, with defining ourselves by contrast with everything around us. We try to set ourselves apart by creating something out of nothing, by out-reaching or out-racing others. But sooner or later, obstacles throw us off course, and the first versions of our life plans, always dear and precious, are broken. Then we're sent into a passage of not-knowing, unsure where to go and what to do. Less certain, we're challenged to inquire into a larger view of life that includes us but is not defined by us.

At this point, we're ready to discover who we are a second time. With nowhere to go but here, with nothing to do but open the one life we're given, a journey begins in which we experience life rather than dreaming that we can escape it. We start to invest who we are and all our care into where we are and slowly become one with everything we encounter. By now, there's been enough suffering that we can feel our kinship with others, and the depth of our care is closer to the surface.

In time, the heart works its way into the presence of grace by showing up completely, no matter the circumstance. We learn that meeting life with an open heart is how we can feel where everything is joined. Our call, then, is to let the soul out and the world in. Where soul and world touch, we spark alive. When our soul expresses itself in the world, our aliveness shows, and we begin to do our part in sustaining a Universe that keeps unfolding.

When the soul expresses itself, we experience enlivened arcs of grace in which we feel the force of life that runs through everything. Anything that moves us to carry our soul out into the world is a catalyst of grace. In this way, love, friendship, creativity, pain, and loss are agents of grace, as are surprise, beauty, grief, and wonder. And while experience wears us down to what's essential so the soul can stop being encased, it also takes daily effort to let our soul out and an open heart to let the world in, so we can spark ourselves alive and finally be of use. Like it or not, we're opened by the hard, sweet journey of being human, until we're sparked and worn into a gateway for life-force.

Seeds to Water

&. In your journal, describe a time when you defined yourself by contrast with everything around you. How did you set yourself apart? At the time, how did defining yourself this way help you? How did setting yourself apart from others hurt you?

&. In conversation with a friend or loved one, describe a time when you were asked to discover who you are a second time. What have you learned about your own nature? How is this second self different from the first version of yourself? Do you feel that you're arriving at a foundational sense of who you are? If so, what does the foundation of you look like?

■ ■ ■ ■

Loving What
You Do

■ ■ ■ ■

Will you ever bring a better gift for the
world than the breathing respect that you
carry wherever you go right now?
                              — William Stafford

Sometimes we seek refuge from our pain in the habits of life, as if sheer routine can put our wounds to sleep. But the habits of life can make us all a little squirrelly, and soon enough, we don't want our little nest messed with. We don't want anything unexpected or different to disrupt the little box we live in. We don't want anything to unearth the pains we've buried. And just about the time we're most inflexible, some great wave of love or suffering crashes over our little box, opening us to the unalterable fact that all the little boxes we construct are tiresome illusions. There is only one home, only one sea in which we all swim. That home is the common, eternal heart we are all a part of. I've always found more comfort and strength in that common sea than in all the habits I surround myself with.

Surviving the Great Wave of love or suffering is how we begin to make our way. Once tossed about by life, we seek out those who speak the language of the Great Wave. Then we greet each other with offerings of truth and compassion: Was the Great Wave kind or harsh? What did it break down or open in you? What did it give you or take away? What have you chosen to rebuild with? Who did you reach out to? Who showed up? Who ran away? Who keeps muffling the questions? Who wants to know what you see?

The chapters in this section explore in more detail what it means to make our way and to love what we do. We begin to engage the world by committing to a life of questions and swimming through our pain and sorrow until we make a career of awakening. In time, we may become skilled at the art of being sensitive, which can help us move past insecurity. Making our way means having faith in the authority of being that informs our soul. This leads us back to solid ground. Though we're blind and sighted by turns, though we stumble through the trance of our fears and the intoxication of our dreams, we remain touchable and capable of love. Ultimately, making our way means staying very close to life, until we begin to feel intimate with all things.

And bringing love to what we do, no matter what is before us, is an act of courage that can right-size our pain and sorrow and worry. Loving what we do may or may not bring us success, but it will reanimate our kinship with everything living, and this will restore us.

Bring Up the Lights

A troubled widower made his way to ask a wise old woman about his troubles. The old woman received him and they walked along a stream. She could see the pain in his face. He began to tremble as he asked, "What's the point? Is there any meaning to life?" She invited him to sit on a large stone near the stream. She took a long branch and swirled it in the water, then replied, "It all depends on what it means to you to be alive." In his sorrow, the man dropped his shoulders and the old woman gave him the branch. "Go on," she said, "touch the branch to the water."

As he poked the branch in the running stream, there was something comforting about feeling the movement of the water in his hand through the branch. She touched his hand and said, "You see, that you can feel the water without putting your hand in the water, this is what meaning feels like."

The man grew tender but still seemed puzzled. She said, "Close your eyes and feel your wife now gone. That you can feel her in your heart without being able to touch her, this is how meaning saves us."

The widower began to cry. The old woman put her arm around him, "No one knows how to live or how to die. We only know how to love and how to lose, and how to pick up branches of meaning along the way."

Every book and form of art, every keepsake and treasure we pass from generation to generation, every story told — these are the branches of meaning that help us along the way. And though we develop over time, there is no logical progression of steps by which our lives grow. Instead, each life unfolds the way rainwater fills the contours and grooves of the ground it lands on. No two patches of earth are identical and so the rain must fit each particular stretch of soil: trickling, pooling, and settling, as it will. In the same way, meaning fills the particulars of each life.

Let me tell you how I try to make sense of my own experience. Two things I'm sure of are that we gather meaning through relationship, and that we understand life by working with what we're given. I've never imagined my books as outlines to be filled.

Once complete, not one of my books has ever been the book I started. Like everyone else, as I move through the days, I'm stopped by wonder and pain, and by worry and surprise. With each stopping, I listen for the story, the insight, the question, or metaphor that is my next teacher. As I travel to be in learning circles, I find that speaking to the honest questions I'm asked causes thoughts and associations to surface that I didn't know I knew. So I record them in order to listen to them and work with them later. After months, I have pages and pages of fragments, rough-cut gems that I have to work with to understand their meaning.

Then I take the questions that won't leave me alone and turn them into possible chapters. Next I reflect on all the fragments that have risen from conversation and circumstance along the way. And based on what I hear from each, I place them like shards or beads into the chapter files. Months later, I dump all the shards and beads from each chapter like rough pieces of mosaic before me. Then I hold them and put them together like chipped stones or riddles I have to decipher. In this way, the light on a tree in Vancouver three years ago and a quote from a little-known painter I discovered last month rub against the breathing of my father in his last days. And in the crucible of a patience that's always hard to sustain, the meaning imbedded in each heart-instance starts to reveal itself. This is when my work as a poet truly begins: in weaving the things that I could have lost over time into the fabric of what matters. I'm always humbled to retrieve insights and patterns much greater and more useful than my small mind could have imagined. As the conversation of a lifetime keeps unfolding, I uncover meaning.

Regardless of what you do for a living, the only important vocation is listening to the heart when it says: this is vital, this is alive, this can't be lost. For me, the vitality and aliveness always precede my understanding of them. Making sense of our experience demands a faith in knowing what matters before we understand what it means. Making sense of what we gather demands a conversation with what we've found and with what has found us.

As the wise old woman says in the story above, "No one knows how to live or how to die. We only know how to love and how to lose, and how to pick up branches of meaning along the way."

In a dream I had eight years ago, I was waiting to be introduced for a poetry reading in an auditorium before a large crowd. I was going over the first poem I was to read, seeing its lines in my head as the lights went down. Then I was introduced. But instead of standing behind a podium, I walked onto a stage that was arranged like my study at home. In one corner, there was a dusty stone, ready to be sculpted. Nearby, my wood-block boards were spread on a table, my carving tools askew amid small shavings. Upstage was a piano with a jazz songbook on it. And in the middle, a worn desk with my open journal surrounded by my favorite books.

With everyone watching, I began to chip at the dusty stone and stopped to jot down a feeling too big to ignore. At this point, all sense of performance had vanished. I'd forgotten the lines I'd rehearsed. As I grew more involved in what was calling me, I was just doing what I do: entering, listening, and staying in conversation with life. It was then that I looked out into the audience. I realized instead of going out into public, I was letting others into the sacred creative space and being transparent about sharing that space, which suddenly seemed more important than sharing whatever I might create there.

After a while, someone asked a question

and without stopping my work, I said, "I don't know." I asked the house manager to bring up the lights, so we could see each other. Then someone else asked a question and I invited them up to get closer to what I was doing. Several people came onstage, at which point the stage was no longer a stage. The focus was no longer on me working but on the sacred thing moving between us all — which no one can see.

In just this way, I hope at some point this book stops being a book and becomes a branch of meaning. Let's bring up the lights, so we can see each other, and enter this together.

Seeds to Water

❦ In your journal, describe three moments of heart that over time have had meaning for you. Look at them together and listen for the insight or lesson that they open together the way three notes might form a chord.

THE STORY BEHIND THE STORY

Like musicians who wait in silence for the music to come out of the forest of their hearts, we wait on each other's stories.

There's always a story behind the story. There's always a thread to pull that will unravel what matters between us, always an opening to look through that will change everything. But the nature of daily living distracts us. So to find the story behind each story we need to search for the larger truth behind our pieces of truth. There the wisdom of connection waits, beneath our immediate circumstances. When we care enough to pull the heart's thread, we uncover the one common story we all come from.

What we see of others is just a snapshot, without any history or depth. Everything and everyone bears looking into. When I was in graduate school, we were influenced by a theory called New Criticism, whereby any piece of writing was treated as a self-contained expression, separate from the life and thoughts and story of the person who created it. This rigorous approach was meant to ensure that the work would stand on its own. While this way of thinking helped us hone our craft, it also truncated our understanding of the human condition.

Since then, life has taught me that nothing is self-contained and that the ways we struggle with love and suffering can reveal a more complete understanding of a person. Finding the story behind the story opens our humility and compassion, which is more important than any well-crafted piece of writing.

In researching my book *Finding Inner Courage,* I came across a powerful quote from the German philosopher Friedrich Nietzsche, which reads, "I want to learn more and more to see as beautiful what is necessary . . . then I shall be one of those who makes things beautiful." I was deeply moved by this and also puzzled, as it seems counter to the steel-edged Nietzsche I'd been taught in college. I suddenly realized that while I'd read Nietzsche, I really knew nothing about his life or his story. I discovered that in 1889, at the age of forty-four, he suffered a breakdown of sorts that softened his insistence on will and opened his compassion.

Around the same time, I found a quote from the Renaissance poet Petrarch, which said, "It is more important to want to do good than to know the truth." This seemed much deeper than the sonnets I'd read. In searching for more about the life of the poet, I was surprised to discover that in 1336, at the age of thirty-two, Petrarch set out with his brother to climb to the top of Mont Ventoux in the Provence region of southern France, a trek of over a mile (6,263 feet). Because of this, Petrarch is considered one of the fathers of mountain climbing in the West. I believe it was the perspective of climbing with his brother that opened him to the power of goodness over truth.

Meeting the more human Nietzsche and more vital Petrarch changed how I look for meaning. I've become a student of this beautiful, entwining truth: no matter how particular our pain or joy, our unfailing closeness to what matters reveals a kinship we're all born with. The particulars of our lives can be unique, and yet when faithfully listening for what we have in common, we all dip our faces in the same luminous pool of grace. It seems the purpose of story is to lead us back to what matters and to show us how everything is connected as part of something larger. The stories of our individual lives keep showing us how we all go together and come together, once we put down our stubbornness.

Come with me now to the Lascaux Caves, near the village of Montignac in southwestern France. This underground labyrinth contains nearly two thousand cave paintings, thought to be over seventeen thousand years old. There, along the inner walls, is a softly etched painting of two small deer, one carrying the other on his back. We can only imagine the story behind this drawing. In prehistoric times, during such harsh terms of survival, among a people we've sketched as underdeveloped, someone was sensitive enough and imaginative enough to merge his or her survival with that of the deer. What a tender symbol of the centuries to come and, no doubt, of the centuries that had passed: one carrying the other. This is a symbol of life on Earth, the truth we come to underneath all the different stories: no living thing can make it alone.

The survival of this small cave painting is miracle enough. Its depiction of how we need each other is even more remarkable. Even seventeen thousand years ago, we were looking for ways to carry each other, looking for ways to participate in a lineage of resilience. This is why we tell stories.

But all these years later, we seem cut off from the larger perspective of time, history, and Eternity. Every event seems to be old news ten minutes after it happens. We live in an era where our attention is so scattered that we just skim events, bouncing from one to the next. But storytelling has always been a deeper, more connective art, preserving the story of life that's at the heart of all news. The most important stories show how we're connected. The most useful stories show how these connections work. News bears witness to circumstance, while the story that lives beneath that circumstance always has a context and a meaning. And the heart of every story takes time to surface.

Now come with me to the suburbs of Boston where a painter is struggling to be true to her vision, though her work is unrecognized in the world. Like many artists, she's suffered rejection and indifference, and has wondered deeply whether to continue. She quits painting for a time, but when her mother dies, she begins again because it comforts her. Whatever the subject, she says she now paints out of love, because it keeps her sane. It keeps her in wonder. Slowly, she gives her work away. Unexpectedly, one of her paintings, of two deer warming themselves in the sun, is bought by a hospital. There a blind woman stands before it every day. A month later, the hospital administrator wants to buy another painting.

So the little-known artist who paints out of love brings a canvas of a moonlit stream to the hospital. After they hang the new painting, the artist wants to visit her two deer. As she turns the corner, she finds the blind woman standing before it. The blind woman senses someone nearby and touches the woman's hand, "Are you the painter? Every time I pass by this spot, I feel a wash of sun. I love what it feels like to stand in front of your deer. It makes me feel warm. My nurse told me they were deer. They must be beautiful."

As she drove home, the artist's fear of being hidden began to fade.

We all long to be accepted. And we all struggle with being invisible, while working to stay close to what matters. The great sculptor Auguste Rodin was shaped by his unwavering commitment to stay close to what matters and to find the story behind the story. In 1891, Rodin was commissioned by the Society of Men of Letters in Paris to create his now legendary sculpture of the French novelist Honoré de Balzac.

Rodin immediately immersed himself in understanding who Balzac was; he researched Balzac's character and personality and read all his books. He traveled repeatedly to the author's hometown, and sketched and fashioned clay studies. He even had clothes resembling those of Balzac made by the late writer's tailor.

Rodin worked far beyond the eighteen-month deadline the Society had set. The Society grew impatient, but the sculptor felt compelled to make more than fifty studies. In 1898, after seven years, Rodin proudly presented a plaster model of Balzac, larger than life, to the Society, which rejected it because it was not a physical likeness of the novelist. They completely missed the sculptor's gift, as gallery owners of the same era rejected the early Impressionists because their trees didn't look like trees. Rodin felt misunderstood despite his fame and moved his model of Balzac to his home in Meudon, France. His companion, his muse, his larger-than-life model of Balzac stood covered in his studio for years.

Across the Atlantic, the young American photographer Edward Steichen, all of nineteen, viewed a photo of the Balzac model in a Milwaukee newspaper and remarked, "It seemed the most wonderful thing I'd ever seen. It looked like a mountain come to life."

Steichen went to Paris in 1908 to meet Rodin. They struck up a friendship and Rodin, then sixty-eight, took Steichen to his home. Quietly, the sculptor pulled the cover off his Balzac and asked the young man to photograph it in the moonlight. And so, Balzac was wheeled out into the blue light of the moon and Rodin watched in silence as Steichen framed the statue awakening before them.

Balzac was never cast during Rodin's life. But on July 2, 1939, twenty-two years after the sculptor's death, a bronze cast was placed on the boulevard du Montparnasse at the intersection of boulevard Raspail in Paris. Looking into Balzac's bold stare, you can see Rodin's unwavering certainty of his own vision. The statue is masterful, but it was the search for Balzac that shaped Rodin himself into the fullness of his gift.

We're all compelled to live our stories and tell our stories in our own way. It's how we keep making sense of life. And though being seen and heard happens one person at a time, we are more than any one story we tell. In Hindu the word *sat-sang* means "holy talk." The story behind the story is holy talk. The story we carry under all our situations opens the space of intimacy and truth in which we can compare notes on what it means to be alive. The place we enter through our stories makes us friends on the journey. We can only fully know our own story if we dare to listen to all stories.

So listen to your life, the way you would listen to a sage too humble to call himself a sage. Look for the story behind all you've been through, the way you would search for the calming silence in the middle of a forest. Stories carry what keeps us alive the way veins carry blood.

The story behind the story reveals a common holy moment, when something within us is moved so deeply by all that is around us that we try to touch it and speak to it. We try to capture what will help us live, the way an anonymous, prehistoric man or woman painted two small deer, one carrying the other through all Eternity.

Seeds to Water

🌰 In your journal, describe a situation in which you were seen out of context. What caused this limited understanding? What is the larger story that led to this situation? How are you dealing with being mis-seen and misunderstood?

&❧ In conversation with a friend or loved one, describe a person or a situation in which you sense there is a story behind the story. Discuss how you might pull the thread and uncover the larger truth waiting there.

WHAT IT MEANS TO BE AWAKE

During the summer, I was staying in a lodge near the foot of the Rocky Mountains. Every morning I'd stroll along the path behind the lodge, watching the tufts of grass stretch to meet the dew. The sun hitting the wet grass seemed an illumination. In that crisp early light, I was reminded that everything in life has an inner quality that emanates from its center. That emanation of life-force coming out of everything is Spirit. And the sensation of that life-force moving out of us into the world is the sensation of being fully alive.

The sun gives flowers light, but what makes them grow to the light comes from within. In the same way, aspects of nature stir us until the life-force within us moves into the world. When we blossom this way — when we come alive and open — we are awakening. As the sun spilled over the face of the mountain, I realized that just as gravity will always pull things to the Earth's center, the life-force of the Universe will always emanate from its center into the world.

Two weeks later, I was in New York City, marveling at the stream of humanity rushing everywhere. I was near Bryant Park, standing on the corner of Forty-third and Sixth, in the swell of hundreds whose moods flashed up and down the outcrop we call a street. I stopped as I had on the mountain path behind the lodge. I closed my eyes, feeling how fragile and magnificent we are. And in that crisp early light, I was reminded of something else I've known forever: that being thoroughly human, we can't remain in a permanent state of awakening.

We emanate a light from within, though the mud of the world covers it while we're breaking trail, getting groceries, getting stuck in traffic, misunderstanding each other, and living with pain. Yet just as light will make its way through a canopy of trees, the light we carry within will break through whatever we put in its way.

I found a small table in Bryant Park and watched the maples and elms stretch and bend toward the light, as they have for decades. I felt beautifully alone in the midst of so many, at a perfect intersection of nature and all our yearning. Sitting there, I realized that awakening is the result of any process that lets Spirit emanate out of our being into the world. That process can be a willful commitment to learning and growing and listening and loving; or it can be a process we don't look for that breaks us open, wears us down, or jars us into seeing.

Across the walkway, a reggae-man and a Hasidic Jew were playing Ping-Pong, and next to me a young Asian woman was reading a Chinese newspaper. Suddenly, a patch of light flooded the Ping-Pong table and spilled across the story she was reading. The ever-present light was coming through. And I was grateful that, regardless of the task or practice we involve ourselves in, we're blessed with these moments in which love softens us and suffering wears us down until our light comes through.

I moved my chair to be directly in the sun. I couldn't help but smile at the diversity of life around me and at the diverse ways we can awaken. It could be love that awakens me. I can be so moved by your beauty — your life-force emanating from you — that my spirit is stirred and drawn out of me — through my heart, through my mind, through my eyes, through my body, ever toward you — and I tremble to be so alive.

It could be suffering that awakens me. I can be broken open by pain or grief so that the life-force we call Spirit can find its way through the walls I've constructed to guard it. Either way, one purpose of consciousness is to gain access to the light of life in the muddy times that we don't feel lighted.

I walked around the block and stood near one of the stone lions that guard the New York Public Library. I stared directly into its resolve and thought, *So many lives, and each a world unto itself. So many personalities, and each with a particular psychology.* But under it all, each of us is a living container that carries the emanating force of life.

Along the way, the pain of living can make us identify with the container — our body, our circumstance, our way in the world — and not the life-force that moves through us. When our body is broken, we only know ourselves as broken. When our circumstance is torn, we only know ourselves as torn. When our way in the world feels uncertain, we only know ourselves as uncertain and confused. But our enduring identity resides in our kinship with the life-force or Spirit that moves through us, and not in what is done to the container.

It's been months since I was walking in

the foothills of the Rockies, months since I was sitting in Bryant Park. Now, as I write this, I'm sitting by the Pacific Ocean, watching the lazy surf curl into itself. And in this crisp early light, I'm reminded that though my container can change, the Spirit it carries rises like these waves from the life-force that entered me when I was born and that will leave me when I die. Tending my true identity is more than mending the cracks in my outer container, more than what you think of me. It's more than how others see me — as a poet or teacher or husband or son. Tending my true identity is staying in relationship with the force that gives me life.

How we relate to what keeps us vital determines whether we're battered by life or whether we move through life's difficulties. We're more than skin and bones, though there's no escaping the sensitivity of being contained in skin and bones. Though we experience what is done to us deeply, we're not defined by what is done to us.

I listen to the waves as they crest and swell, as they've done for millennia. Everything alive is drawn to the sea, as everything alive is drawn to be awake. As individual beings, we're portions of Spirit born in bodies in time, tumbling through this messy and tender journey of being human. And awakening — surfacing the Spirit that gives us life — allows us to discover Heaven here on Earth.

I just walked a mile along the shore because I felt compelled to sit on the rocks at the turn of this coast. Their steadfastness makes for a beautiful spray. Our steadfastness makes the forces we meet glisten like the spray on these rocks. Though I confess I'm not always steadfast. There are days I struggle to find the aliveness I cherish so deeply. But right now, sitting on these ancient rocks facing the sea, I'm opening and closing this miracle I call my hand, knowing I'm not just the muscles that make my arm lift, but the life-force that inspires my arm to reach. This urge to reach is an intrinsic form of awakening, in which the Spirit we're born with is fulfilling its purpose by emanating into the world.

If you look at anything long enough, you will sense life-force emanating from it. If you stand still long enough, your heart will open and you will feel life-force rising within you. You are ever awakening. We are ever awakening.

Seeds to Water

❧ In your journal, describe one thing in your life that, like the undergrowth in the forest, is blocking the light within you from shining forth. How has it grown in the way? What can you do to move it aside or prune it back?

❧ In conversation with a friend or loved one, tell the story of a person, place, or experience that has awakened you, and how you've been changed by that encounter.

Heart and Path

Any path is only a path, and there is no affront to oneself or to others, in dropping it if that is what your heart tells you. . . . Look at every path closely and deliberately. Try it as many times as you think is necessary, then ask yourself, and yourself alone, one question. . . . Does this path have a heart? If it does, the path is good; if it doesn't, it is of no use.

— Carlos Castaneda

In many ways, my life has been spent simply allowing my heart and soul to guide the process of my becoming. Becoming what? Well, let's just say, becoming more fully human.

— Henk Brandt

As all of life is encoded in the strands of DNA, all of life is reflected in the face of a clear heart. Our journey asks us to discover the relationship between our heart and path by extracting lessons from what we feel. Because feeling is the only way to know that we're truly here. We try to make further sense of everything by turning what we feel into ideas, conversations, and words. When confused or lost, we can only be restored by the original experience of our heart and what it says to us directly.

Though you may find a common language with others, the goal of uncovering the language of your heart is not to have everyone speak your language, but to help *you be you,* to be the small sun you are, so you can emanate in all directions. And though you may be heard by others, the purpose of uncovering the language of your heart is not to be heard, but to inhabit life and embody your aliveness.

Beneath all our noise and trouble, the secret of life is waiting to be discovered, the way a pearl grows in a shell at the bottom of the ocean long before the diver enters the water. In just this way, the things we're born to love are waiting to complete us. We sorely need to listen to life and follow our heart, to find the things that will complete us and to uncover the meaning carried in our feelings. This lifelong conversation between the heart and the rest of our gifts will bring us alive, though the path may appear differently to everyone.

To have our heart become the conductor of all our gifts is the inner work of everyone drawn to a wakeful life. As the humanitarian Jean Vanier said:

I began to discover that human maturity comes as we begin to bring our heads and hearts together.

As we begin to bring our mind and heart closer together, we begin to know our worth. As our heart becomes the conductor of our life, we enter the long journey of finding our place in a mysterious world.

How do we begin? By showing up and giving our all, which are the purest forms of effort. And while we think of grace as a sudden gift of understanding, a moment of epiphany or revelation, effort is often revelation in slow motion.

Consider the value of exercise. Though it's sometimes hard to exercise, I never regret it once I've done it. Because the embodiment makes use of all my parts and brings me alive. Effort and work bring our heart and mind and body together. Effort and work refresh and enliven us, regardless of what we accomplish.

There are two fundamental kinds of work. First, the work necessary to survive: to be fed and clothed, the work of inner and outer hygiene, the work of creating and sustaining some form of home. This is the work that keeps us well and safe. And though the work of surviving may be difficult, it's how we meet adversity.

The other kind of work is the engagement in life that lets us thrive. This is the creative, loving work of care that has us get up and dance when we imagine a dance. It has us climb a mountain because we've dreamt of the view. It prompts our kindness when we meet someone in need. It has us carry a puppy in our coat in a thunderstorm or sing for no reason other than the sudden light at the end of the day has lessened a darkness we carry inside.

The work that brings us joy isn't necessary to survive, but it's necessary if we're to fully come alive. The path we cut helps us survive, but the heart with which we walk that path enables us to thrive. This kind of work — when the heart and mind and body conspire to completely enter the world — is the effort that opens us to grace.

Life is full of distractions that estrange us from both heart and path. It doesn't help that, in our time, we've been technologized away from direct, first-hand living. This makes the heart seem distant. Today, "to know by heart" has been reduced to memorization. The original sense of knowing something by heart is to be touched by what we meet so completely that our compassion is awakened. When we memorize things, we live in our heads and tend to track life rather than enter it. To truly know something or someone by heart means we will, no doubt, be changed for the experience. Ultimately, as prepared as we try to be, the aim of life is to be surprised into a greater depth of connection and being. Ironically, to be touched by life, we often have to put down what we know in order to be refreshed and revitalized by what we don't know.

My dear friend Margo told me this story:

Last week I spent the afternoon here in Victoria wandering through these beautiful gardens, including a rose garden, which is part of a path of flowerbeds. I overheard a little girl say to her friend, as she stepped into the garden: "We're in a maze!" But I heard it as, "We're in amaze." And I started thinking about the attitude of wonder, which is available to us, but which we don't often choose.

Our call is to stay in Amaze!

At times, we may feel numb and enervated and the language of our heart may seem foreign to us. This happens to everyone. Losing our way and refinding our wonder is part of the journey. When feeling lost, which is inevitable, we can remember that the physics of the heart are timeless; that giving is tied to life-force; and that being kind revitalizes us while leading us back into our kinship with other life. Wonder is how the heart meets what can't been seen. The simplicity of direct living can return us to the path of our heart when we're tired and confused. And listening to life is the most intimate way to uncover the heart of things.

No matter where we are in life, we come to an edge at which we're asked to grow. It's the heart that leads us to that edge. I've stumbled at that edge my whole life, only to accept that there's no one way to grow, and no one shape to the path that keeps us alive. But I've learned that to strive is the work of apprenticeship. To trust is the work of mastery. And only a practiced heart can know the difference.

Seeds to Water

🦜 In your journal, describe a time when speaking from your heart let your inner beauty be seen in the world. What caused you to speak from your heart and what did this process feel like? Will you speak from your heart again?

🦜 In conversation with a friend or loved one, tell the story of a time when someone you love gave you well-intended advice that was steering you away from your true path. How did you process this advice and deal with this situation?

THE COVENANT OF LOVE

In the West, we're eager, even anxious, to choose names for babies before they're born. In other parts of the world, the naming process unfolds differently. The Yoruba people of southwest Nigeria wait for a child to arrive before considering a name. There's a need to meet the new being, to keep company with the child, before sensing the name the child carries. After the first three days of life, the infant is brought into a community circle, where the child's feet are held to the earth. The elders then *receive* the name the new life has revealed, fully expecting that in time this being will fulfill and transcend his or her received name.

This speaks to a way of knowing others. We're too quick to name or label people we meet without taking the time to experience the spirit they carry. And we seldom allow for those we know and love to transcend the name we've given them. Then, when they outgrow the silhouette we've put around them, we're surprised, and even see their change as betrayal.

The covenant of love is to *expect* that those we care for *will* grow and change and blossom. The covenant of commitment is to celebrate the soul transcending its given name and love what that soul reveals over time. Through the work of love, we can keep the spiritual commitment to support each other in finding our true name.

Some years ago, my oldest friend, Robert, was visiting, and we experienced a session of sand-tray work together. Sand-tray work is a form of expressive therapy in which you place seemingly random objects in the sand of a tray to create a landscape that might convey an image of your unconscious mind. After creating a symbolic landscape, it's possible to interpret what that landscape is revealing about where you are in your life.

Whenever I've created a sand tray, it's proven uncanny, full of intimate meaning. Robert and I created our landscapes opposite each other and, after reading the symbols tucked in the sand, we had the impulse to remove the objects one at a time in silence, until the only objects left were figurines that felt indispensable to who we are.

Robert's figurine was of a sage-like man with a bird on his head, and mine was of a horse running. Knowing each other so well, Robert smiled slowly and named me, "Horse Running." I laughed and named him, "Bird on Head." At the time, we weren't sure exactly what these new and deeper names meant, but they felt absolutely true.

Now, we're close to thirty years of friendship, and the spirit names we received that day have unfolded as attendant spirits for the direction of our souls. For in his essence, Robert is a quiet sage, so still at times a bird might land on his head and share its secrets of the sky. And I have always found what I know by running freshly, like a horse chasing light.

In modern times, we've drifted from the true purpose of naming, often labeling things to quiet our discomfort with uncertainty. But we don't name things to pin them down or to keep them in place or even to have them bleed their meaning. We name things to feel and be led by what can't be named.

Seeds to Water

🌿 Explore in your journal what you might name your true self, in the spirit of how Native Americans name themselves, by phrases glimpsed from the natural world. What phrase or two would you start with?

🌿 The Abenaki elder Joseph Bruchac says, "A friend is a person you tell your true name." In conversation with a friend or loved one, share this newfound name for your true self and tell one part of your story by which you have come to befriend and know your true self.

THE POWER OF HOLDING

A rheumatologist at a workshop at the Cleveland Clinic spoke of a twenty-one-year-old woman she was treating who was dying of cancer. The medical team caring for her was running out of treatment options, and the sight of this young woman withering was weighing on everyone.

On a sun-filled September day near the end, the young woman was curled in her bed in a fetal position, her family around her, the blinds closed, the room dark and silent. Entering the room, her doctor felt their despair. She could see her patient staring into all the years she wouldn't have. It was heartbreaking. Moved beyond all the standard protocols, her doctor felt compelled to climb in bed and hold her. This unexpected, quietly heroic offering broke death's hold, for a long moment, and brought everyone closer.

After a time, the young woman sat up and

asked for the blinds to be lifted. Light came flooding in, and her family began to speak and listen. They brought her juice. They all began to live again.

For all our skills, for all our training, and for all the miraculous advances in medicine, we caregivers are left, finally, with what we're born with, the capacity to hold. When leading with our heart, we can mitigate the pain and despair that the sharpness of life can render, if we softly dare to get as close as we can and simply hold.

Of course, this moment of grace and connection did not prevent the young woman from dying. But it powerfully affirms the power of holding. To hold another is the oldest form of heart-to-heart resuscitation. It can change how we live *before* we die. Holding someone in his or her pain or despair can allow the life-force to return. It can let light back into the room. And letting light back in, though it might not cure us or keep us from dying, is at the heart of all healing.

Seeds to Water

&❧ In conversation with a friend or loved one, describe a time when you were held

196

by another and how being held affected you.

❧ In your journal, describe someone you know who is struggling and how you might hold them in their pain.

Swimming Through Pain and Sorrow

> You will earn your bread with the sweat of your brow and your light with the sorrow of your eyes.
>
> — León Felipe

It was my second time speaking at the Phoenix World Burn Congress, a national gathering of over a thousand tender beings whose lives have been maimed and disfigured by fire. Entering this community of survivors was very raw and moving. I could feel their pain, their courage, their love — all mixing in the room.

Later, when guiding a discussion group, a man with no arms almost yelled, as if from a raft at sea, that life is still a blessing. And right next to him was a young woman who'd lost her face. She was sinking below life as we know it, right before my eyes. Both in the same moment. Regardless of whether they were looking into the light or the abyss, their presence made me honor each of them by holding their stories. I listened, then offered softly, "I don't know why we're given what we are. I only know that we're still here and that I'm more alive for knowing you."

This is true for everyone. One of us proclaims, despite our hardship, that life is a blessing, while someone nearby sinks before our eyes. Over a lifetime, we get to play each part, more than once. And the only honest thing to say is, "I don't know why. I only know that I'm more alive for knowing you."

The unspoken contract with joy is that to taste it, we have to swim through pain and sorrow. Though no one likes to have a broken heart, the bareness of being we find inside the heart gives us access to our gifts. When broken-hearted, I wonder if the seed packed in the ground feels the dark soil is a form of hell before it blossoms into a flower.

One of the noble bonds of love is how we lift each other from the limited vision that presses on us when we're shut down by pain. Being there for each other means that we take turns affirming that there's more than our pain, more than our despair. Even when swimming through pain and sorrow, we can bear witness to the depth of truth that shows itself through our pain and sorrow.

When my father was first in the hospital, he was in a wheelchair and I was holding his hand as he began to doze. He was startled awake by some kind of pain. Alarmed and helpless, I rubbed his head and called the nurse. As we waited, he felt the pain a second time. I told him I was there, though there was nothing I could do. The nurse came and tended to him. When she left, he dozed off again. As he slept, I remembered sitting with his mother, my grandmother, when she was in a wheelchair, almost twenty-five years earlier. Then I thought of my own tumble through cancer. I was in the same wheelchair, waiting in the hall, three days after my rib was removed, dozing and being startled awake as my missing rib poked me sharply. No one was there and I felt adrift and yet glad to still be able to feel. Just like my father and my grandmother.

Under everything we know, feeling it all is the most heroic fate of all. Why? Because like a worm that eats the soil to aerate the earth, the soul must eat experience, must have it move through its bowels in order to be cleansed and renewed, *and* to make spaces in this life so that Spirit has a place to enter, the way rain will reach further into the tiny worm holes, feeding the nearest root.

But feeling pain and sorrow has its danger, too. Cut too deeply with no way to process what we feel, our wounds can fester. If I'm hurt at a tender age, burned by accident, my first sense of relationship is to avoid being burned again. Emotional accidents take hold like this, and one painful experience early on can compel us to project our fear and pain onto other experiences without good reason. And so, the world of our wound can cause us to find all potential relationships untrustworthy and burning, doomed before they start. Of course, we're burned in many ways by living on Earth with imperfect others. The paradox is that the deeper the trauma, the greater our need to remember the world *outside* of our wound, in order to restore our sense of wonder.

Often, our wound determines our preoccupation. If suffocated, we long to be free. If abandoned, we want to find home. If abused, we don't want to be touched. If ignored, we want to be held. If wounded deeply enough, we tend to forget what we know to be true about everything other than our wound. The press of our trauma initiates an unhealthy kind of forgetting. Preoccupied with the soreness of our wound, we can forget our place in the Mystery. We can forget there *is* a Mystery. We can forget there is a larger Whole to drink from. None of this minimizes the legitimate pain of the wound.

When traumatized, our wound can become the entire world we wake in. We begin to think there's nothing beyond the world of our wound: the sky is wounded, the water we drink is wounded, the silence we can't bear is wounded. Once the all-encompassing wound takes over, we try to relieve the wound by reliving it, hoping it might turn out differently. This is how people return to those who have abused them, hoping against all logic that this time they will find kindness. All the while, we need a larger sort of remembering that reunites us with everything that is *not* our wound; so the larger Universe in all its mystery and splendor can heal us and restore our sense of safety and possibility.

My early wound was the anger of my mother. It moved like a sudden flame, burning everything she touched. For so long, my woundedness made me think the world was about to ignite. And so, for much of my life, my wonder has been rimmed by a guardedness. I've always felt wired to be on alert. As strong as my love of life has been, I've always had a lining of mistrust, as if a fire could erupt at any time. It's taken sixty years for me to right-size this guardedness. Trauma is a powerful influence, and the markings of woundedness stay with us.

I finally got below the trauma of my mother, who was simply an insecure young woman, not ready for a son. And while the early eruptions and unexpected flares instilled a certain fear in me as an infant, I kept this wound alive in me long after I left home. But now, I work with myself to put all that guardedness down. And since my father's death, my mother, at eighty-nine, has lost her anger in the swamps of dementia. She can't seem to find her anger and even forgets what she's looking for. She's softer now. And so am I.

This brings me to a law of emotional nature about what we want and what we need. When in pain, we want the company of those who understand what it is to be in pain. Yet in order to heal, we also need the health of everything around us that is not in pain. This is akin to how white blood cells rush to the site of a wound. Likewise, when in fear, we want the company of those who understand what it is to be in fear. *And* we need the safety of other life from beyond our fear to cure us of our fear. When broken, we understandably want the company of those who know what it is to be broken. *And* we need the foundation of everything not broken in the world to repair our brokenness. When experiencing grief, we sorely need the company of those who understand loss. *And* we need the kind outreach of those who are, for the moment, free of loss. We need both: heartfelt company and strength from beyond our pain to bring us back to health.

Regardless of what is fair or just in any situation, if we can't face our pain, we will nurture offenses and cultivate love through being a victim. No matter how skillfully we might do this, relationships will fall away till we are sadly left alone with the pain we won't face.

I've had three important friendships dissolve over the years because we couldn't relate beyond their wound. Each had an argument with life brought into sharp relief because of their woundedness. One felt life was unfair and he was trapped forever in comparing his misfortunes with the blessings of others. Another friend felt he was secretly unworthy, and to keep the secret, he made the whole world about him. His love always came with a price, two for one, so needy was his secret want to be loved. And the third friend was so frightened to face the anger she'd experienced as a child that she, like my mother, became angry with the world and everyone she'd meet.

Though I loved each of them dearly, it became impossible to stay in relationship with them, because I stopped being a person to them. I became an object of envy to my friend who had to compare himself with others, and a prop in the drama of my friend who had to have the world be his stage, and the recipient of rage from my friend so frightened of the anger that shaped her.

So in addition to experiencing pain, we're asked to accept and correct the many ways we mishandle and deny our pain. This is an inside job and a difficult one at that. On any given day, we can be thrown under by the rapids. Yet, difficult as it can be, swimming through our pain and sorrow can cleanse the heart enough to keep us afloat.

It's all very daunting. How do we begin? I recently learned that before the stethoscope, physicians and healers would place their ear directly against a patient's chest to hear their heart. The earliest form of stethoscope appeared when healers discovered that holding a hollow tube or container between their ear and a patient's chest amplified the sound of the heart.

In this small piece of medical history is a way to begin. Can you put your ear to the heart of those around you and listen? Can you put your ear to your own life and follow what you hear? Can we hollow out what stands between us so we can hear each other's truth? Can we hollow out what life has done to us? Can we clear out the buildup of our wounds? Can we scour the pretense and denial that keep us from hearing the wind of life funnel through? Can I put down my preoccupation with my smaller self so that nothing is in the way of feeling what joins us?

Hollowing out the sediment of our pain and sorrow so that compassion is possible is a personal reckoning each of us must undertake. We often mistake the journey of healing as one that covers over a wound. But as wounds need air and light to knit and heal, our pain and sorrow need to be brought out into the open so we can be healed by life.

Coming of age, we realize we have to make our way to an unseen shore on the other side of a vast sea. With no boat or paddle, we learn that the only way to live our life is to swim through the years and all they bring. At first, this seems impossible, and while on the way, even unfair. But far enough along and we're surprised to discover that being carried by the sea of life is what we were born to do.

Seeds to Water

๛ In your journal, describe the last time you paused to help someone in pain. What caused you to stop and help? What did you see there? How were you received? What did you learn from this?

๛ In conversation with a friend or loved one, describe an early wound and how it has shaped the way you meet life. How has this woundedness impaired the way you think? What can you do to begin to put down this way of seeing? What might life look like beneath your woundedness?

BLIND AND SIGHTED

We are like someone in a very dark night over whom lightning flashes again and again.

— Maimonides

I came upon this quote when I was barely thirty, and the image changed my understanding of awareness. Maimonides was a great rabbi, philosopher, and physician, born in Córdoba, Spain, in 1135, during a long period of harmony between Jews, Muslims, and Christians. In this one sentence, he offers a profound instruction about the nature of consciousness. He suggests that the human journey is a constant trek through the bump and grind of our days, informed repeatedly by flashes of unified sight. And so we make our way under the temporary flare of the totality of life.

Implicit is the notion that we are all blind and sighted repeatedly, that there is no permanent state of lighted understanding. What's most important is the practice we each develop by which we bring more and more of what we see during those flashes of unity to inform our trek through the phases of darkness, until the next flash or revelation of Wholeness presents itself. Then we add a bit more to our map of what it means to be alive.

Entire philosophies have been constructed to uphold the extremes of living in the light or living in the dark. Some believe that we're only truly alive in the illuminated world, if we could just find a way to transcend the dark, bumpy trek of reality. I felt this way when I was young. I only wanted to stay in the light. I was barely tethered to this life. Of another mind, there are those who believe that the illuminated flash is only an illusion. To them, there is only the dark, bumpy trek. I confess there were weighty passages during my cancer journey when I could barely lift my head and feared the light might be an illusion. But all these years ago, Maimonides tells us that being human is to navigate both the light and the dark, and to have the particulars of life and the totality of life inform each other.

So it does no good to pine for the light or bemoan the dark. Our nature is that of a spiritual amphibian, living through the recurring illuminations that help us find our way along the rough and textured geography of life. In fact, the very purpose of consciousness is to retain more and more of what becomes visible when a flash of lightning shows us the Whole of Life.

We can understand the flash of lightning as the transforming instance of great love or suffering that breaks our trance of isolation, that jars us with wonder or pain into feeling our connection with everything. We're illumined when we least expect it by great beauty or truth. For me, one such flash of understanding came while watching the stars on a warm summer night on the other side of my cancer journey. Everything was so still and quiet. The stars seemed to pulse in place and I realized, in that moment, that there's nothing between the stars and us. The sky is not a ceiling. Briefly, I could feel how connected everything is. This flash of Wholeness passed, but my felt awareness of this connection has informed the rest of my life.

Yet how are we to endure the time between these flashes of light? Well, questions are lanterns we swing ahead of us to see in the dark. And friendship is a lantern held by a loved one when we're too exhausted to light our own way. And wonder is a lantern that waits to be lit inside the heart. We flicker and glow and illuminate each other and the depth of the world. Along the way, we pulse like human stars.

The truth is that things are often dark because they're deep, not because they're forbidding. The purpose of spiritual lightning is to illuminate the deep. The soul's journey is to bring the totality of life and the depth of life together. This is the work of consciousness: to go from being blind to being sighted, to illuminate the dark, and to bring the totality of life and the depth of life together, again and again, as long as we breathe.

Seeds to Water

&* In your journal, explore which part of the journey you are in these days: are you feeling blind or sighted or in between? Describe what conditions make you feel blind and what conditions make you feel sighted. Name one step you can take that will remove a condition that makes you feel blind and one step you can take that will bring you closer to feeling sighted.

In conversation with a friend or loved one, describe a flash of understanding — a moment of lightning — that overcame you and how that moment of greater seeing has informed the rest of your life.

THE TRANCE

We can fall into a trance by over-identifying with our past or the work we do or our dream of the future, all of which can keep us from the bare peace of presence that is always near. No matter their importance, we are not our past, we are not our work, and we are not our dream. If not careful, whatever we enshrine from the past or devote ourselves to or whatever we long for in the future can become a substitute for direct experience. When no longer aware of the difference, we're in a trance.

In my case, my devotion to work insulated me in a smaller world that I mistook for the larger world. And so, losing my job when I was fifty-nine was more than losing my employment. I was thoroughly knit into the fabric of a community for sixteen years, when I and eight other senior staff were let go in fifteen-minute intervals on a Wednesday. Our key cards were turned off that day

213

and we were told to vacate the building by Friday. I was jettisoned out of a world I had loved for years. After tumbling in loss and uncertainty for months, I had a sense of waking from a trance. I began to remember my life before coming to this world. I'm not saying the world I helped build for sixteen years was false, but in immersing myself so completely in that world, I had suppressed parts of myself in order to belong. By doing so, I lost touch with the larger, deeper, more original world. I've done this with relation-ships throughout my life, too. You may have, too.

Beneath the pain of being cut off and the fear of being jobless, which made a crack in the trance, I felt a sense of liberation. I felt a sense of return to something more founda-tional, as if these sixteen years had been a journey within a journey. While in the trance, I'd only seen the world through my immersion in work. Until something ter-rible happened that restored the miracle of sky as sky and dirt as dirt. Suddenly, the life shattered revealed the life it was resting on.

No one is exempt from this process. Yet thrown under and tossed ashore, we keep breaking into something durable and pre-cious. The way a shell I found on Lake

Michigan was scoured by the sea, tossed ashore to bake in the sun, retaken by the night tide, scoured smoother, spit out again, and reclaimed, again and again. It barely resembles what it began as. And like this shell, I barely resemble what I began as.

We're always pulled between the surface and the deep, between the fear and pain of any sudden rip in our lives and the bare presence that waits below any history we've endured.

Seeds to Water

ช In your journal, describe a time when you over-identified with your past, your work, or your dream of the future. What defined you during this time, and what did you have to do to maintain your sense of worth?

ช In conversation with a friend or loved one, tell the story of a time when you felt you were in a trance, when you experienced a way of being or living that kept you from directly experiencing life. Try to narrate the history of how you became entranced and how you recovered from this state.

OUR AUTHORITY OF BEING

Alex is a trial attorney who knows how to be assertive and use the authority of his position. He began as a public defender, and his closeness to people under the thumb of authority has always made him fight for the underdog. A few years ago, Alex became obsessed with mountain climbing. After immersing himself for eighteen months, he began taking trips around the world, trying to conquer legendary climbs.

Last spring, he traveled to a western province of Mongolia to climb Mount Khuiten, which stands on the edge of the Gobi Desert. All expeditions up Mount Khuiten begin in Ulaanbaatar, which sits on the edge of a barren landscape. The trek begins with a day's walk across the open, green steppes that approach the Altai Mountains. Along the way, Alex saw yaks, sheep, and double-humped camels. He was eager to stand on the 14,350-foot snow-capped summit, from which you can see Russia, China, and Mongolia.

By the second day, Alex was already weary. His determined intent to conquer the mountain began to fade. He was settling into the tired rhythm of planting one foot in front of the other. Talk drifted away into the uneven rhythm of everyone's heaving breath, and there was only the sound of the ponies carrying their gear.

On the third day, they camped on a plateau, and Alex was no longer sure why he was there. As he told me his story, Alex grew tender. He said that everything began to drop away that afternoon. Camped out on the plateau, he felt that the wind of centuries would not slow for any living thing. His obsession with climbing, his work, his career, his training, his history, his dreams, all began to fall off like frozen supplies too heavy to carry. As he focused on his cold breath, he even let his name slip away for a moment. All that was left was the bare fact of his own existence, the fact of his breath connecting him to the fact of all existence. He was a piece of life living — that was all.

The weather worsened and the climbers had to come down without cresting the summit. It didn't matter to Alex, as he'd found what he didn't know he'd come for.

As he descended, he put back on all the aspects of his life: his name, his history, his training, his career. But as he tried to put his will back on, it no longer seemed to fit. With each step down the mountain back into the world, Alex was remade.

Of course, to live in the world we have to wear clothes and have an identity in order to make our way. But it makes a difference when we can show our heart's face without any covering. Though we can't stay this naked, we're sanctified in such moments to have the ancient air touch our soul. Alex encountered the authority of his own being and the authority of all being on the side of that mountain.

This inner quality of authority invokes the touchstone of certainty by which we know first-hand that we're alive. Our inner authority emanates from the nakedness of our soul. Once we remove our masks and opinions, our authority of being resides in whatever point of stillness we can no longer question. Our authority of being resides in the fact of being here, regardless of what circumstance surrounds us, regardless of what we have to put back on to live in the world.

Our awareness of our depth of being is fleeting. Yet just because we close our eyes doesn't mean the sun has disappeared. And just because we can't keep the unquestionable fact of being alive in view doesn't mean that the inherent vitality of life has disappeared. We are more than what happens to us. We are more than what we think or fear. The turbulence we encounter is very real, but underneath what happens to us is the inherent, unwavering fact of life filling us from within.

Under all the tension to belong and fit in, under all the psychological weather, there is a place of stillness that is immune to our submitting and resisting. When we can put down all our reasons and excuses, it's from this inner plateau of being that we begin to experience life directly again. This sense of utter being doesn't come from willfulness or determination. It comes when the bottom of our personality nakedly touches the common center of all life. When life-force enters us directly and moves through us completely, our authority of being can't be denied.

In discovering your own authority of being, you may want to spend time with the great poem *Song of Myself* by Walt Whitman. I urge you to read it slowly, and to be in conversation with the places it awakens in you.

And the next time you're told you're good or bad, the next time you're ignored or rejected, I encourage you to practice your inner resolve; not by criticizing yourself or finding yourself wanting, but by climbing to that place in you that is immune to both submitting and resisting, that place of unquestioned certainty about the fact of life, which Walt Whitman confirms in *Song of Myself* when he says:

> I do not trouble my spirit to vindicate itself
>   or be understood;
> I see that the elementary laws never
>   apologize.
> I exist as I am — that is enough;
> If no other in the world be aware, I sit
>   content;
> And if each and all be aware, I sit content.

Beyond all vindication and blame, the fundamental truth of our existence — the bare fact of our being — can outlast our doing, as Alex discovered when exhausted on the mountain.

Seeds to Water

∻ In your journal, describe the settings you experience that crowd out the simplicity of your presence, and describe the settings that let the simplicity of your presence fill you. In which settings do you spend most of your time? How can you silence the crowd in you and let the simple presence in you have more space?

❧ In conversation with a friend or loved one, describe one place in you that feels both fragile and unbreakable. How did you come to know this place in you?

THE GREAT THRESHOLD

As two eyes are necessary to see and two legs are necessary to walk, being and doing must work together. In this way, we know the certainty of our own existence. When we can inhabit a very personal unity of being and doing, we enable our ability to love, to hold, to carry, and to care.

We travel great distances to learn that loving is how we blossom wherever we are, opened by care until we know who we are. Just as a wildflower doesn't choose what it opens to, our blossoming depends on loving everything and everyone. And opening to everything can dissipate our personal darkness.

When completely true to our own nature, we touch and join with everything we meet. In such moments, we are beyond persuasion, debate, control, or manipulation. In such moments, we live and breathe beneath any agenda. In such moments, the emanation and influence of our authentic presence removes the need to go anywhere.

Of course, like the man coming down from the mountain, we'll be drawn back into the world, into the expectations and judgments of others, for that's what it is to be human. But it's our direct experience of being that leads us back to all that matters.

Along the way, we can learn from each other. But great teachers always encourage us into the work of direct experience. Great guides always ask us to quiet our yearning so we can listen to our own gifts. For great sages are not a light to be stared at and revered, but serve as a light to illumine what matters. In an often-told story of Buddha, it was a summer night and Buddha was prompted by his students into a long conversation. The warm breeze circled their talk until, noticing the moon, Buddha stopped and said, "My teachings are only fingers pointing to the moon." After everyone gazed toward the night sky, he added, "Don't get distracted by my fingers. Make sure you look at the moon!"

So the greatest threshold to an awakened life is the courage to say yes. Not yes to what others dream for you or to being abused or mistreated, but yes to the challenge to live your own life, vulnerably and directly, until your own being touches the sea of all being. To be this vulnerable is even harder in a society that views saying no and staying hidden as a form of sophistication, as some necessary way to be more practical and less innocent. Yet all the while, it's the innocence of direct knowing that returns us to wonder.

In the Middle Ages, alchemists viewed the heart as a sun shining forth within a human being. Such an understanding holds that the light that comes from within each of us is not self-contained. Rather, the heart connects us to a greater central light that informs all life. Feeling our authority of being is feeling the light of all life as it comes through our heart. At some point in our journey, whether in a café in New York City or on the side of a mountain in Mongolia, we're called to expose our soul so we can know the light of all life, even though we have to put the things we carry back on in order to live in the world.

This explains the moments of calm I feel sometimes in the midst of great pain and loss. This calm doesn't replace my pain or grief, but it sits like a mountain beneath all my trouble. Touching that mountain of calm, despite what I'm going through, lets me feel the certainty of life. The irreducible fact of our existence doesn't take away the need to meet the days and the dangers that living brings. But the authority of our being makes trouble bearable, and casts sunrise as something I feel waiting within me.

Seeds to Water

- ❧ In your journal, describe one truth about your life that has nothing to do with being seen or heard.

- ❧ In conversation with a friend or loved one, describe a situation in which you're struggling with submitting or resisting to what others want of you. What is pulling you into this situation? What do you fear will happen if you submit or resist? What aspect of who you are is already complete as it is under all of this?

Understanding Success

I can no more count the ways we connect than I can count the stardust in Orion's belt.

— Sue Caulfield

We all want to be successful and we all struggle with what that means. Someone tells a young man running track that he'd be good at jumping hurdles. So he trains and finds himself in the blocks, nervous, wondering if this is right for him. When the gun goes off, he's running as fast as he can to beat the others, to stay in his lane, to clear every hurdle. Legs burning, he pushes harder and strains to cross the finish line. Out of breath, hands on his knees, he wonders briefly, *How did I get here? Is this where I need to be?*

Often, our struggle with success is like that of a young hurdler. We find ourselves on a track we may or may not have chosen, working to stay in our lane, straining to clear every obstacle, and lunging to beat others to the finish line. It's all very confusing and hard to unravel when the gun keeps going off and we feel an urgency to keep racing.

But let's go back to the beginning. The word *success* derives from the Latin verb meaning "to come close after." What success really means for each of us depends on what we're after and what we come close to. The soul of success centers on our very individual journey as we struggle to come close to what we want or aim for. But the success of the soul centers on the part finding its place in the Unity of Things. This deeper journey is revealed through the life of experience as we humbly come close to the very pulse of life and how all things are connected, no matter what we start out wanting or aiming for.

Wanting influences and empowers the typical notion of effort: we work toward something we want, and we get it or we don't. But along the way, we discover that working with what we're given is a deeper journey, because that allows us to experience our connection to all life. This doesn't mean we shouldn't want or work toward things, for wanting and working help us reach for our better selves.

But we often confuse our wants as needs, and in doing so, we elevate or deify our wants as requirements to be happy. We often install or enshrine our dreams, goals, and ambitions as end points: *I'm going to do everything to make this dream come true, to arrive at my goal.* While dreams, goals, and ambitions are wonderful tools, they're not destinations. I now consider dreaming a *process,* not an end point. The dream is kindling used up in the fire of aliveness. The goal disappears or leads us to an unexpected goal. Our ambition dissolves when we encounter realness on the journey.

I like to tell a story about how our understanding of success can change. A bicyclist had trained long and hard to race in an event similar to the Tour de France. He was very disciplined and focused; he even shaved the hair off his legs to streamline his body and trim seconds off his time. At the beginning of the race, he pulled so far ahead that he couldn't see the other cyclists.

Then, just as he was descending a long hill, a huge heron, with its magnificent wings fully spread, swooped down in front of his handlebars. The cyclist was stunned and stopped in the road. The encounter with the heron opened something in him that he'd been chasing. He stood there, straddling his bike as the others caught up and passed him. He lost the race.

Years later, on the porch of his home, someone asked him, "What cost you the race?" He stared off and said, "I didn't lose the race — I left it."

A pragmatist can say, "That's nice, but he did lose after all." But I see it differently. I think all his training and effort were done so he could meet the heron. If he'd known that was the goal, he probably wouldn't have trained the way he did. We often work toward things, not knowing what we're really working toward. Isn't that a blessing? We can trust our *effort* more than what we're working for.

In another story, a Hindu sage is offering teachings in a huge field to the many who have gathered. He tells a parable about two monks who have studied many years, preparing themselves to climb a mountain so they can meet with Buddha. They begin the arduous climb, and halfway up the mountain, one of the monks breaks his leg. They both stop to rest and the other monk makes the injured one comfortable. They need to stay overnight and in the morning it's clear that the monk who broke his leg isn't doing well. He's developed a fever and shouldn't be left alone.

The teacher stops the story and asks the crowd, "What would you do? Would you leave and keep your appointment with Buddha or take your fellow monk back down the mountain to be cared for?" One earnest student replies, "I'd make him as comfortable as I could. Then I'd leave to keep my appointment with Buddha." The teacher looks at him and says, "Well, I'm glad I wouldn't be traveling with you." The earnest monk is embarrassed.

The teacher then explains that, in every era and every generation, when we have more who would leave that monk to keep their appointment — no matter how sacred — we have an age of cruelty. When there are more who would take the injured monk back down the mountain, we have an age of compassion.

What if making it to the top isn't the summit of our journey? What if making it as far as we can go is the summit? What if putting down what we're after in order to care for another is the heart's destiny? What if our grand dreams are only meant to start us on our journey until our love awakens us? Perhaps caring for another — wherever we're stopped along the way — *is* the summit.

So what really constitutes success or

failure? Are we open to where our effort, if we trust it, will bring us? We're both the monk who would go up to keep his appointment with Buddha and the monk who would take the injured one back down the mountain. We're the cyclist who would finish the race and not be touched by the heron and the one whose life will change because of the heron. We carry all these voices within us. How do we start to discern whether we're trapped by success or open to the life of the soul? How do we move beyond our insistence to go after only what we want and allow ourselves to come close to what matters?

Whenever we feel unseen or unheard, invisible or less than — and, being human, we all go through this — the first thing to do is not to want more things but to give our heart's attention to the first thing we see. Rather than asking for attention, we need to give it. That exchange will affirm who, where, and what we are. By giving our full concern to what's before us, the soul loves the world into view.

Often our dreams don't come true, but sometimes we do. And working toward our dreams and through them enables us to inhabit our truth, which is much more important and life-giving than whether we get what we want or not.

Seeds to Water

☙ In your journal, describe a time when you felt a tension between what you wanted and what you cared for. Did you finish your race or follow your heron? Did you finish your climb or bring your wounded companion back down the mountain? What did you learn from your choices?

☙ In conversation with a friend or loved one, discuss what you currently want and what life is bringing you close to. How are these different? How are they the same? Which is more life-giving? Where does your success lie?

WALKING TOGETHER

When the heart breaks, it takes only one soul-friend to help it break open instead of apart.

— Parker Palmer

I've listened to burn survivors from around the world who carry great wisdom. These people changed my life and made me think deeply about the courage that rises in us when we're broken. I remain in awe of the resilience we carry inside our wounds.

Being with these brave souls led me to realize that I don't spend time with the broken because I like pain, but because I need to feel life from inside its shell. I've known this truth first-hand, because of my experience with cancer. In our fear, we think we might lessen the strain of our journey by sorting experiences into good ones and bad ones, which only keeps us from the one encompassing truth of Wholeness that can heal us.

We're ripened by what we go through until some crack lets all of life in and our sweetness out, the way a coconut must be opened to let its sweet milk flow.

And the sweetness we carry within often shows itself in a quietly heroic want to help others. When we dare to reach for each other as we are, pain and all, we walk together in a way that heals us all. Though this kindness can be modeled, I believe we're born with it. How else to explain the young woman I met who'd lost her arms in a fire. She sought me out because her best friend had cancer. She wanted to ask me, as a cancer survivor, if I thought it would be all right if she bought groceries and made her friend dinner. I looked into her magnificently giving eyes, took her prosthetic hands in mine, and told her she was a gift and how much I admired her. As she awkwardly went to the store, I sat in the hallway and wept.

A few months later, while walking in the woods, I thought of the armless giver and wondered where she was. A hawk began to glide overhead, and I realized this is what happens when we let ourselves love — our kindness carries us.

Seeds to Water

 ❦ In your journal, tell the story of someone you know and how they've endured
being broken. What have you learned
from their journey?

 ❦ In conversation with a friend or loved
one, tell the story of a time when you
were called to give when you thought
you had no more to give. Were you at
your genuine limit? Or were you opened
to a deeper resource you weren't aware
of? How has this experience affected
your understanding of what you have to
give?

THE WORK OF INTIMACY

The experience of intimacy requires that we stay in tune with the needs of those we love, honoring their reality, without losing touch with the center and foundation of our own reality. This is the true practice ground of compassion: how to keep our heart open while not losing ourself in the trouble at hand.

I'm still learning how to do this, how to live this. In my thirties, I wasn't yet individuated; that is, parts of me were asleep, even dormant. I was most at home with my inner life and creativity, but was afraid of the challenges of daily life and annoyed by them. And so, I relied on those around me to help me be in the world in ways I should have been shouldering myself. When living as half a person, it's easy to look for your other half when entering a relationship. This is how I entered my marriage to Ann. Our time together became a codependent adventure that I helped design, in which neither of us was whole. We each relied on the other to complete us.

This arrangement worked for eighteen years, but it never let either of us grow in the areas where we were dormant. All that changed when my cancer journey split us open, like a tornado breaking up a home. We were left standing, but all our patterns and ways of being had been leveled. It forced me to inhabit all of myself, and the part of me so reluctant to live in the world had no choice. I don't blame Ann. We were both young, forming ourselves slowly, and we did the best we could. But waking in the rubble, my dormancy was broken. Rawly and awkwardly, I was starting to live my life directly, and the ways I'd asked Ann to complete me now felt controlling and parental, even though I'd co-created the whole thing. After a heartbreaking struggle, I had to leave to build a new foundation in order to inhabit the half of me that had been dormant for so long.

When my wife, Susan, and I met, I was a whole, if unformed, person. And for the first time, I entered a relationship not wanting to rely on someone else to complete me. Now I wanted someone to live their life while I lived mine, and to share the journey.

Susan and I have been together now for over twenty years.

Regardless of whether you're looking for someone to live half your life for you or if you're struggling to live your own life and share in another's, every relationship has its knots and tangles. Individuation is not a cure for struggle and suffering. But being a whole person — striving to inhabit and integrate your entire self — does make life more meaningful and relationships more tender.

Sooner or later, the work of intimacy presents itself like a fast-moving river between two distracting banks: the weeds on one side, where we can over-identify with the pain and struggle of those we love, and the stones on the other side, where we can step away when a loved one's pain and struggle frighten us. But to be intimate is to stay in the fast-moving river of feeling in between. To be intimate is to stay close to another *and* stay who we are.

What this looks like on a daily basis is that if Susan or a friend or a family member is anxious or sad, it doesn't mean I need to be anxious or sad. Rather, I need to understand what it feels like for them to be anxious or sad. Likewise, if I'm in pain or filled with doubt, it doesn't mean that Susan or my

238

friends need to be filled with pain or doubt. Rather, they need to understand what it feels like for me to be in pain or doubt. I now try to understand what my loved ones are going through, to be intimate with their struggles, *and* still feel whatever peace or separate struggle I may be waking with.

Imagine you're with a friend in a rowboat on a beautiful day. As your friend slips over the side to swim, you lean back in the boat to feel the sway of the lake under the warmth of the sun. For a long moment, it feels like heaven. Then your friend in the water has trouble climbing back on board and you have to help. While grounding yourself in the boat, your attention and focus immediately go to offering a hand over the side. If your friend were drowning, you'd have to jump in. But either way, the long moment of heaven under the sun is still happening. This is how we practice intimacy: jumping in when we need to, but mostly stabilizing our weight in the boat that carries us to heaven, so we can lend a hand to those who've jumped or fallen over the side.

Seeds to Water

❧ In your journal, describe a time when you lost yourself by empathizing with someone you love. Then describe a time when you turned away from a loved one because you were overwhelmed or frightened by the intensity or depth of what they were experiencing. Where did each of these experiences leave you? How did your reactions affect the relationship?

❧ In conversation with a friend or loved one, explore the pattern of your intimacy; that is, discuss what it's like to stay close to each other and still stay centered in your own reality.

THE PRACTICE OF RETURN

The ocean is smart — the waves recede
to gather energy for the next one.
— Carole Starkes

Despite all the blessings of an awakened life,
and all the support we can give each other,
we can stumble and lose ourselves in a
second. I can leave home tomorrow and trip
into an old insecurity and flounder for days.
And you can become lost, no matter how
many times you've found your way. Accepting how quickly our course can change
opens each of us to the practice of return.

Being human is to always be in return: to
sacredness, to wakefulness, to the fact that
we're on the same journey, alone and
together. We're safe, then afraid. We're calm,
then agitated. We're clear, then confused.
We're enthusiastic, then numb. We long for
the moments of lift, and run from the moments that weigh us down. But the inescap-

able rhythm of life lifts us and weighs us down by turns, just as the ocean swells and dips with each wave. When we lose our way, each of us is challenged to discern and embody a very personal practice of return — to what matters and to what has heart.

Sometimes, our return to what matters depends on how we break old patterns and loosen old habits. When I was a boy, my father took my brother and me sailing. Straightaway, he taught us how to coil a line so we wouldn't trip on the excess rope or get tangled in it. He learned this in the navy. After a few years, the line in the bow that we'd use to dock would almost coil itself. Then, on a breezy day, my father said we needed to use that line for something else and taught us how to work it in our hands, a little each day, in order to break its habit of coil. It took over a month for the line in the bow to loosen and soften enough to be of use. All these years later, my father is gone, and I can see that the habit of coil applies to more than just rope. It takes time to soften the habits of our heart and mind and work them in our hands, a little each day, in order for the heart and mind to be of use somewhere else.

I've noticed that when coiled too tight, my fear makes me shrink till I feel like a little boy in a man's body. When I'm able to soften my fear and quiet it, I return to full size. What's more, when I can assume my full stature — not larger than I am or smaller than I am — I'm more alive. When I assume my full stature, I'm closer to life and can see more clearly. When I'm a little boy in a man's body, it's harder to see, for I'm nowhere near my eyes.

I'm trying to uncoil. I'm trying not to over-prepare for tense situations, encounters, or conflicts. When my fear occupies itself in the endless rehearsal of what to say or not, of how to respond or not, it prevents me from showing up with who I am. I'm learning to trust that I can meet these situations simply with my being, my self, my soul. I may not be articulate. It might be awkward. But I'm learning to trust that if I'm integral, the encounter will be authentic.

Recently, I had a chance to practice being real at the health club where I swim. Because of the chemo I had years ago, I get cold easily, a common condition for cancer survivors. So I wear a wet suit. This particular day, Tim, a lifeguard my age, began teasing me for using a wet suit in an indoor pool. At first, I ignored him. But when he persisted, I thought, *I'll take a risk and let him know a bit more about my journey and see what happens.*

But after I shared that I'm often cold due to the chemo I had, he barked at me, "Keep telling yourself that!" I was stunned and hurt and retreated inwardly. He left and I swam for thirty minutes, furious. I left the pool, feeling certain I had to voice myself. I didn't know his last name but got it and his phone number from another lifeguard. I was also certain that I wanted to speak my heart before I considered what to say and how to say it, before I talked myself out of it, before I diluted my truth.

I opened my locker, pulled out my cell phone, and, dripping wet, called Tim, who was at home. I told him how rude I thought he was, and he became belligerent. I began to yell at him. After a while, he hung up. Not used to being angry like that, I was shaking. I had no illusions of changing Tim's behavior. But I felt it was imperative not to remain invisible, or I would diminish myself.

Though I voiced myself awkwardly, loudly, and even inappropriately, I assumed my full stature and stood for the truth of my experience. I left trembling but in absolute integrity. From that day on, there's less between me and the world, and I trust I will become more skillful at being authentic in the moment. This raw experience freed me from a great deal of rehearsing before meeting others.

Blessed now to have a sense of what it means to be authentic, I aim to return there when I stray. Often, the smallest moment will catch my heart and reawaken me, like a quiet angel calling with its beautiful whispers. By simply lingering with the whispers, I can rediscover what matters.

Returning when we stray makes me think of a friend who worked in Denali National Park in Alaska for a summer, when the sun is out for twenty hours a day. She found it hard to sleep and learned that, even when our eyes are closed, something within us still tracks the light. Likewise, even when I'm not aware, something deep within me is — something I can trust and return to.

But how we return when we stray is pivotal. It's well known that divers who come up too fast from the deep can injure themselves, not allowing their bodies to decompress slowly. Organs can rupture, bones can suffer lesions, and hearts and brains can literally pop. Whales surfacing too quickly can suffer the same ruptures. Often, fear chases whales to the surface too quickly, as when they're frightened by the stark and sudden loudness of military sonar.

Fear also rushes us out of the deep at a dangerous pace. For divers, the sudden panic that they're running out of air — that they might die in the deep — makes them rush into trouble. While that possibility is real, it's frequently unchecked fear that is the killer. Unwarranted fear is something we all need to resist. While any moment of suffering or joy can drop us into the deep, it's crucial that we don't ascend back into normal time too quickly or we'll suffer mental or emotional ruptures.

Clearly, life-transforming lessons can happen in an instant — this is epiphany — but it takes time to integrate meaning and depth into our lives. Patience — the courage to let time carry us — is important for our survival.

It takes time for us to reach the deep and time to surface with each other. It takes time to listen our way beyond our cuts into the depth of each other's experience. This is a mysterious physic of the soul: the deeper the cut, the redder the blood. The deeper the experience, the richer the wisdom.

When we can invoke our practice of return, we're reminded that everything is alive and that everything has something to offer. In the press of daily life, we often ignore these teachers, though they're everywhere. Still, our connection to life can be renewed by these recurring aspects of practice: uncoiling our habits and returning to what matters; assuming our full stature and speaking our truth; and entering the deep and having the courage to let time carry us.

Developing a practice of return can help us regain clarity. One way to return to what matters is to put all the urgency of a situation, with all its difficult decisions and impending implications, on an imaginary shelf, to be looked at later. Then, without the weight of your situation, you can simply see and feel where you are. In time, your direct connection to unscripted life will be renewed. Yet sometimes it's only through extended stillness or exhaustion that we finally stop and go clear like water. When stilled of all that stirs us, we can see what is life-giving. When quiet and still, we rediscover that regardless of where we search, life is never somewhere else.

Despite the hardships that life throws at us, despite all the pain and loss we endure, life keeps growing us and shaping us. Life keeps living. Not always in the form we expect, and not always in a way that's recognizable. But life keeps pulsing under everything. Despite the pain or confusion I face, something in me keeps reaching for that irrepressible force that lives under everything.

Instead of making progress from here to there, we're asked to penetrate the layers that cover what matters in any moment, so we can inhabit what is vital. This is how we find our place.

Seeds to Water

❧ In your journal, describe a situation you currently face in which you're being asked to surface in the world, even though it's painful. What are you being asked to bring up from the deep? What are you being asked to move through? What is keeping you from breaking surface? Who can you reach out to for help?

❧ As a way to personalize your own practice of return, try sitting in the sun when you're afraid. Locate your fear, if you can, and let it wait for you in the future, where fear mostly lives. Then try to feel the sun on your face, your neck, your shoulders, your arms. When you feel your fear reassert itself, return to the moment you are in and concentrate on the feeling of light and warmth on your body. Practice this movement from fear to warmth for five minutes three times in the coming week.

❧ As another way to embody your own practice of return, try leaving your house or apartment when you're feeling numb or enervated, though it's hard to get moving. Enter the world on a small experiment of wandering. Follow the trace of anything that interests you, however briefly. If it's a bright tree full of wind, go closer to that tree. If it's a song on the radio, give your full attention to the music. If there's a street that seems to call, park and walk down that street. Try to return to a moment of unrehearsed living as a way to re-energize your connection to life about to be lived. Try this small experiment three times in the coming week.

THE CAREER OF AWAKENING

By staying in relationship, we gather
    meaning.
By staying in relationship, our Spirit draws
    closer to the surface.
To follow our aliveness is the career of
    awakening.

Inevitably, certain experiences rearrange us.
These unexpected events puncture life as
we know it and turn us inside out and
upside down. For me, this rearranging event
was cancer. It could just as easily have been
wonder. For you, it might appear as being
loved completely when you've never been
loved before. Or discovering what your work
is and giving yourself to it wholeheartedly,
whether that's gardening, fixing cars, caring
for children, writing, painting, or being a
great listener.

Whether our transforming event is dramatic or subtle, once our gift is exposed,

it's our job to keep it in the open, though no one can stay permanently awake. We take turns being clouded and clear. Today I might be awake for a time, then trip and fall, while you're awake longer. While you're awake, you're the teacher. Tomorrow, you might shut down. You might get something in your heart's eye, and you'll be squinting, unable to quite keep it open. That day, I might be clear, and I'll be the teacher.

No one can avoid the turbulence of being alive. Just as everything in the natural world faces friction and erosion, human beings face the erosion of experience called suffering. There's no escaping this. Though being awake and wholehearted can help us move through difficulty and suffering.

From an early age, we're taught to sort, prioritize, and choose what's most important as a way to negotiate difficulty. Yet while sorting, prioritizing, and choosing can help us get through life, they don't always help us retrieve meaning from life. Over the years, I've been continually broken open beyond what I thought possible. And with a larger, more open heart, I've been challenged to let things in, rather than sort them out, and to let what I experience mix into a potent synergy of life's energies. Drinking from that synergy, I am renewed.

Despite what we're taught, we don't have to choose between meanings. Rather, we can absorb and integrate many meanings. So I invite you to let the many things we're exploring gather and open you to an experience of Wholeness. You don't need to choose among them. One of the rewards for staying awake is that we start to swim in what we experience, rather than separate and isolate what comes our way.

In Baghdad, two Iraqi brothers survived the war and emigrated to Spain. The war had closed one brother while opening the other. The closed one was forever on alert, anticipating danger and sorting, prioritizing, and choosing his way through the days. He couldn't let down his guard. The war had blasted the other brother open to how fleeting life can be. He could no longer close. He let everything fill him. He couldn't plan or be other than where he was.

This difference came between them, even though the open one relied on the closed one to survive and the closed one relied on the open one to thrive. These two brothers are emblematic of traits we each need to integrate if we are to both survive and thrive. For all we go through is meaningless if we can't stay awake and be touched by life. This is the career of awakening — to be touched by what we experience, while staying out of danger, and doing no harm.

Given our fluctuations of wakefulness, we're asked to find ways to get strength from what we know, for the times we don't feel quite awake, for the times we're bumbling around. You may pull over to the side of the road and blurt out, "My God, I was so clear yesterday and today I feel like a fool!" That may feel true, but there's more to it than that. As your eyes dilate and constrict, as you blink countless times each day, as your lungs expand and contract every time you breathe, the heart and mind expand and contract. When the heart and mind expand, we're more awake. When they contract, we feel less than and lost.

Consider how the waves at sea crest and dip. At the top of a wave, we can see forever. But in the belly of a wave, we can't see very far. These are the rhythms of wakefulness. So, in the expansion and contraction of the spiritual journey, we can't place too much importance on any one movement.

It's our commitment to follow our aliveness to the common center we all share that lets us thrive in the midst of our survival. When I can enter a moment to the bottom of my feeling and follow that feeling to the bottom of my personality, I touch into the

Eternal Well of everyone who's ever been. When the bottom of what I'm feeling touches the place where everyone who ever lived has felt their own intimate yet common version of that moment — that mysterious place of joining conveys resilience.

In Denmark, two sisters were born conjoined. Once surgically separated, they shared a special bond. Each was uniquely aware of what the other was feeling, no matter how far apart. When together, they were able to amplify their empathy for those around them.

These two sisters are emblematic of our innate bond with life. For we're all mystically conjoined at birth and separated by experience, led to inhabit our individual lives, always looking for how we can come back together. Yet when awake and aware — when living with an open heart — we become conduits for everyone who ever lived.

In these moments that are both personal and universal, we're both alone and not alone. Imagine standing outside on a winter night, beyond the cast of streetlights, staring at the stars until you begin to sense others around the globe staring at the same stars at the same time. Imagine staring longer still, until you begin to feel everyone throughout the ages who ever stood outside in the cold to be awed by the heavens. We touch into resilience by opening what we're given and entering it wholeheartedly, where we find the mystical company of everyone who's ever lived.

Seeds to Water

❧ In your journal, describe the history of your own career of awakening. Begin by naming three significant moments of wakefulness, whether painful or joyful, that expanded your experience of being alive.

❧ In conversation with a friend or loved one, describe someone you admire for how awake to life they seem. What traits do they exhibit that lets them be so awake? What habits and commitments do they invest in that lets them meet life so fully?

THE SIREN OF INSECURITY

I was recently in a social setting where a small group motioned for me to join them. Yet when I approached, they made no effort to include me. It seemed a small thing. Perhaps they were immersed in their conversation, but I immediately felt invisible. I don't think anyone meant any harm. They were unaware at best. Nonetheless, the situation felt very adolescent, and though I didn't know these people well, I left feeling a little insecure, not even sure about what.

A week later, I was in conversation with a woman from that same group. While she was warm and gracious, I felt diminished for being in her company. As others joined our conversation, I felt like we were all props in her drama. This was puzzling until I realized that she could only relate to others as either above her or below her. In order to keep herself up, she held everyone she met below her. It took enormous presence on my part to resist her draining energy.

My learning here came precisely because I didn't know this person well. We had no personal history to muddy what I was experiencing. It was stunning to me that, though I hardly knew this woman, having been in her company only twice, I felt excluded, less than, and invisible, even though there were no harsh words, no incidents, no conflict of any kind.

We all emit energy patterns and, because we're sensitive, we're all affected by those patterns. The current of our presence is powerful, whether we realize it or not. And we're responsible for the energy patterns we emit. Beneath all our words, we either welcome others as equals or we distance and judge them. When under the influence of such judgment, we're challenged to stand firm in our own worth without accepting what others are projecting and without shutting down our sensitivities.

In Homer's epic poem *The Odyssey*, Odysseus is on his way home from the Trojan War, when he is instructed to pass by the island of the Sirens whose call is so compelling that no one hearing them will ever leave the island. He has himself strapped to the mast of his ship, and has his men fill their ears with wax. He then has them pledge not to untie him no matter what happens. Even strapped to the mast, he has a hard time resisting the call of the Sirens. But he does.

This ancient story warns us of the power of seduction and addiction, but it can apply to any pattern of energy that is against our true nature. Insecurity is such a siren that appears in many disguises. For me, it appeared in the social gamesmanship of this woman I hardly knew.

We can't deny the feelings that overtake us as we move through the world, but we can stand firm in our true nature. Like Odysseus, we can withstand the Sirens we encounter while staying on course as we find our way home.

Seeds to Water

ଆ In your journal, describe a time you felt overcome with insecurity and the circumstances that led to this. How much of this mood came from others and how much did you contribute to your own diminishment? What did you do to move through the insecure feeling? How long did it take to pass?

When in a social situation, with friends or colleagues, allow yourself to feel the moods and energies of those around you. Who is nervous? Who is sad? Who is positioning themselves above everyone else? Feel these moods wash near you and over you. Then, while in the middle of the gathering, take a deep breath and feel the ground you are standing on, feel your own presence and mood. Take another breath and remember that all these moods and energies are not you. Take a third breath and feel your own presence, as if you are alone. Then look to the company around you, meeting their presence with your own. Practice grounding your own worth in the company of others two times in the coming week.

REMEMBERING

The proper function of memory is to re-member, to put the members or parts of our life back together. We often get lost in reliving the past, when the gift of memory is to knit things back together, to re-member the whole.

In my thirties, I had a powerful dream that showed me this. I was stopping by my grandparents' home in Baldwin, New York. They lived in a small brick house, just off Sunrise Highway. In the dream, there was a serial killer on the loose and I wanted to check on the little boy staying with my grandparents. It was mid-morning and the front door was ajar. I called as I entered. No one was home. I was frightened that something bad had happened. I could sense the trouble was upstairs. The house was completely silent. I climbed the stairs, afraid what I might find. The handle to the upstairs bathroom was broken. I opened the door to find the little boy dismembered on the floor. It was a horrific scene. I woke with a scream.

It was Father John Malecki, a kind priest who was a Jungian analyst, who led me back into that metaphoric bathroom to see that I was returning as an adult to put the members of my inner child back together. He said that dreams often arrive in graphic terms to get our attention. He suggested that the dream was telling me that I was now strong enough and individuated enough to face the wounds of childhood and mend them, putting myself back together.

From the outset, we're imprinted by our early experience. Many of us suffer as we try to escape this imprinting. Yet we have to face it, if we are to truly live our lives. It can be very daunting to undo what pain and fear have taught us. Like a dog trained to fight, some of us are brutally trained for a game of survival that someone else created. But it's possible to remember what we were born with.

Whether smothered or abandoned, or lost or found, the unfolding of our lives has us uncover or peel away what gets in the way, so we can recover the essential nature of things more deeply. This uncovering of what gets in the way is how we learn. Because we fall down and get up again and again, we're called to pick ourselves up, dust off our habits, and sustain our authenticity.

Because we form patterns along the way, we need to scour and break those patterns in order to stay freshly alive. Dreams, insights, and honest friends help us break our patterns. To keep us going, we need an inner practice that will help us remember when we forget. Why? So we can return when we stray and soften when we harden. So we can put to rest the things we dwell on, and come alive and participate fully in the days once more.

There are times we can feel the vastness of life and grasp a larger sense of things. And times we get lost in the details, entangled in problems and old patterns. But when love or suffering return us to the depth of life, the days become precious and familiar and everything feels new. Expanding after being small, the weight we carry lessens and the smallest effort matters again.

In Japanese lore, a pearl of a child was born in poverty and left in an abandoned hut. She managed to survive and until she realized she was all alone, the light she attracted and reflected was enough. But inevitably, she felt the weight of being an orphan. And so her lifelong struggle began.

When looking in the world, she always felt rejected and bereft. When looking in herself, she felt received and complete. This is the struggle we all face. No matter what circumstance we're born into, our trial of individuation is to see through our circumstance and remember the pearl we are.

Seeds to Water

✤ In your journal, describe in detail a time when your fear made you forget what you know or who you are or what you understand about the gift of life.

✤ In conversation with a friend or loved one, describe a time when love helped you remember what you know or who you are or what you understand about the gift of life.

✤ We tend to forget the meaning of things when we move too fast. To practice remembering — to practice putting the parts of life back together — pause after a friend speaks to you and ask them to repeat what they've shared, so you can truly take it in. Remember who this person is to you, and respond from your heart.

LOVING WHAT YOU DO

Work is love made visible.
                                    — Kahlil Gibran

Kurtis Lamkin is a poet praise-singer from Charleston, South Carolina, who plays the kora and the jinjin, stringed instruments of West Africa. But mostly, Kurt plays his heart. I fell in love with Kurt the first time we met. Watching Kurt play the twenty-one strings of the kora, his eyes closed and his head back, I knew I was witnessing someone who loves what he does. So much that it was hard to know where his fingers stopped and the strings began. Centuries of living came pouring through his praise singing.

As I got to know Kurt, it became clear that this is the way he loves everything and everyone. He's one of those who glows, a lamp to everything he touches. And loving what he does is what keeps his lamp lit. This is a great lesson. When we can love what we do, it keeps our lamp lit, which lets us bring light to everything we touch.

Whatever we touch bears the mark of our heart, because our hands and heart are forever connected. I was amazed to learn recently that as we form in the womb, the first sign of our arms, known as arm buds, grow directly out of the heart. Before we even arrive, our arms are small branches stemming from our heart. This is why when we feel love, we have the impulse to reach and touch. This is why when speaking from the heart, we tend to speak with our hands. And when having a heart attack, we feel the pain in our arms.

Our hands carry whatever we feel into the world. We can't know the tenderness of touching another without taking the risk to be touched. We can't know care unless we let the care in our heart spill out through our hands. We can't know love from outside of loving.

The visionary educator Parker Palmer suggests that vocation is that which calls us into who we truly are. Underneath all the professions and job descriptions, our vocation is to embody our authentic self and then to live that self in the world. In this way, our vocation — our call — is to find what we love and to love what we do. The philosopher Howard Thurman said:

> Don't ask what the world needs. Ask what makes you come alive, and go do it. Because what the world needs is people who have come alive.

Yet how do we discover what we love to do? How do we maintain it? How do we recover it when it changes? Loving what we do involves a continual alignment of inner with outer, a commitment to place our care in the world. When we can bring enough of ourselves to bear on what we do, the smallest task will open its drudgery and show us its seed of truth. It's the depth of our care that rinses the drudgery from what must be done.

The power that comes from loving what you do waits inside the doing, which means we have to enter what we do and not just handle it. As long as we force the wrench to fit the pipe or worry the saw through the lumber, the world remains a problem to be solved. Once we can feel the pipe through the wrench and feel the lumber opening as the saw and our hands are one, then we join with what we do — and love begins to show itself.

I remember picking corn with Ed, my

former father-in-law, in the August sun. I didn't care for it at first. I trailed behind him feeling very inept. In one motion, his old arthritic hand swiftly snapped each ear of corn from its stalk and tossed it in his canvas bag. I couldn't keep up. Finally, I just watched him for a while. I noticed a tender hesitation before each snap, as if he were quietly thanking the corn for growing so tall. This was his love affair with the earth.

Later, I watched him eat the corn he grew, and thanked, and picked. There was a big grin on his face, which others thought was because the corn tasted so good. But having loved him enough to watch him in his care, I could see that he was eating the earth, the rain, the seed, and the sun that were all wrapped together in these juicy kernels. Ed was always more himself during corn season. It was tending the corn that kept his lamp lit.

Yet because we live in a disposable age obsessed with the new, we seldom put our hands in the earth or hold the objects we build and give to each other. Though it's easier to throw something out rather than repair it, we lose the history of objects and tools and the presence they accumulate, when we toss them away without a thought.

As long as we remain instrumental — that is, intent and fixed on using whatever we touch to gain us some advantage — we won't be open to the life that moves through whatever we touch. The vitality of life reveals itself when we can be present enough to become a conduit for other presence — like Kurt when he's playing his ancient instruments, and Ed when he's watering the small stalks of corn.

Every tool has a story of what it's fixed, every stone in a garden wall that's been hoisted into place holds the story of those hands, and every pair of earrings has heard all the secrets whispered in its ears. The objects of the world are like notes of music on a page, silent and waiting for us to play them.

So when you can, pick up an object, any object, and hold it as you would a beautiful shell you've found by the sea. Feel its edges, hold it to your ear, and listen for its story. Love whatever you hold so it can reveal its history and its presence.

Everywhere we turn, we're asked to remember that our hands have grown out of our heart. With everything we do, we're asked to enter what's before us with immediate hands-on effort. By loving what we do, we invoke the effort to stay present, the effort to restore our trust in life when we lose it, the effort to open our heart especially when pain and fear close it, and the effort to do small things with love, as Mother Teresa would say. These offerings of heart through our hands keep our lamp lit.

There is no greater healing agent than loving what you do. My father, lifelong craftsman that he was, worked in our basement whenever he could. He was always covered with sawdust. In the midst of all his tools, with an irrepressible smile on his face, he'd say, "If you love what you do, you never have to work a day in your life."

Seeds to Water

🕊 Bring to mind and heart someone you admire who loves what they do, whatever that might be. In your journal, describe in detail this person doing what they love. Describe the motion and rhythms of how they work. Describe the nature and music of their love.

🕊 In conversation with a friend or loved one, describe this person and tell the story of their doing what they love. Follow this by describing in detail something you love to do.

A Song for Pilgrims

I wanted to journey with a group of inner pilgrims over time and so convened a small class of willing souls who agreed to gather four times a year. We bonded quickly and at each gathering picked up as if no time had passed. We just kept going deeper. We became a tribe of seekers and agreed to meet for a second year. Gathering like this, we entered the one conversation of life that we all approach uniquely, though once inside it, we find our common journey. Along the way, we developed a spiritual vocabulary, a language of symbols and phrases that served as shorthand for insights and experiences we worked hard to understand together.

Over time, each of us shared how we'd been forced by life to shed some form of mask in order to live closer to what matters. We quoted the Greek poet George Seferis, who said:

Like a bird with broken wing
that has traveled through wind for years . . .
I sleep and my heart stays awake . . .

How the bird continues for years with a broken wing and how the heart continues for years despite its breaks became part of our inner vocabulary. When we'd gather and share difficult questions, we found comfort in remembering that "like a bird with broken wing," we all continue despite our brokenness. It was uplifting to realize that we're part of a timeless journey that everyone participates in, and that having a break in our wing is part of the journey.

I shared my deep connection to herons, how they've appeared as guides for me, how we finally wait like a heron, standing on one foot for all the troubled waters to clear, so we can see through to the bottom, where everything is still.

I spoke about a South American custom called *E daí* (ay-die-ee), which is Portuguese for "And then?" Regardless of the story told or hardship conveyed, the custom is for the listener to ask three times, *"E daí?"* with a tone that implies: "And so, what does this mean?"; "And so? What now?"; "And so, what is your next step?"

We learned about the Chinese sage Seng-

Ts'an, who, no matter what his students asked, would say, "Not Two, One!" This phrase became a cornerstone for our conversations around problem-solving, when trouble kept trying to make us separate life into good and bad or right and wrong or light and dark. During our first year together, Susan from Minnesota had refrigerator magnets made for each of us that said, "Not Two, One!"

We discovered together how the bird that flies with a broken wing reminds us that the heart can stay awake no matter how troubled. We can stand like herons, on one leg if necessary, and wait for all trouble to settle. No matter the story we find ourselves in, we can listen to each other and ask, "And so, what is your next step?"

This happens between true friends: a hard-earned vocabulary reveals itself by which we can help each other stay close to all that is life-giving. And under all the conflicts and dilemmas we face, we can discover over and over that everything and everyone in life is connected. We can discover that resilience begins with feeling the Oneness of which we are a part.

This blessed journey with these honest souls came to an end last summer. It was beautiful and difficult to say good-bye. Just last week, one of those kindred souls, Megan, sent me a handmade leather journal. The cover was burned with two images: a heron waiting on one foot and the phrase *E daí.* I was deeply moved.

I began using this journal on my next trip, which was to Seattle. On the plane, above the clouds, where the sun shines no matter the weather, I ran my hands over the burned images on the cover for a long time, feeling the presence of our small tribe, feeling the place in my heart where all my loved ones live, feeling the presence of everyone I admire who keeps living, no matter the break in their wing. They all began to speak to me, and the following poem revealed itself:

The Slow Arm of All That Matters
I have fallen through and worked into
a deeper way — one step at a time,
  one pain
at a time, one grief at a time,
  one amends at a
time — until the long, slow arm
  of all that matters
has bowed my estimation of heaven.
  Now, like a
heron waiting for the waters to clear,
  I look for

heaven on earth and wait
  for the turbulence to
settle. And I confess, for all the ways
  we stir things
up, I can see that though we can stop,
  life never
stops: the lonely bird crashes into
  the window
just as the sun disperses
  my favorite doubt, a
sudden wind closes your willing
  heart as the
moment of truth passes between us,
  and the
damn phone rings as my
  father is dying. All
these intrusions, majestically unfair,
  and not
of our timing. So we spin and drop
  and catch
and land. And sometimes,
  we fall onto these
little islands of stillness, like now,
  from which
we are renewed by our kinship
  with all and that
irrepressible feeling resurrects our
  want to be here,
to push off again into the
  untamable stream.

I wrote this poem, but can't say that I authored it. True expression rises through us. In this expression, all the conversations and honest sharing that passed through our small tribe over those two years permeated my consciousness, the way the ocean saturates a sponge. A sponge doesn't create the water it holds. Water passes through the sponge. So, too, with all we learn in this life. We soak up the deepest meanings from each other and the water of wisdom passes through us.

As the poem suggests, life never stops unfolding, sometimes harshly, sometimes gently. And though we're cast ashore from time to time, stunned and exhausted, convinced we can't go on, we can find these sacred inner islands of stillness on which we know what it is to be alive. Truth is such an island. Tenderness is such an island. Friendship is such an island. The quiet space we enter after putting down our history and wounds and principles is such an island, where the song of two birds circling the light introduces us to our goodness.

Seeds to Water

> ᔰ In conversation with a friend or loved one, tell the story of someone you ad-

mire because of their kindness. Once you've shared this story, create a symbol that honors this person and their story.

❧ As a meditation with your hands, create two versions of this symbol. If the person you admire is still alive, tell them what their kindness means to you and give them one of the symbols. If the person you admire is no longer with you, tell someone else what that person's kindness means to you, and give them one of the symbols.

STRENGTH FROM
WHAT WE KNOW

To get strength from what we know means that when we're afraid we don't forget the power of truth, that when we're mistreated we don't forget the light we were born with. It means that when we get caught in a lie we don't give up on honesty and become a liar, that when we're hurt we don't give up on kindness and become cruel, that when we're rejected we don't give up on love and find fault with everyone. It means that when we fall down we don't give up on standing tall, that when we don't have enough we don't give up on the certainty that we are enough. Getting strength from what we know means that when we're in pain we don't give up on the kinship of all things.

Still, in times of pain and confusion, it's hard to trust that the Whole of Life waits beneath our trouble. At each turn, getting strength from what we know depends on the conversation we sustain between who

277

we are and the rest of life.

This is as elusive as it is necessary. Each of us paddles like a surfer in search of a beautiful wave, so we might catch the power of the deep and be carried by it, for as long as we can. Being lifted and carried by the swell of the deep is the appearance of grace. For the time we're riding the wave, we are at one with the sea. For the time we're one with the sea, we're getting strength from what we know. Effort leads to grace.

After we put ourselves in a position to wait for a wave, a second effort is necessary to catch the wave and ride it. But like all waves, all moments of grace subside to rejoin the larger sea and we're left with the need to make our way safely back to shore, so we can re-enter our lives.

In our efforts to make it from day to day, every one of us will catch a wave and fail to catch a wave, and everyone will have a wave crash over them. And each of us will have to find our way back to shore, where we will try to make sense of both the lift and the crash, and how to go on from there.

Day by day, we're each reshaped by the rough and gentle currents of life. The things we care for and the things we lose excavate a new depth in us, until we sense that our heart has a new bottom. This happened to me when I survived cancer. In that excavated depth, I felt a new reservoir of being under all my difficulty, sadness, wonder, and grief.

While trying to catch the next wave of life, this new depth brought me closer to the foundation of being we all stand on. It took a few years to understand the wisdom of this added depth. That wisdom can be phrased like this: When we can meet what we're given and see it through and not skip over it or deny it or minimize it, we enter a more elemental state.

In this new depth of being, I also began to feel more than one thing at the same time, as my heart was now swimming more deeply in the current of life. One of the tasks we face on the other side of suffering is not to identify completely with any one feeling. We're each a worn-open container that holds all feelings. The farther we go, the more we're asked to absorb all that comes our way and let it integrate within us.

Being worn open while drifting at sea led me to the strength of what I know, part of which is that we each arrive as a beautiful, wholehearted, worthy human being, complete as we are. Inevitably, we spend a lifetime summoning the courage and commitment to face and accept our worth, being shaped as we go by whatever we're given.

This cycle of transformation is still shaping me. During the past two years, I lost my father; my wife, Susan, and I lost our beloved dog-child Mira; and we lost Susan's sweet mother, Eleanor, and my dear friend and mentor Joel. These losses have excavated a few more inches under my heart. Mysteriously, this hollowing has brought me closer to the depth that lives under all we go through. I'm in awe that life has no bottom and strengthened to discover that the heart has no bottom. I feel more resilient and tender by the day.

The force of life's sea has unearthed another sediment of knowing in me. Everything seems new and ancient at once. In New York a few weeks ago, Susan and I went to Central Park. We were drawn to sit near a man who was playing a steel drum. As children gathered to listen, I began to weep to see Susan laugh again, the sun on her face. And in my weeping, I was getting strength from what I know.

The waves come and go. We ride them and they crash upon us. But we're still here. We're still being opened, able to love each other and try again.

Seeds to Water

ᘰ In your journal, describe an experience of lift and wonder when you caught a wave in life. Explore this experience as a case study in your own sense of effort. Using the analogy of the surfer, describe in detail the paddling you did to wait for the wave, the effort you made to catch the wave, your effort in riding the wave, and the effort you made to return to shore. What does all this say to you about the nature of effort?

ᘰ In conversation with a friend or loved one, describe a time when you felt you were getting strength from what you know about the nature of life. What enabled you to access such a deep knowing? How did this strength show up and help you?

FEELING THOROUGH

The effort to look closely
until the inside of any moment
reveals the ocean of all care.

I love how I feel after swimming. For the
moment, I'm no longer catching up; inner
and outer time are moving at the same
speed and my breath connects them. I feel
thorough. The word *thorough* means "complete in all respects." When I feel thorough,
it's an indication that my life is complete,
however briefly, in sync with life itself.

Not surprisingly, I think and see with
added clarity during these moods of completeness. Whether it's exercise that flushes
out the circulatory system, or meditation
that flushes out the clogged-up thought
system, or honest conversation that flushes
out the buildup that aggregates in the heart,
it's this sensation of thoroughness we're
after. It's what dance and song and pure

music do for our vitality — they flush out numbness and enervation. These are all powerful ways to clear our pipes.

It's crucial to note that *being thorough* requires *investing extraordinary care, and tending to every aspect.* Now we can see the self-evident way this works. If we want to *feel* thorough, we have to *be* thorough. If we want to feel complete, we have to risk extraordinary care and invest in every aspect that is before us. It seems rather obvious, but just as it's necessary to open our eyes in order to see, it's necessary to care in order to feel complete.

My dear friend George is thorough in everything he does: in the rattle he's carving out of cherry for his granddaughter, Evie, in the strawberries he picks from the garden he and his wife, Pam, plant every spring, in the way he listens to each of us with his whole being. George tends to every aspect of life that comes his way. And so, everything's of interest to him. He has his likes and dislikes, like the rest of us. But without any intention of turning what he meets into something else, his thoroughness of care leaves him excited and enriched by whatever might happen next.

Such thoroughness is both revealing and contagious. Having witnessed it in others, I want to experience that kind of complete care myself. I remember my own early moments of such thoroughness: the first time I got lost before a waterfall, the first time I got lost in someone else's eyes, and getting thoroughly immersed in the strange melodies of the Torah when studying for my bar mitzvah.

Yet growing up, a certain clutter started to surround me. It kept me from being immersed in my own care. Then other people's opinions began to hang like a veil between my care and the world. And thinking with other thinkers' thoughts, it became hard to dive into the Original Ocean that gives rise to all thought. Twisting myself and bending my personality to please so many, it became hard to love simply and directly, the way a lion licks her cubs. It's hard to recover, but the whole world is in that lick.

Many years later, after two marriages and surviving cancer, I understand that when we dare to put down everything we carry and open ourselves to what we're born with, clarity is the tear of being that cleanses the heart. Such clarity permeates who we are until we recover that sense of complete care. And one or two such moments of heartfelt clarity are enough for a lifetime. Now I know that feeling thorough is the recurring sensation of living in rhythm with all of life.

There's no lack of chances to care completely. Great intensities of pain, grief, and wonder bring us to this edge. And great open spaces can animate our thoroughness. But to live deeply and freshly, we need to roll up our sleeves and lean over the thing we care about, so we can keep remaking the world, the way my good friend George uses a tool to carve another tool, as if some angel guides his hand with the steadiness of a surgeon.

Seeds to Water

❧ Center yourself and breathe slowly. Reflect on what is going on inside you. As you breathe, reflect on the life around you. Inhale slowly and honor your breath as the inlet between who you are and the world. Exhale fully and stop catching up. Let your breath flow in and out. Let the rhythm of your breathing meet the rhythm of the life around you until your inner world is moving at the same speed as the outer world. At this moment, notice what it's like to feel thorough.

❧ In conversation with a friend or loved

one, describe one person, place, or activity in which you invest extraordinary care. What does caring so completely look like? What calls you to care so deeply? How does caring in this way affect you?

■ ■ ■ ■

FINDING WHAT CAN LAST

■ ■ ■ ■

Before the inexplicable mystery of the universe, we are all the village fools. But in our choice to reveal our hearts to ourselves and to each other, we can all be masters and healers.

— Agapi Stassinopoulos

As I get older, I see my life more and more in terms of stories, stories that have been lived, and stories waiting to be lived. And then there is the sense how these stories of the soul are like threads in a tapestry of a much larger story.

— Llewellyn Vaughan-Lee

Two brothers were on an urgent journey. Their father was ailing and one had a dream of a potion that would cure him. The other listened closely and made a map of the dream. Though they weren't sure where they were going, they were hopeful they would get there and bring back the medicine that would heal their father.

On the second day, it became cold and windy as they reached the foot of an enormous mountain, too steep to climb. The brother who had the dream said, "I'm certain we need to travel east." The second brother strongly objected, "No! Don't you see? The map calls for us to travel west." They spent the rest of the day quarreling in the cold wind at the foot of the mountain. Not able to agree, they parted ways, never to find each other again.

You might wonder if their father was ever healed. But the story ends here. I think the point is that while they quarreled, their father's life depended on their ability to accept that they were at the end of all they knew. The brothers needed each other to find a new way. On one level, the brothers represent our intuition and our reason, which always quarrel over where we're going. Our life often depends on our ability to find a new way by accepting that we're entering the unknown.

This inevitable struggle between what we intend and what life provides is how we apprentice in the art of acceptance. The chapters in this section explore in more detail what it means to accept our way. This is how we begin to belong to the world. After the exhilaration of beginning any journey, we settle into the tense struggle when where we think we're going clashes with where life is taking us. The strain of this struggle can occupy us for years. During this in-between time, we're asked to exhaust all the ways we don't listen. At some point, we may feel like a failure because we think we've fallen off course. Feeling lost, we may think we're unworthy because getting where we thought we were going is taking so much longer than we imagined.

Eventually, we're drawn to what we need to learn, so we might find what can last. In time, we can discover the truth that lives at the center of every feeling. Asking for our turn to drink from that well, we can be healed by the

paradox that while life at times feels unbearable, what we are made of is unbreakable.
Only acceptance can lead us to this potion.

LETTING ALL THINGS IN

In March of 2013, I went to Long Island to see my father, who at ninety-three was slowly leaving this Earth. He'd just been moved from a rehab center back to the hospital. I sat with him for hours, holding his ancient hands. The morning I left, he was slouched in a wheelchair by his bed, looking like God about to touch Adam's finger on the Sistine Ceiling. Except reaching into the air, my father was giving his life back. Slumped in that wheelchair with his hand draped over a tray, he looked 150 years old.

We were alone and I rubbed his arm and ran my fingers through his white hair. He was in between worlds and didn't seem to know I was there. He was breathing steadily and, hard as it was to see him like this, there was something holy about it. I took a picture of him with my cell phone. Strangely, it is the one picture I return to.

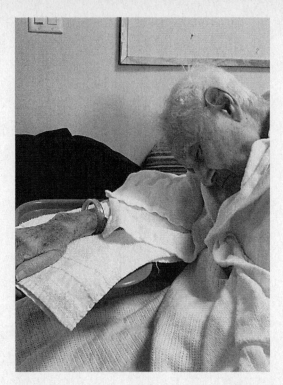

My father in the hospital, March 2013

Seeing his soul almost leave his body after close to a century of living was haunting and beautiful.

An hour later, he stirred and we talked for a while. When it was time for me to leave, he gripped my hand and I kissed his forehead. I cried in the parking lot and began to drive to New York City to attend the Books for a Better Life Awards ceremony as a finalist the next day.

On the drive from the hospital to midtown, I began to feel the pull of joy and sorrow at the same time. We spend so much of our life bouncing from one to the other, so much effort trying to cheer up or distract ourselves from our sorrow, pain, and grief. But letting joy temper sorrow is how we endure, and letting sorrow temper joy is how we remain compassionate.

There I was, eyes filled with tears, on the Southern State Parkway, still seeing my father slouched in his wheelchair. How could winning an award even matter? Yet after all my years of inquiry and writing, I also felt good about being recognized for my journey. My heart bounced back and forth for much of the drive, feeling the weight and lift of each, feeling tightly wound between the two.

My wife, Susan, and some close friends were arriving the next morning. I checked into my hotel and went by myself to a small Italian place in Hell's Kitchen. Being with my father had brought the nerve of life rawly to the surface. Now everything was aglow. I sat in a booth, had a glass of wine, and stared at the reflection of the candle in the glass for a long time. The flame glowed from inside the glass. I thought, *When we feel so deeply, is this how the flame of our soul makes the heart go clear? Is this how the soul burnishes the heart from inside?* I could feel my father's small flame flickering inside his laboring heart, could feel my own flickering. I stared at the flame in the glass and tried to feel our hearts rise and fall in rhythm. I was back in the stream of life.

A few tables away, a plate of tuna arrived and the sheen of the sauce seemed full of a truth we seldom see. And beyond the strangers eating truth, through the window, across the street, a homeless man was carefully going through a trash can and the yellow street light on his shoulders made him seem like a character walking out of a Rembrandt. I ordered the tuna. As I ate the sauce filled with truth, I couldn't stop thinking of my father slowly giving his life back to God.

The next day, I was still being pulled between my father dying and the anticipation of the awards ceremony. Susan and Rich and Michelle arrived and we took a cab to the Times Building. Suddenly, we were in the buzz of a lively reception. I spoke to many, seeing the glow in each, while feeling my father's ancient figure hovering somewhere within me.

In the auditorium, the ceremony began. The awards were announced Oscar-style, the envelope please. As the first recipient expressed her gratitude, I felt her sincerity.

These were good people giving and receiving. It's such a simple and real thing to do, to honor books that help us live. I wondered what could have given my father a better life. Could I make his life better now? The kindness in the room now made me want to win.

All the while, my father was sitting in his wheelchair in the back of my heart. I began to speak to him in silence, "I know it doesn't seem fair, Dad, but life keeps going." His glow pushed back into the moment, as if to encourage me to go on.

The next recipient was Gail Sheehy, for her book *Passages in Caregiving,* in which she deeply shares the journey of caring for her husband Clay Felker for years until his death. When Gail spoke, the world of my father, the world of her husband, and the world of that evening all became one.

My category was next. In that moment, I stopped choosing between sadness and joy, between pain and wonder, between things that matter and things that don't. In that moment, my heart widened and deepened to make room for them all. Strangely, just before my name was called, I flashed on the day before when my father wasn't sure who I was and I gently whispered, "I'm Mark, Dad. I'm your son." Then I heard my name announced. As I stood and walked to the stage, my father in his wheelchair was in the back of my heart.

I looked on the kind faces in the auditorium. And though they didn't know him, I let their applause rush on through my sense of self, the way water rushes through an inlet, so it could lift the face of my father in his hospital bed, fifty miles away.

That night, I began to understand that all things are true, everywhere at once. That night I learned that the heart *can* be in two places at once. That night I learned to open my heart to include what I don't understand, instead of working to solve it as a problem.

It's been three years since that night. My father has died and the glass award is next to one of his tools. When the light is right, the tool and the award reflect in each other, just as sorrow and joy do. And I've been practicing ever since: to stretch the heart, not to wall it in; to let all things in, not to sort the good from the bad; to let the ups and downs of life merge, not to bounce with urgency from one to the other. When I can do this, a depth of aliveness appears. In those moments, it seems as if my father — slouched in his wheelchair like God about to touch Adam's finger — is touching me from the other side, giving me a jolt of life, encouraging me to go on.

Seeds to Water

- 🪶 In conversation with a friend or loved one, tell the story of a time when you felt torn between joy and sorrow and how you dealt with this tension. What would it look like if you were to let both feelings in, rather than bouncing from one to the other?

- 🪶 In your journal, explore a situation in which you're being asked to feel more than one thing at the same time. How is it affecting you? How might you let all things in?

FOLLOWING LIGHT

The Impressionist painter Claude Monet followed what he was drawn to and had an unwavering devotion to a life of seeing. He continually tried to paint light and stayed committed to painting what he actually saw.

Monet's masterful *Water Lilies,* a series of approximately 250 oil paintings of his garden at Giverny during the last thirty years of his life, were mainly painted while he had cataracts in both eyes. Though Monet was consciously dedicated to painting light as revealed by his water garden, the garden he created is a living work of art itself, to which he was equally devoted. Often, devoting ourselves to the creation of one thing leads us to the creation of something we couldn't have imagined, and what we think we're seeing is only an entry point into a deeper way of seeing.

Monet would leave five or six canvases up and move from one to the next as the light of the day progressed, returning day after day to the morning-light canvas, then the midday canvas, and so on. All the while, he wrote detailed instructions to his gardening staff, sketched precise designs and layouts for plantings, ordered varieties of flowers, and extended his collection of botany books. As Monet's wealth grew, his garden evolved with its water lilies, pond, and bridge. He remained its architect, even after he hired seven gardeners.

As his garden matured, his vision slowly broke down, though his devotion to painting what he saw never wavered. After his second wife, Alice, died in 1911, Monet's vision began to be affected by the cataracts in his eyes. In 1923, three years before his death, he underwent two experimental operations to remove these cataracts, but the operations failed.

There's speculation that the paintings done through his cataract-vision have a luminous reddish tone because after these failed surgeries he was able to see certain ultraviolet wavelengths for a time. Through the veil of his cataracts, he also repainted some of his water lilies with bluer tones. Others surmise that after a lifetime of seeing, he was able to paint the light inherent in all things. Whatever the cause of his deeper sight, his lifelong friend Georges Clemenceau described Monet as a human microscope, magnifying through his love and attention the inside of light and how it illumined the things of this world. I think both insights are true: that seeing through his cataracts *increased* his soul's capacity to *reveal* the light inherent in all things.

It's inspiring that after a lifetime of dedication to seeing more and more clearly and painting exactly what he saw, Monet's masterworks came as he painted what he saw through a vision that was breaking down.

It's uplifting that Monet's lifetime of seeing was preparation for what he was born to perceive once his learned way of seeing was undone. Our passion for learning may be an inevitable apprenticeship to a deeper, more fundamental way of seeing once we reach the end of all we know. When we love things dearly enough, in time they reveal their light in response. Until we're left with the noble effort to voice and affirm what we see and hear when closest to life, for as long as we can.

Monet's struggle to see is inherent to the life of the soul, whether you're an artist or not. The questions life puts before us, daily, are: How can I keep my heart open and my mind from hardening into its cataracts of opinions and suppositions? And how can I surrender years of work and hard-earned conclusions for a greater, fresher engagement in life that suddenly becomes clear? And when I fail, how can I persevere and see what is true through the film of my cataracts?

Paradoxically, it takes a tremendous strength of surrender to put down whatever has led us to what is most real, as one puts down the weight of the climb for the view from the summit. Where do we get the strength for such surrender? For me, it comes from a faith that life is leading the living into ever-deeper waters, into ever-greater awareness; the way gravity brings all rivers to the sea.

Seeds to Water

 This meditation explores the gift of seeing: Go for a walk, if possible. Whether you're outside or inside, stop before something you're drawn to: a tree, a bridge, an old fence, or a window filled with light. Seat yourself nearby and simply look in silence at what has drawn you for at least thirty minutes. Notice how what you're looking at opens. Notice how you begin to relate to what you're looking at.

&. Later, in conversation with a friend or loved one, describe this experience of seeing more deeply and how it has affected you.

FIRE IN THE TEMPLE

Here is a story of how I was drawn to what I need to learn. I began to search, not sure for what. I thought of Tetsugen (1630–1682), the monk devoted to publishing the first translation of Buddha's Dharma talks into Japanese. He collected funds for many years, only to twice give away the money in order to help feed and clothe those sick and starving around him.

In trying to find exactly where he lived, I stumbled onto the history of the Yangtze River, whose name comes from an ancient ferry crossing, Yangzi Jin. This same river downstream was named by others the Tongtian River, which means "River Passing Through Heaven." This led me to artists who had painted the river and somehow I came across the phrase *the Three Brushes of Ōbaku.* What a beautiful phrase. There was no logic to my search. I was just following threads of light, like Monet. One thing that felt alive led me to the next.

The Three Brushes of Ōbaku (*Ōbaku no Sanpitsu*) referred to three revered Zen teachers who were each master calligraphers; one seeming to have taught the other. Sokuhi (1616–1671) was the youngest and perhaps the most accomplished poet and calligrapher among them. Along with Mokuan (1611–1684) and their teacher Ingen (1592–1673), the three were known as the Three Brushes. I found the notion of such a living lineage compelling. I wondered about their conversations and their luminous connections, as well as the friction that no doubt surfaced from the authority of their own personalities.

Then I came across a brief description of a transformative event in Sokuhi's life. In 1650, at the age of thirty-four, Sokuhi was badly burned while fighting a forest fire and nearly died from asphyxiation. In the midst of the fire, he was suddenly enlightened. This stunned me. I wanted to know more, but couldn't find any more. I went through my chores that day wondering about Sokuhi and what happened in that fire.

I couldn't let go of this detail of a monk's life. It seemed to glow like an ember flickering 350 years later. That night I dreamt of Sokuhi caught in the unbearable heat of

flames as tall as the trees around him. The
next morning I entered this poem in his
voice:

There I was, unsure if the fire was
    supposed to
fill the temple the way life fills a body.
    Others
were frantic, swatting robes at the base of
    flames,
but I was stopped by the beauty of the
    yellow
heat embracing the trees. It made me think
of my father's funeral pyre. How I miss him.
Where did the fire take him? In the heart's
long look back, I wanted to run into the
flames and go after him. There's something
in us that wants to join the flame. It was
    then
master Yuan stood before me, flames
    everywhere,
the forest crackling, the empty temple
waiting, master Yuan calm as the lake
    before
dawn. He spoke softly. "Now you have to
choose, Sokuhi." A burning limb fell behind
us. He stepped closer. "Will you bring in
    there
out here? Or keep watching from the rim?"
His robe caught aflame and I cried out,

knocking
him to the ground, smothering the heat.
Though his back was burned, he stared
  into
the small fire I'd been guarding inside for
years. Something in the truth of his love
brought me into the world. I began to weep.
The flames moved past us closer to the
  temple.
I ran through them to get more water and
  the
smoke of centuries made my eyes burn
  and the
veil between worlds made my legs heavy. I
  couldn't
breathe. I grew light-headed in the midst of
  flames
taller than the temple and began to sing
  some
song that rose from my small fire so eager
  to
join the fire around us. I didn't understand
what was happening. But the harder it was
  to
breathe, the more I understood my breath.
  The
harder it was to keep my eyes open, the
  more I
understood the moment of true seeing. The
  last

thing I saw was the temple waiting for the
   flames.
When I came to, the earth had been
   cleared and the
temple seemed less a refuge and more an
   oasis.

Being drawn to write so thoroughly in the
voice of others doesn't happen often, but I
felt in this case that I'd been led to serve as
a brief conduit for Sokuhi across the years,
as if his story was waiting to be told. At this
point, I realized that, in trying to write
about the mystery of how we're drawn to
what we need to learn, I was drawn to this.
Now, as when meeting a koan, I'm left to
decipher what it is *I* need to learn from
Sokuhi and his moment of being undone.

I have stopped writing poems with the illusion that I have something to say. I write
with a faith that in following a feeling, a
question, or an image, I will discover my
next teacher. In this case, I found Sokuhi.

The felt experience of surfacing Sokuhi's
story left me breathless, and I went to my
friend David to read him the poem. I was
taken by the moment when master Yuan
confronts Sokuhi as the flames are rising
around them. "Now you have to choose,
Sokuhi." David and I looked at this as a mo-

309

ment we all must face sooner or later; a moment when we need to bring all of who we are into the world.

Once giving voice to the poem, I realized that Sokuhi's teacher was Ingen, and yet the name Yuan appeared in the poem. I've learned to trust such discrepancies and left it as it came. I now claimed Sokuhi as part of my personal mythology, part of the constellation of voices I turn to as teachers and kindred seekers across time. As I told David that I needed to find out more about Sokuhi and this fire, but didn't know where to look, he smiled and went to his bookcase to take down a large book called *The Art of Zen.* The author was his cousin, Stephen Addiss, an art historian who specializes in this period of Japanese calligraphy.

We quickly looked through the book, and sure enough, there was a chapter on Obaku Zen with a section discussing the Three Brushes of Obaku and a passage each on Ingen, Mokuan, and yes, Sokuhi. We were stunned. It was there I learned that master Ingen's Chinese name was Yuan.

David's cousin had unearthed more details surrounding the forest fire:

A deeper enlightenment came to Sokuhi in 1650 during a forest fire on Mount Huangpo. Sokuhi was helping to fight the fire, which was fanned by a strong wind, when he burned his face, arms, and legs and fell into a trench. His colleagues came to rescue him, and at that moment he experienced satori. When he presented himself to his teacher, Ingen said, "You have had the experience of a great death and have come alive." The first month of the following year, Ingen gave Sokuhi a whisk in recognition of his understanding, and Sokuhi declared, "With the power of this whisk I will work for the Buddha by going out to teach." Ingen composed a poem for Sokuhi, and from that time on the young monk was considered a Zen master.

What are we to make of such connections? That there is always a story behind the story as we have talked about? That "we are each other," as the traditions say? That we all share a common element of being, that "Thou Art That," as the Hindus say?

Personally, I keep exploring the moment in the fire when the master challenges the student to bring all that he is to bear on the messy tangle of living. I think this is my challenge. I think this is a challenge for all of us. I keep trying to open this moment so I can stay in conversation with it and in conversation with others about it. This is how the education of our soul unfolds: moment by moment, story by story, as we bring our souls to each other and hold them to the light, trying to make sense of their markings.

I found two of Sokuhi's seminal ink drawings. Not surprisingly, they have the waver and feel of flames. One is called *Ocean of Good Fortune,* the other, *Mountain of Longevity.* These drawings make me think about the moment *after* Yuan confronts him, the fire rising about them. It's only when a blazing limb falls on his master that Sokuhi stops contemplating and leaps into the world. Did he, after being burned himself, understand this? Is he saying with his drawings that leaping through the fire, into the world, to save the things we love is the key to good fortune and longevity?

Mysteriously, we're drawn to what we need to learn. We're drawn to live in the world till the fire within meets the fire without. We're drawn to move through all the invisible barriers to find what we love, to love what we love, and to save what we love.

I'm drawn to this conclusion, this beginning, this spirited refrain: that the inevitable journey of being a spirit on Earth is to love things dearly enough that in time we become a nameless part of what we love. Until we're left with the noble effort to voice and affirm what we touch and know when closest to life, for as long as we can.

Seeds to Water

🐦 Intuitively open a book you've wanted to read and meet whatever passage speaks to you. Center yourself and reflect on the passage. See what it stirs in you. Throughout your day, follow the thread of curiosity this passage has opened and see where it leads you, pausing to reflect on each connection that is revealed along the way.

🐦 In conversation with a friend or loved one, describe how you are currently being called to bring who you are out into the world. How are you facing this call? What scares you about this? What excites you? What might be your next step?

THE SACRED GROVE

Walking is the great adventure, the first meditation, a practice of heartiness and soul primary to humankind. Walking is exact balance of spirit and humility.
— Gary Snyder

What is it like when one has broken through? A thousand miles, the same mood.
— Yun-men

I am a teacher. That means I shine a light here and hold a mirror there. It means I walk in wonder and sit in truth. It means I love stories and follow where they lead. My father was a teacher. My brother is a teacher. Like them, I love to sit with others around questions that can't be answered because they light our way. The lineage of teachers says that everyone has a gift, and that along the way everyone meets an obstacle to their gift. I'm a teacher because I believe that the obstacle is there to ignite the gift. And so I devote myself to how and not why.

I've always been interested in the lives of teachers and how they gather. I was born into the Jewish, Talmudic tradition, where meaning is gathered through relationship, and God appears through the fire of dialogue. I once saw a Roman Vishniac photograph taken in a small, Jewish town in Poland in 1934. The viewpoint is from a stairway above a large, open room. The room is packed with students, nowhere to move. Behind a desk, a *rebbe* (Yiddish for *teacher*) is in mid-question. All the young lives in the room are focused on the space into which the *rebbe* is about to speak. That space is sacred and dynamic. We all come alive in that space of meaning where a true question is about to be asked.

Two great teachers in ancient Greece gathered with their students to enter that space of meaning: Plato, a student of Socrates; and Aristotle, who studied with Plato. Plato inherited a grove of olive trees near Colonus, about a mile north of Athens, where in 387 BC he began his school, the Academy, and convened informal gatherings. From the outset, there was no clear distinction between teachers and students. Plato had no particular doctrine to teach, but posed quandaries of living to enter and study together. Students and teachers alike would walk throughout the olive grove trying to find meaning in their time on Earth. It's profound to realize that the original meaning of the word *academy* is "Sacred Grove."

There is a Sacred Grove waiting to be inhabited between us. It is less a physical sanctuary and more a gathering place for those on the journey. True education depends on a covenant that all teachers make: to gather and walk around life's great questions with their students. The holy space that comes alive when we truly behold each other has always been a source of transformation in the world.

The land where Plato gathered his students was considered sacred to the goddess Athena. Even when the Spartans conquered Athens, they left the Sacred Grove untouched out of respect. But in 86 BC, the Roman general Sulla axed the sacred olive trees to build fortifications.

In this history lives a stark choice at the heart of all education: Do we preserve the Sacred Grove as the safe, restorative center where discovering meaning together gives us the strength to meet the world, or do we axe the sacred grove to build fortifications against the hardships of the world?

Each of us is born with a restorative place that is safe and life-giving. That safe place is our Sacred Grove. But the abrasions of living agitate us out of this restorative place until we no longer feel safe. Now fear infiltrates our sense of being. When we find ourselves in this agitated state, which no one can avoid, we're faced with a more personal form of the same choice. We can invoke the ancient effort to recover our safe resting place and restore our trust in simply being. Or we can axe what is sacred to build new fortifications in hopes of lessening our fear. But regardless of the protections we build, it's restoring our trust in life that opens us to the Sacred Grove, that place of true meeting, always possible between us.

Aristotle was a student in Plato's Academy for twenty years. When his mentor died, Aristotle wasn't chosen to succeed his teacher, because his views had already diverged significantly from Plato's. Eventually, he founded his own Peripatetic school in Athens. *Peripatetic* comes from the Greek word that means "given to walking about." Because Aristotle wasn't a citizen of Athens, he couldn't own property, so he gathered his students on the grounds of the Lyceum, a public meeting place, also situated in a grove of trees, where they would amble through the colonnades and covered walkways, exploring life's questions.

By walking, we take the Sacred Grove with us into the world. All cultures have traditions of walking as a way to seek spiritual guidance and to clarify purpose: the Camino de Santiago in Spain, the Native American vision quest, the Christian tradition of walking labyrinths, and the long, silent, meditative walks that Buddhists revere. Walking bring us into the open. When we walk in silence and then talk, we let life become part of our conversation.

The urge and call to walk is an inborn way to come out of our smaller selves and heal. Walking is symbolic of how we meet others, of how we move through the world. If you're feeling insular, take a walk and it won't be long before you encounter other life. Walking reminds us that we're in a constant struggle to deepen and trust our own direct experience of life *and* to stay open to the lives of others.

There are Sacred Groves and walking paths all over the world. They mark a lineage of gathering places across time, all brought into being so we can remember what matters, touch the sacred, and exercise wisdom more lovingly in the world. If you can't find or travel to traditional pilgrimage routes, you can create your own. It's not the doctrine we follow, but the path we discover. As Carl Jung says, "Learn your theories well but put them aside when you confront the mystery of the living soul."

Fittingly, as I'm writing this, our new dog Zuzu interrupts. It's time for our morning walk. And once striding among the trees, I can see that, more than what we arrive at, it's walking in the Sacred Grove, together and alone, that matters.

Learning is a chance that appears when we're drawn to a patch of sun and for a second all seems clear. Meet me in this clearing where we can walk together until some sense of truth appears. We have a strength that longs to make its way into the world, if we can only find it. I am a teacher. You are a teacher. Anyone who longs to sing the song under everything is a teacher.

Seeds to Water

    ❧ Take a walk, alone in silence. Walk until you begin to feel the lineage of those who gather around life's questions. Walk until you begin to sense that you are entering the Sacred Grove. Upon your return, journal about this experience.

❧ Take a walk with a friend or loved one, only speaking when moved by life's questions. Discuss whether you preserve what matters in order to gain strength to meet the world, or whether you cut up what matters in order to build fortifications against the harshness of the world. What are the value and cost of each to you?

OUR SPIRIT PATH

After four months of aggressive chemo, I had to have a test known as First Pass, in order to determine if the chemo had damaged my heart. Through an IV, I was injected with a radioactive dye, which made me feel flush and hot. Then I watched the screen as the first pass of blood moved through the chambers of my heart. It was the only time I've seen my physical heart. Ever since, the heart and how it works has been a teacher for me.

Recently, I felt my heart beating in rhythm with the larger network of life, and I could feel how we all fit together. With my hand on my heart, I realized that beneath the intensity of our inevitably personal journey, we're part of a larger pattern of life fulfilling itself. With my heart pumping, I could see that as blood flows from every part of the body to and through the heart, each life follows its mysterious path to and through the

Center of All Life. Each of us is born with an instinct to flow to and through that Center. And the heights and depths of our experience form the Spirit Path that brings us through that Center.

We think the Spirit Path we discover is special and unique, though all paths lead to the same Center of Life. Some of us try to map the flow of life and name it physics, psychology, spirituality, nature, or biology. Others want to understand the flow of life as mechanics and dedicate themselves to engineering, meditation, or pragmatism. Still others feel certain the flow of life is entered through art, painting, music, or dance. Some find their Spirit Path through the life of expression. I come alive through the inquiry of writing. But no one path or flow of aliveness is more important than another, any more than the liver's understanding of blood is more important than the kidney's.

Just as the heart keeps the blood in circulation, the Center of All Life that draws us to it and pumps us back into our days is the beat that keeps the world together. When following this beat, we're drawn into the Heart of Oneness. When we pass through that Center, all the principles and names we've given to what keeps the world together are cleansed of their self-importance in favor of a more common, nameless immersion into life.

Being human, however, we can't stay in the Heart of Oneness but must live in the world, the way our blood can't stay in the heart but must return to the hands so they can do their work in the world. Once freed of our self-importance, our hands are filled with a mysterious aliveness that conveys the strength of the world. Taking the chance to touch and be touched, we can inhabit the flow of aliveness we're born with and become a conduit between it and the work that needs to be done. I stop now to look at my hands, thinking of all they've touched through the years.

So what is your Spirit Path? How do you come alive and help keep the world together? How do you receive the flow of life that draws you to its center? Discovering this, personalizing this, and relating to this is how we gather our being into a force that can be of use.

This is another way to say that we're born with a dormant set of gifts that we need to inhabit in order to help each other become complete — through our absorption of what is life-giving, through our reaching with open hands to meet the needs of the world, through our effort to stay connected, and through our courage to remain kind.

I place my hand on my heart and can feel the first pass of blood through its chambers. I open my other hand, accepting that it's this circulation of aliveness from heart to hand that emanates healing in the world. In this deeper state of involvement, we *are* goodness.

Seeds to Water

   ❦ In your journal, tell the story of a moment when you had the privilege of looking into the canyon of another's heart. What did you see there?

MAKING HONEY

Bees are drawn to gather nectar and pollen from flowers. Landing on a flower, a honeybee will suck the nectar of the flower and store it in her second stomach, a stomach for carrying honey called a *glossa*. She carries almost seventy milligrams of nectar, close to her own weight, back to the hive. A single bee must visit fifty to a hundred flowers to fill its honey-stomach before heading to the hive.

When returning to the hive, a worker bee sucks the nectar from the honeybee's glossa, chewing the soft nectar for almost an hour. Then, the worker bees spread the nectar in the honeycombs. In time, the worked nectar turns into a thick syrup, drying faster as the bees fan their wings. The bees seal off the honeycomb cells, which store the nectar until it becomes honey.

The process of bees making honey is how we follow our sense of aliveness. We're drawn to what we need to learn. And what we extract from what we go through is our nectar, gathered by rubbing our face in the center of a hundred encounters with life. Through the engagements of our heart, we help other things grow, leaving care like pollen wherever we go. Then we chew on each other's nectar until it breaks down into something essential through friendship and honest conversation. Chewing what life brings us makes honey of our troubles. In time, the nectar of our love becomes the honey of wisdom. Often, what we struggle with so deeply in such a personal way, once voiced and shared, becomes food for everyone.

When I find that problems and doubts are gripping me and interrupting my connection to what matters, I stop and imagine that this is my last hour on Earth. If that is so, how important is anything on my list? How important is anything but the effort to gather love like nectar and leave care like pollen wherever we go?

In a letter dated November 13, 1925, the great poet Rilke writes to his Polish translator, Witold Hulewicz: "We are bees of the Invisible." Our soul seeks aliveness in the nectar of the world. Then we're on our way: bringing life to others who will chew on it with their love. We are meant to pollinate the world with love and presence, chewing on what matters until it sweetens into wisdom.

Seeds to Water

🐝 In your journal, identify three examples of nectar you've retrieved from what you've been through. By nectar, I mean something that has helped you live. Describe each example in terms of how you were drawn to it and where you keep what you've learned.

🐝 In conversation with a friend or loved one, share these examples of nectar and chew on them together. What kind of honey are you creating?

THE SERPENT KING

Seeds incubate in the dark
so they can break ground
and grow toward the light.
For the seed we call Spirit
in the ground we call human,
being held in the dark
can last a long time.

For years, I had a fear of snakes. I didn't
grow up with it and I wasn't born with it.
Though we're wired at birth with fear as a
built-in warning device, the things we fear
are often acquired and fertilized like dark
seeds we tend when no one is looking. My
fear of snakes took hold in my marriage to
my former wife, Ann, more than twenty
years ago. Ann grew up on a farm and had
some bad experiences with farmhands who
dangled snakes to scare her and watch her
run. When we lived in upstate New York, I
tried to protect her from snakes, which she

never asked me to do, and slowly, I began to take on her fear, in a shadow form of empathy.

One day, in early spring, when the frost was thawing, I noticed how our front stoop had cracked and, in the crack, a snake had wintered nicely. It was larger than any snake I'd ever seen, thick as a pipe, and about five feet long. Ann was at work and I was terrified for both of us. All I could think was that I had to make our home safe, that I had to seal up the crack in our home and bury the thing for good. I ran out and bought some liquid concrete and carefully filled the crack thickly, burying the snake alive forever. I hoped. I thought I had been resourceful. I wouldn't even have to tell Ann what had happened.

Shortly after lunch, the sun came out and somehow the snake had found a way out and was now coiled under our rhododendron, next to the stoop. My fear escalated and I thought, *The only way to be certain is to kill it.* I didn't know how and really didn't have the stomach for it, but I kept thinking of Ann coming home in panic. And so I got the hoe from the garage, put on some work gloves and boots, swallowed hard, and awkwardly and basely began hacking at the snake. It was ugly and prolonged. Once the snake was dead, I cleaned it up, and even as I write this, I can still feel the weight of its dead coil in the Hefty bag.

Trembling, I drove to a nearby field along a back road and dumped the remains and went home. To my surprise, my fear was not relieved but intensified. I couldn't calm my heart. I came close to vomiting several times, and wondered why it had never occurred to me to call someone to take the snake away. I'd let my fear create a life for itself.

That was more than two decades ago. I now live halfway across the country. The autumn before last, my wife, Susan, and I took a walk with our dog Mira to see the orange leaves against the pines in a wood we've come to love. It was a mild October day and, on the path, I jumped at the sight of a small garter snake and felt the old fear rush into my throat. It was hard for me to calm down. Fifteen minutes later, another small snake appeared. I saw the huge old snake in my mind, writhing under my hoe. On another trail, a third snake appeared. Finally, I dropped my shoulders and faced my dark history in the sun. I had traumatized myself all those years ago, and the anguish of my karma has been to relive the pain I inflicted by needlessly taking the life of that snake.

Squatting in those autumn leaves, I was certain that I was no longer the young, inexperienced man who kept switching the hoe, trying to escape a fear I'd taken on and made my own. Nonetheless, I'm responsible for all that he did.

I became weepy in the orange grove, and our dog, sensing this, ran to lick my face. I knelt closer to the earth and asked the snake I had killed in another life to forgive me. On that autumn day, it became clear that much of the harm we do on this Earth comes from trying to remove or cripple what we're afraid of, rather than face what stirs us within to be afraid. For when we kill what we fear, we often close the door to what we need to know.

Within a month after our walk in the woods, I found myself in a museum in front of a Cambodian stone carving from the second century. It was a statue of Buddha and Muchalinda. It represents a moment in Buddha's process of enlightenment. It's said that Buddha, on the verge of illumination, was drawn into a deep meditation, so much that he was unaware of the torrential rain and rising waters surrounding him, which were sent by a demon in an effort to drown him. But using his thick coils, the Serpent

King Muchalinda raised Buddha above the rising waters and protected him with his seven cobra heads. Now I'm forced to wonder, what protections have I foregone by hacking what I fear? What teachers might we bow to, if we could only withstand the urge to eliminate what frightens us?

Seeds to Water

❧ In your journal, describe in detail a fear or worry that you have absorbed and taken on from others. How did this happen, what has it cost you, and how can you face it?

❧ In conversation with a friend or loved one, discuss an unnecessary harm you inflicted out of fear. How might you have handled the situation differently?

READING THE CRACKS

Legend has it that in 1899 in China, a man suffering from malaria acquired a turtle shell in order to pulverize it in hopes of concocting a traditional remedy. As he began to break it apart, he found inscriptions engraved on the shell that were more than three thousand years old. And so, a lost culture, the Shang dynasty (1766–1122 BC), was discovered. As archaeologists pieced the Shang culture together, they discovered a ritual known as Oracle Bones. It appears that each Shang king had a diviner who was charged to use a turtle shell or the shoulder bone of an ox to foretell the future. The back of the shell or bone was carved with notches. Then the diviner would heat the shell or bone until it cracked, and bring the cracked object to the king, who would read the cracks like a palm reader. The questions and predictions were then engraved into the shell or bone as some form of retrieved wisdom.

Reading the cracks that life opens in us reveals meaning. The Jewish tradition speaks to this powerfully. In Deuteronomy, it's written that the word of God is placed like honey *on* the heart. When a student asks his rabbi why the word of God is not placed *in* the heart, the rabbi replies that, being human, we ignore the word of God unless we're broken open to it. So the word of God waits like honey to enter our heart through the crack made when change or sorrow forces us to open.

The cracks that lead to growth appear throughout nature: stems of flowers and vegetables grow out of cracks in the earth and their growth aerates the soil. Rain streams through crevices that part the face of a mountain, providing water for those who live in the valley, and small flowers work their way through cracks in stone to show us how to stay strong.

The psychoanalyst Lou Andreas-Salomé, a peer and inspiration to Nietzsche, Freud, and Rilke, wrote in her memoir:

We cannot imagine God except personally . . . according to (the opening of) our own personality . . . (the way) light falls into a room in the form of the opening through which it enters.

Being human, we can't help but crack. And where we do, the Divine Life-Force known by many sacred names pours through our cracks, illuminating who we are. We learn along the way that the beauty of life also enters us through our cracks. If we can't accept this fundamental law of how light and beauty enter us through the ways we're opened, we will misread the initiations of experience as a cruel avalanche of unfairness.

Part of our inner work is to endure the pain of being broken in order to receive whatever light might enter us. Since the beginning, we've always been compelled to read the cracks, wherever they appear, trying to make sense of what comes through.

This is how Linda shared her story: "I can only tell you of a time when I held out, when my husband wasn't working and I was supporting both of us, as well as our two little kids. I was working very hard. We weren't poor, but we were watching things. My husband's father was living nearby. One day, my husband came home and said, 'My father would like a new suit. I'd like to buy it for him.' It cost three hundred dollars. I was put off that he would ask such a thing. I thought it frivolous and not essential. So I said no. I was the one working. My husband said, 'It's not about the suit but about his finally respecting himself.' I didn't want to hear it and turned away. My husband was hurt but didn't ask again. Well, it wasn't six weeks later that his father was diagnosed with cancer and within a month, he was gone. My heart cracked open. What was three hundred dollars? What was my objection, really? What wall was I maintaining? Was it really important? It was too late, but I insisted on buying the suit he so wanted. It was blue with wide lapels. We buried him in it."

We sometimes hide behind our principles, as if they will protect us from those rare moments that crack us open. Though we often think we're protecting ourselves, we're more often, as Parker Palmer says, "conspiring in our own diminishment." For Linda, her father-in-law's request was the crack she tried to refuse, and his death was the honey of God that finally softened her heart.

We encounter more of these chances than we'd like to admit. If we deny enough of them, we go numb and lose our access to beauty. The Jungian analyst Robert Johnson describes a time when he was refusing to

336

accept how deeply estranged he was from his own life. He tells the heartrending story of rushing to Grace Cathedral in San Francisco to listen to Handel's *Messiah,* one of his favorite rituals. Though he was front and center, he couldn't feel a thing and left midway, driving down Highway 101 with the stark realization of how removed he'd become. Johnson painfully concludes that "the inability to feel in the presence of beauty" is the deepest of psychological pains, a devastating sign that we've slipped into a numbing corner of hell.

A quiet crack like this can let us see the truth of how we're living. Hard as this is to face, it's an opening through which we can heal. For at least, at last, we can admit that we're removed from what is beautiful. The worst hell of all is when we don't even know what we're missing. An old saying in the twelve-step rooms among recovering alcoholics is, "I was so sick, I thought I was well."

Sometimes, the weight of things brings us to our knees, and we're forced to see into the cracks, where the light of God is awash, breaking all principle. When we hide from or resist the truth that comes through us, we stunt our growth and fail our inborn promise. In time, our want to hide or resist makes surrender necessary as a way to love the cracks we're given into openings. And there's never a dearth of chances to do this. For experience and suffering crack us open constantly.

When love does its work, it cracks the illusion that we're separate from each other. When experience does its work, it cracks the illusion that we can sidestep time and pain. When all our thinking fails, it cracks the illusion that analyzing life allows us to control it. But when we can keep *breaking through* what has hardened and keep what is alive soft, the cracks turned into openings fill us with an undying light.

Seeds to Water

❦ In your journal, describe a time when some experience of breaking let more light in. Discuss your pain in being broken open. Speak to how the light that came in affected you.

❦ This is a street meditation. Center yourself and breathe slowly. As you inhale, try to feel the Spirit you carry rising from your center. As you exhale, feel your Spirit trying to move out of you into the world. Breathe fully and feel the container of your life that lives between your Spirit and the world. As you walk down this street, look for the cracks in your walls that will let your Spirit out. This may appear as a moment when your guard is down and you feel vulnerable. Or when what you planned to say in a certain situation no longer seems relevant. Or when a moment of nature slips through a crack in your worry. Notice how you feel during these moments of being cracked open. Take the time to read your cracks.

ASKING FOR OUR TURN

Karen's father never listened to her. When her college friend, Iris, came home for Thanksgiving to meet her family, Karen's father began to drift away from their conversation as he always did, dismissing both of them. But Iris immediately said, "Mr. Hollins, we're here, please." This awkward call from Iris broke a dark custom between Karen and her father. After a brief and difficult silence, Karen's father said, "Oh, sorry. Yes, where were we?"

Later, Iris said to Karen, "It hurt me to see you so disregarded. Why can't you ask for your turn? He probably won't change, but you don't have to muffle yourself." It had never occurred to Karen to say a word.

It's hard to remember that we are filled with light, and that we have choices. To emanate our light in the presence of others is a struggle that everyone faces, more than once. Unlike animals, we as humans can muffle our light and do so every time we let others block us from being who we are. We do this to ourselves each time we don't ask for our turn: to come out from behind our masks, to speak our truth, and to honestly share our feelings.

Some people are so blocked from their light that they can't bear the light of others nearby, as it painfully reminds them of the absence of their own connection to the Truth of the Universe. They become light-mufflers rather than light-seekers. In the face of all this, we're asked to grow toward the light the way trees and plants do. Each branch grows toward whatever opening is available. Branches grow around each other and through each other. Some branches grow down before growing up. Some grow sideways, while some twist through the smallest openings. But together, all the branches form a majestic, unrepeatable latticework of trees. Growing toward the light is asking for our turn.

In my own struggles to ask for my turn, I've always had to take the simple yet hard step of saying what is true in the moment it is true. Saying what is true always seems extremely dangerous before doing so. But when I do speak the truth of what I'm experiencing, the ground of the relationship

I'm in shifts and growth becomes possible. Saying what is true is an earnest way to grow toward the light.

A common example of our light being blocked is when someone, often meaning well, interrupts our sharing in an effort to advise or fix us. In this situation, one way to speak our truth might include saying, "I know you mean well but I'm not done sharing," or, "I really need your company now. I'll be glad to listen to you later." Each time we can do this, even in the smallest way, there's more room for our soul to come out of hiding and simply breathe.

Under all our attempts to be heard is the basic fact that we don't need the other person's permission to honor what is true for us. We don't have to pretend that they haven't interrupted us or been hurtful. Another more challenging level of speaking our truth is to say, "I know you mean well, but I don't feel you're giving me space to speak," or, "Are you able to listen right now? If not, we can talk about this at another time."

You don't have to stay in a life-draining situation, pretending it is other than what it is. And you don't have to explain yourself. You can just remove yourself from the situation. If someone doesn't honor your need for space and truth, you can simply leave. I know how hard these affirmations are to actually inhabit. I still struggle to do this myself. But each time we say what we feel and speak what we mean, our soul and the light that enlivens our soul come out into the world a little bit more. And like a branch growing toward the light, the growth of our life slowly unfolds.

Seeds to Water

♣ In your journal, describe a time when you needed to ask for your turn. Did you do so or not? If so, what made that possible? If not, what kept you from asking for your turn? How has this experience affected the way you share what you truly experience?

♣ Go for a walk and find a tree whose shape in reaching toward the light feels akin to your own. What do you see in the pattern of the tree's growth that mirrors your own?

NOT LISTENING

It's not what you don't know that hurts you,
but what you know for sure that just ain't
so.

— Mark Twain

We often miss what matters because we're
preoccupied with the weight of our past,
the press of the present, or our worry about
the future. These preoccupations are all
forms of not listening. Yet under all the
weight, press, and worry is the fundamental
truth of our existence, if we can reach it.

Moving through the forms of not listening
till we can hear the truth of our heart, the
truth of our experience, and the truth of
existence is an initiation that has gone on
forever. In the Assyrian tale of Gilgamesh,
over seven thousand years old, the lost and
empty king doesn't listen to the pain in his
heart and so mistakenly declares war on
Nature, projecting his pain as something to

be conquered in the world. His insistence on striking out rather than looking inward leads to the death of his only friend, Enkidu. In his grief, he seeks to bring Enkidu back to life by making a pilgrimage to the Assyrian god Utnapishtim.

Along the way, Gilgamesh falls prey to another form of not listening. The sad king is told that he will come upon a set of stones that he must bring to the ferryman who will read the stones in order to bring him to Utnapishtim. But three times in his journey, Gilgamesh comes upon the stones and each time — in his grief, in his impatience, and finally in his anger — he smashes them. Of course, he finally meets the ferryman who says, "I've been expecting you. Where are the stones?"

How many times do we project our pain onto the world, rather than face the emptiness in our heart? How many times have we all been given a sign of what might help us find our way, only to smash the sign, out of grief, impatience, or anger?

We may also give away what we know to be true about our gifts and our strengths in deference to the insistence of a loved one. How many times does not listening to our own truth throw our most intimate relationships out of balance, leaving that intimacy at risk?

There is also this example of not listening from the history of my own family. In 1933, my grandmother and grandfather, eking their way through the Great Depression in Brooklyn, New York, had heard rumblings of great danger for the Jews in Europe. My grandmother's sister lived in Romania with her husband and small boy. Somehow, over the coming year, my grandparents saved enough money to purchase and send steamship tickets for the Romanian family to come to America. But my grandmother's sister sent the steamship tickets back, saying that everything was fine and Romania was their home. They all died in the concentration camp at Buchenwald. While no one can foresee the future, this tragic exchange stands in my family history as a cautionary, if heartbreaking, tale of not listening to the world around you. Here, not listening looms as the want to deny difficulty in hopes that it will go away.

These stories are not curiosities of history. More deeply, they reveal ever-present challenges that we each face in our personal journeys. Projecting our pain, grief, impatience, and anger on others, abdicating our gifts to please a loved one, rejecting new learning because it challenges what is familiar, exiling others because they threaten our position or identity, and denying difficulty in hopes that it will go away — these are all forms of not listening that can undermine our aliveness in any given moment.

Seeds to Water

- ❦ In your journal, describe one form of not listening you participate in and tell a story of your not listening as an example.

- ❦ Explain to a friend or loved one this form of not listening, and explore what you fear would happen if you truly opened yourself to listen to others, yourself, and life.

Keeping Our Eyes Open

According to Buddhism, there are three poisons — ignorance, greed, and delusion — that make us forget why we're here and what really matters. Turning away from what we don't understand, wanting more than we need, and pretending things are other than they are — these reactions to life can stymie us. But the antidote for ignorance is our courage to face the unknown. And the remedy for greed is to accept that who we are and what we have are enough. And when intoxicated with the shimmer of our dream, we can stop and open our hearts to the truth of the moment — which is all that matters. These are simple actions, and yet they're as demanding as sitting in silence until our mind runs out of ideas.

We're often kept from meeting the truth of our experience by our urge to count and compare, to measure who we are and where we are. As soon as we begin to count and compare, we're removed from the life of presence. You can't count and be immersed in life at the same time. We're also frequently distracted by our urge to worry and to please others. These preoccupations form a dark net that prevents us from seeing ourselves, others, or reality accurately.

Each of us is challenged to uncover our personal way of restoring what matters. When we face impediments and reclaim who we are and what we know to be true, we mature as souls. We learn to live a full life. The artist Corita Kent, a former nun who lived in Montecito, California, said, "Damn everything but the circus." I think she meant that, hard as life is, we have to love the carnival of being here. For it's only through entering the many games and rides that we fulfill our potential. Only by moving through life's absurdities can we find meaning and each other.

For centuries nuns and monks were taught not to look up when they walked and not to look each other in the eye. Life was thought to be a distraction from God. This practice was called "custody of the eyes." This monastic inclination to withdraw from the world upholds a false separation of the inner life from the outer life.

Here, custody implies that an individual is

unable to engage with what he or she sees and must be blinkered to it, that we must be quarantined from experience or we'll lose our way. This mistrust assumes that we are unequipped to search for God *and* live in the world. There is some truth to the fact that we must withdraw from the world at times to know the Source, but not to avoid reality. A deeper look at all traditions shows that after inner reflection we must engage the world to live what we know. Experience is the teacher that inevitably leads us to what is sacred. Engaging our inner and outer selves is how we find our way.

We often create our own forms of blindness. What particular custody do you invoke in the name of courtesy or propriety, or even holiness, in order to avoid facing and engaging life? What is the nature of your doubts about your ability to engage what you see? Do you face these doubts or do you avert your eyes, feeding a distrust of yourself that only makes you feel sorely unequipped to enter the stream of life?

One custody can lead to another: a custody of the eyes, then a custody of the mind, then a custody of the heart, and then of the hands. First, we don't meet another in the eye. Then, we don't look up when we walk. Then, we change the channel when the talk is different from our own. Then, we turn away when we hear someone cry out in pain or laugh too loud. All this leads to a custody of the hands in which we make sure we touch nothing when we move through the streets, or remove all traces of contact when we do. Eventually, we can mistake watching life for living life. We become like work-horses who wear blinders to keep them on task, to keep them in the furrow of the plow and away from the breeze in the field. Yet so much of being human is asking more than once, "What are we here for?" The work-horse of the soul needs to plow the breeze as much as the earth.

We're meant to look beyond our blind-ness — no matter its form — in order to unearth a deeper way of seeing. So, if there's a strain between your being and your do-ing, a strain arising from being inwardly not where you are, stop and face what is con-gesting your heart. Make what you need to tend be where you are going. Stop, breathe, and let your inner and outer attention go in the same direction. Keeping our inner and outer attention aligned is a practice that can cleanse the heart.

When in doubt, stop looking at yourself and *be* yourself, and whatever form of blindness you're suffering will start to lessen. You will meet yourself like a river flowing into the light.

Seeds to Water

🌰 In your journal, explore what kind of illusion or blindness you have created that has been an impediment. What steps can you take to recover from it?

🌰 In conversation with a friend or loved one, discuss when you had to overcome your own custody of the eyes and look directly into a situation or into another person's life. What did you learn from this experience?

WORKING OUR WAY
INTO GRACE

The other day I missed my grandmother who's been gone for almost thirty years. The ache was with me heavily. I was in the Chicago airport and through my ache I saw a mother and daughter reunite on the G concourse. Though we never spoke, their ache and my ache, sweet and sour, spilled into each other, and the boundaries between us vanished. They walked away, and as I looked at others I didn't know, I could now feel their hearts beating for all the loved ones they were en route to.

Feeling our experience thoroughly can give us access to what others feel. When we can inhabit the reality of our full and ordinary lives, the boundaries between us vanish. If we can keep our heart open, just a bit longer, the boundaries between yesterday and today vanish as well, and our effort opens into the grace of a timeless communion with all living things. This is how we experience Eternity, by being completely authentic in our particular moment until it opens into all moments, until who we are pools with the presence of all hearts.

At times, like in that airport, I've fallen into the presence of all hearts when too exhausted to avoid my own pain or sorrow. The older I get, the more I understand that courage is a form of openness that calls to us to step into what's necessary. When I can face what's necessary, I discover what we all have in common.

Living with an open heart can be liberating and renewing, but it can also be draining and overwhelming. We can become emotionally overloaded and even deadened, if we can't break out of the replaying of our pain. Regret can plague us. In our pain, we can fix on one detail or mistake and replay that event over and over, as if reliving that moment will change what happened or lessen our pain in being flawed and human.

When I fell backward on our dog Mira, I injured her right paw. I was beside myself with worry and guilt. Her foot was swollen for days and didn't mend. She had to have surgery and had early arthritis from that point on. Every time I saw her limp, I replayed the moment of stepping on her. There was no way out of what I'd done.

When she was older, I'd massage her arthritic paw and feel the pang of my regret. She'd look at me with her timeless innocence, not sure why I was sad, but happy I was close to her. When I'd tear up, she'd start licking my face. It was her lick that stopped my mind from replaying what I'd done. It's the touch of new life that stops the replaying of old life.

There is a practice that helps us move through our pain: the effort to feel and *not* hold on to what we feel. Often we pair the two, certain we're not feeling or being present unless we're holding tightly to what we feel or to the situation we find ourselves in. But under our brokenness, the heart feeling deeply is like a flag that surrenders to the wind. A flag doesn't hold on to the wind, yet it couldn't be more immersed in it. Our job is not to stop or gather the life of feeling but to let it keep moving through us, the way a flag opens itself to wind.

Once we let what we feel move through us, no matter how difficult, the life of feeling — ever coming our way — enables us to recover our aliveness. Such wholeheartedness empowers us to go on. When I hold on to one feeling, whether pleasant or painful, I'm holding my breath inside my heart. When I can let the life of feeling continue to unfold, I begin to welcome grace. When I can meet my pain wholeheartedly without drowning in it, I fall into the one long moment of life, and there I know the ache of being human. When I can stop fixing my ideas as assumptions and conclusions and enter what hasn't yet happened with complete wonder, I fall into the endless stream of aliveness that has been flowing since the beginning of time. Letting life continue to unfold, despite our longing or regret, is how effort turns into grace.

When we push off of others, we remain lonely. When we admit our frailty, we're never alone. And though what saves us for tomorrow is the courage to get up when we fall down, what saves us for today is how we pause while on our knees to feel the weariness of everyone who's ever fallen. It's remembering our kinship when undone that lets us discover that there's nowhere else to go.

Within the acuteness of any one feeling, life can be overwhelming, but once feeling our kinship with other living things, the tide of all feeling lifts us with its depth and buoyancy. Such deep knowing doesn't eliminate our struggle or pain. Yet feeling our place in the human sea introduces us to grace.

When exhausted of my resistance to my feelings, I sink into the weightless depth of all feeling. When that opens, I can feel the history of kindness in the moment you place a washcloth on my fevered head. When I put aside my opinions and kiss you with my whole being, I can feel the union of all souls who have ached their way beyond their walls of fear. What else are we here for?

How hard we try, how little we know, how much we love.

Seeds to Water

❧ Center yourself and breathe slowly. Reflect on a brokenness you're carrying. As you inhale, feel the break. As you exhale, feel your way through the break and begin to feel the depth that waits beneath all breaks. Breathe deeply and inhale that depth up through your break into your heart. Carry the strength of that depth with you during your day. That strength of being is the beginning of grace.

❧ In your journal, describe a moment — of love, or pain, or wonder, or a moment in nature, or a moment while helping another — in which you began to feel the presence of other, similar moments throughout time. How did this depth of feeling affect you?

WAITING FOR OUR SOULS

The Nobel Prize–winning writer André Gide traveled through Africa in 1926 and, like most Europeans, hired native guides to travel with him. The morning after a very long day, Gide was eager to set out again, but the guides sat in a circle and refused to leave camp. When Gide told them to get moving, they replied, "Don't hurry us. We're waiting for our souls to catch up with us."

We can't move faster than our presence. Why? Because if we do, we arrive without our soul and never really experience the life we're in. Yet we do it all the time. My dear friend David Addiss, a leader in global health, told me this story about Gide. David went on to say:

> Retreat is a time to sit quietly and wait for our souls to catch up with us, a time to invite our souls back into the center. To do this we must let go of all that is not es-

sential, going ever inward, in silence, to encounter the true Self, and to hear the voice of God. Paradoxically, it's in this sitting, this silent waiting, this "act of doing nothing," that we embark on the inward journey. Despite the outward appearance of stillness, retreat is far from passive or inactive. Rather, the inward work, the inner journey, can be intense. Perhaps as the story suggests, it's only in this stillness that we can reconnect with our soul, that deepest part of our self, which all the while, has been on a journey of which we have been largely unaware. Retreat is becoming aware, once again, of the soul's journey and reconnecting with the soul's Creator.

Retreat is not just time away from the busyness of our lives. Retreat is a way of returning to the deepest part of our self, our soul. Waiting for our souls to catch up with us is how we practice letting the soul remember itself. This all speaks to an undeveloped skill by which we must learn to listen for when the soul is left behind and when it has returned.

It may help to think of André Gide and his guides as two voices within that we need to listen to: the explorer and the native.

These voices always seem to be in conversation and even in conflict. The explorer, eager to discover and achieve, presses us to move on, while that which is native to us knows there's nowhere to go. Both voices work together to bring us awake. To stay awake, we need to remain a student of this conversation, the way meditation makes us a student of breathing.

When impatient, the explorer in us demands that the problem solver in us work faster. But the native in us works more closely with what is. The native in us is in no hurry to get anywhere, wanting only to inhabit wherever we are to the fullest.

All this reminds me of my brother Howard who several years ago visited the Red Pyramid in Egypt. The largest of the three famous wonders, the Red Pyramid was built in Dahshur by Sneferu, the pharaoh who founded the Fourth Dynasty of the Old Kingdom in ancient Egypt (circa 2600 BC). As the tour guide went on, my brother couldn't move. He was captivated by the outer stone of the pyramid, and found himself waiting for his soul to catch up with him. He quietly stepped back from the others to place his cheek against the red granite baking in the sun, till he could feel the hands that put that block of stone in place over four thousand years ago, till he could feel all of life and all of time. As he told me this, I stopped to take it in, to take him in, and for the moment my soul had caught up with me. We were in the river of time together.

When the soul remembers itself, regardless of how or when, it spreads like light on stone to fill us with the presence of all life and all time. So wait, especially when you're worn and tired, wait till you fall open like a small, clear bowl destined to collect rain. Wait in the open for your soul to remember that you are its home. Wait for your soul to rain into you.

Seeds to Water

❧ In your journal, describe a time when you were moving ahead of your soul. How did this happen? What did this feel like? How did you realize you were doing this?

❧ In conversation with a friend or loved one, discuss the tension you each experience between the explorer, eager to press on, and the native, happy to be completely where you are.

Finding What Can Last

Dr. Leonard was about to trim down an old tooth for a crown and I was all numbed up, listening to the Beatles — *Abbey Road* — on small headphones. About halfway through, I began to feel the drilling. It wasn't bad, but I was afraid the drill would hit the nerve and get much worse. Nerve pain in a tooth is such a piercing thing. *There it was* — a sudden jolt of sharp pain overcame my whole being, radiating out. You can never see it coming and there's nowhere to go. I raised my hand while making a guttural sound. Dr. Leonard said, "You feeling that?" and gave me more Novocain and we were back on our way.

As he kept drilling, my mind began to reverberate. At times, I'm so afraid of feeling *anything,* but at the same time I so want to feel *everything.* There — with my mouth wide open, with George Harrison singing "Here Comes the Sun" in my ear, with the soft eyes of Dr. Leonard and his assistant Kari so carefully focused on the exposed nerve in my head — I realized that the tension of living often comes down to this paradox we all carry between our fear of feeling anything and our need to feel everything. I took a deep breath, trying to reach that larger sea of being in which my body drifts like a beat-up raft. Suddenly, I felt both strong and weak at once.

From that strong-weak place, I could see that we're such fragile, resilient creatures, here for just a long unplanned moment, tumbling and waking in this beautiful, harsh, tender existence. Through it all, we ride this call to both stay alive and be alive, which has us running from all the things that might hurt us and break us, while seeking all the things that might wake us and break us open. Here we are: left to dig ourselves out of hiding when we deny life too much, and soothing our cuts and burns when we let life in too much.

Kari dabbed my numb lip and Dr. Leonard told me not to eat anything too hard for a while. He said the place under the tooth where he injected the anesthetic would be sore for a day or two. Even numbing the pain has its pain. They kindly waited to make sure I understood their instructions.

Back on the street, I closed my eyes and lifted my head to the wind, half my face numb, the other half feeling the slight bite in the air. It was still early, sunny but cold. I quietly laughed at how we're each a walking koan, half feeling nothing, half feeling everything. I got in the car and drove on as life kept happening. As I slipped back into the stream of the ordinary, my awareness of our eternal battle between staying alive and being alive crept back below the surface.

Later that day, I came upon this quote by the spiritual teacher Raimon Panikkar:

Dialogue is a matter of understanding, of peeling away the mind to stand under (our thoughts) in Oneness. To understand the bountiful nature of reality, we must open our hearts. For we can't understand, if we don't love.

I rubbed the half of my face that was still numb, and thought, *Everything that matters comes through being opened to life, even at the dentist.* I read the Panikkar quote again. Perhaps when we can stand under our thoughts on the ground of life, perhaps in that moment, we stand on something that can last. And the only way to find what can last is to open our hearts and begin to care, even while we're numb and afraid.

The tooth has healed and I can eat again. But there are deeper nerves to tend. Afraid of what I might feel, I go on, wanting to be touched by everything. This is how we find our way. When tender or sore, we have to be careful not to think life is other than where we are. When afraid, we have to stand under our thoughts to find solid ground. When feeling worn down, our inner beauty begins to show. For underneath the exposed nerve is something indestructible, if we can reach it. Like a song encased in all our flaws, waiting for a singer.

Seeds to Water

🌿 In your journal, describe something you're afraid of feeling and why, and describe something you want to feel and why. How does fear affect you? And how does wanting affect you?

🌿 In conversation with a friend or loved one, discuss what it means to stand under your thoughts and open your heart.

At the Center of Every Feeling

Loss and grief are harsh teachers, though once they have our attention, they can turn gentle. I had a recent lesson with them. I was teaching in Santa Barbara. It was a month after we lost our beloved dog Mira. The sun was setting. The group was having dinner. Someone from Alaska asked me what kind of dog Mira was. How could I possibly say? I started but stopped and closed my eyes. Another woman offered softly, "I understand."

In the morning, there was a man in a wheelchair in our group. He had a service dog, Murphy, a golden retriever. Murphy was beautiful but I couldn't pet another dog, not just yet. I was afraid if I did, it would send sweet Mira farther away. Throughout the weekend, Murphy kept coming to me. I think he sensed my sadness. I think he sensed Mira. On Sunday, while I was talking to the group, Murphy got up, walked to my side, curled up, and leaned into my leg. I started to cry. The next morning I reached for Mira when waking. I missed the softness of her face on my lap and the weight of her body leaning against us as we slept.

The next day, I was alone in a hotel in Pasadena with a picture of Mira on the desk, when I heard Pink sing "Somewhere over the Rainbow." It made me cry for my father who died while I was flying to him, and for Mira who died in our arms at home, and for my wife, Susan, whose heart has been quaked open like the Grand Canyon, and now everything flies through it. It made me wonder, *How can I help them? How can I soothe them? How can I find them? How can I ever let them go?*

I dressed and walked the streets. The day was beautiful and the light swirling behind the clouds made me happy, though I wasn't ready to be happy. This damn miracle of life just keeps coming. Being on the street in Pasadena on that beautiful day while so deeply sad, I was faced with the immediacy of presence crashing its beauty into absence, the way the sea crashes its waves into the cliff that meets it, until the tender spray of awareness is all we're left with.

Sometimes, presence rises out of absence.

I think of how my father was absent for much of my adult life and now he's so present to me after his death. Our closest moments overcame us in the years approaching his death. It was there on the edge between the great presence of life and the great absence of death that we were most real with each other.

In the depths of our heart, where what matters defies separation, presence and absence are one. In the depths of any one feeling, we're led to the unnameable sum and source of all feeling. Grief is a great teacher of this. Losing both my father and Mira in the same year, I fell into the turbulence of grief, where I was tossed in the cool drift of absence away from the world. And feeling the depths of their absence strangely opened me to this unnameable place where all things exist at once.

Exhausted by my struggle to sort these extreme feelings, I settled into humbly receiving them, which led to this poem:

Adrift
Everything is beautiful and I am so sad.
This is how the heart makes a duet of
wonder and grief. The light spraying
through the lace of the fern is as delicate
as the fibers of memory forming their web

around the knot in my throat. The breeze
makes the birds move from branch to
  branch
as this ache makes me look for those I've
  lost
in the next room, in the next song, in the
  laugh
of the next stranger. In the very center,
  under
it all, what we have that no one can take
away and all that we've lost face each
  other.
It is there that I'm adrift, feeling punctured
by a holiness that exists inside everything.
I am so sad and everything is beautiful.

Every poem appears like a beam of light
that calls for me to follow it into the open.
Once there, I'm always surprised the way a
tired seeker, winded by the climb, is stalled
by the sudden view. The sudden view at the
end of every poem is the unexpected
teacher, the reward for following our feelings into the open.

I was led to this poem by my awareness of
how sad I was on another beautiful day. I
was sitting on our deck when the delicate
potted fern was aglow in such a quiet way
that I felt the fragrance of Eden for a moment. It strangely mirrored the delicate

fingers of my sadness, which swayed like a dark fern behind my heart. I was struck again by how these pure states of being are always present at the same time everywhere. I stopped asking how this could be, and in my exhausted, sad, and beautiful state, I could no longer resist my amazement that all things are true and present at all times.

And yes, under it all, what can never be taken away, the grace we're born with, faces all that we try so hard to keep but lose. Like the quivering life-force at the center of every atom, this quivering dance between presence and absence reveals a holiness that is indestructible. Even while I'm enervated and sad, this holiness is quietly sparking inside me. It carries me the way the Sun carries the Earth through every spin it takes into night.

Seeds to Water

   ❧ In your journal, describe a moment in which you experienced both beauty and sadness at the same time. What did this feel like? How did beauty and sadness manifest through you? What did they say?

   ❧ In conversation with a friend or loved

one, tell the story of one loss you've experienced and one lesson you've learned about life for enduring that loss.

UNBEARABLE AND
UNBREAKABLE

. . . because the mind would rather
turn back than let itself go blank
and the heart, like a bodhisattva
goes wherever it's most needed.
                              — Henk Brandt

A difficult paradox in the life of feeling is
that when we are most sensitive, the heart is
at its strongest. In such moments, our
experience of deep love and suffering can
feel intolerable. But this means the heart is
working. Feeling such intense sensitivity is
evidence of what a finely tuned instrument
the heart is. Being so sensitive, life can feel
unbearable even while the heart that guides
us is going strong. Our challenge is to learn
from both the sensitivity and the strength.

When strong enough to endure life's ir-
ritations, the soul we carry can issue a pearl.
If able to endure the pressures that life puts
on us, the heart can be compressed into a

small diamond. The word *diamond,* from the ancient Greek *adamas,* means "unbreakable." When most sensitive, we're being compressed into what is unbreakable.

What's unbreakable waits behind what's unbearable, the way the quenching waters of life wait behind all the dams we build. And all my attempts to love have taught me that resilience waits in the very center for all that's broken to be swept away in order to reveal what can't be broken. Though the process of shedding feels unbearable, we have to endure this in order to uncover what is lasting and true.

Inevitably, crossing into life for love is what saves us. At unexpected times, our care leads us to dive into the world to save something we love by holding it close to our heart. When my first dog, Saba, fell through the winter ice, I jumped in to save her without a thought. I would never have jumped into an ice pond if little Saba hadn't fallen in. I would never have been that close to nature if I didn't love her. This is the baptism of care and how it engages us in the world. Though we curse the mess of being involved from outside every experience, we almost always bless it, once up to our waist in life.

We resist this process of being irritated

into a pearl, of being pressurized into a diamond. Yet each of us has to feel our way into the authenticity of a self from which to meet others and the world, only to be opened beyond the confines of a single self, so we can be renewed and vitalized by what we have in common. For what is unbearable is acutely personal, which when endured leads us to the seed of what is universal, which is unbreakable. When we can earn the presence of being completely ourselves, we join a lineage of those who were completely themselves. Feeling our way into this kinship lets us feel the presence of souls across time.

When wholehearted, we can no longer keep things separate. Then the journey is to see how everything goes together and works together, no longer choosing one way over another. Once open to how everything goes together, we start to see that we're shaped and carried by life itself.

Lou Andreas-Salomé wrote:

> In its inviolable wholeness, [life] lives *us,* it composes *us.* This is something far different than the old cliché "Turn your life into a work of art"; we are works of art — but we are not the artist.

What feels unbearable is how life carves

us into a work of art that is never finished. When in difficult experiences, we fear they will never end. When in wonderful experiences, we fear they will end. But there's no arrival, only inhabiting the journey, alone and together. The cycle of life and our engagement in it never stays the same. It rises and falls. It compresses and expands. And staying committed to this roller coaster that spins us upside down is how we experience all of life and all of time through the depth of our own feeling.

When I can inhabit the fullness of my own humanity, I reach the bottom of my personality, and through the thoroughness of living the one life I have, I touch into the well of all humanity. It's there that resilience lives. And feeling what is mine to feel to the best of my ability enables me to feel the swell of everyone who ever lived. It's there that I know in my bones that I am not alone. It's there that I am buoyed and uplifted by the One Eternal Heart we are all a part of.

It's as if the heart is a wick and the soul is its flame, and the burn of the soul feeding off the air of the world feels unbearable as it shapes us. But as long as it burns, we're alive and unbreakable.

Seeds to Water

❧ In your journal, describe what it means to you to be a person. Ask this question of someone you'd like to know better.

❧ In conversation with a friend or loved one, describe one way your heart has been carved out by time and how you find shelter there.

■ ■ ■ ■

BEING KIND
AND USEFUL

■ ■ ■ ■

It's not our job to toughen our children up
to face a cruel and heartless world. It's
our job to raise children who will make the
world a little less cruel and heartless.

— L. R. Knost

Through conflict and joy, and love and loss, we're asked to craft our soul and weave our journey into the one life we're given. This is how we become instruments of love. A shovel, a hammer, a pair of calipers, a screwdriver, a candle, an altar, a set of worry beads, a crooked divining rod — these tools are never as happy as when they're being used. As are we. To be relied on, to be leaned on, to be asked to give something we didn't think we could give, to be asked to listen beyond our edge of patience, to be asked to carry what others have trouble carrying — these are hard blessings that have us grow for being of use. In learning a craft, any craft, we are crafted. In working to create anything, we are worked and in turn created.

Since living is breathtaking and hard, we need the stories of our own transformation to become the personal myths that guide us, that help us remember who we are and how we're joined to life. Every day, life asks us to accept that we are radiant and broken. And time asks us to uncover what it means to love the world. And love asks us to gather the gifts that come from keeping the window of our heart open, while integrity asks us to continually widen our circle of compassion. No matter what we face, we're asked to stay tender and resilient, so we don't harden to life.

One of the ethical challenges in living is not to betray ourselves while giving of ourselves, tricky business at best. In the end, all the insights we can unravel and all the paradoxes we can enter are meaningless if they can't help us live and be of service to each other.

All we have explored only matters if you can practice it in your own way. If anything we've discussed has touched you or made you consider how you meet the world, I hope that seed of knowing will crack open inside you and blossom in time.

CULTIVATING WONDER

Don't misuse your mind. Don't say there isn't anything extraordinary here.
— *The Blue Cliff Record*

We're all here by a thread, but it's a very strong, eternal thread. On any given day, we can be terrified that it's only a thread and, at the same time, stunned that such a thing as vast as life is held together by this magnificent unseeable thread. If we try to run from the fragile nature of a single life within the indestructible nature of all life, we will suffer the preoccupation of avoiding terror and miss the braid of life that we can hold on to. Our challenge is not to question why this is so, but to find the thread and hold on to it. Our challenge is not to choose between the fragility and strength of life but to cultivate our wonder by holding both in our heart. Life is fragile and unbreakable. We teeter and we soar, often at the same time. Wonder helps us find the indestructible part of the thread.

When my father was dying, I was alone with him in the hospital and found myself feeding him applesauce. The moment opened and my whole being, my whole life, was suddenly concentrating on slipping the spoon with the utmost care into his mouth, waiting for him to swallow, and then sliding the spoon slowly from his lips, so as not to disturb his labored breathing. We repeated this ritual tenderly, spoonful after spoonful. And in the rare quiet of a January afternoon, wonder began to fill the room. I began to cry softly. There seemed to be a glow about us. There was no need for words. I didn't want my life to leave this moment of feeding my father.

Through my thoroughness of care, I'd found a transparent instant in the middle of all our trouble, in the middle of his dying. And in this moment of tenderness, all of life opened. We had fallen into the center, which felt like the dot of clarity cleared in a lake by one drop of rain from which the water ripples in every direction. My father and I were in that still dot of clearness. My sadness had given way to care, which had given way to wonder. Wonder in the center of all that pain.

As I slipped the spoon from his mouth one last time, I felt that I was in the moment of every child who ever fed their dying parent. I kissed his forehead and held his hand, both of us more alive than we could remember, completely covered in inexplicable wonder.

Wonder is the rush of life saturating us with its aliveness, the way sudden rain makes us smile, the way sudden wind opens our face. And while wonder can surprise us, our daily work is to cultivate wonder in ourselves and in each other. Yet we only have a few seconds to love the wonder out of those before us or they will swallow it. Seconds to warm their life-force into the air where it will reveal the kinship of things. Seconds to let the timeless resource of aliveness come into our knowing, so it can soften our fears and save us from the brutality of insisting that our way is the only way.

If, out of insecurity or pride or a need to achieve prominence, we assert our own authority over the authority of life, wonder will go into hiding like a shy animal. The authority of being that connects us to all life needs to be *affirmed,* not *asserted.* Only safety, honesty, and welcome — the servants of encouragement — can create an opening for wonder.

Wonder helps each soul awaken and discover where its foundation touches the foundation of all things. Wonder doesn't just appear as a function of peace or joy or things draped in light. Wonder is a matter of depth, not mood.

That day with my father, I learned that a presence waits beneath our chatter and our pain that can illuminate the world. When tired, we splash water on our face. If you find me half-hearted, please, splash some wonder on my face.

Seeds to Water

ॐ In conversation with a friend or loved one, describe your first memory of wonder and how that changed you. Were you able to speak about this experience of wonder with anyone? How did they react? Did they affect how open or closed you are to wonder?

ॐ In your journal, explore how one small act of openness can bring more wonder into your life.

The Bones of Grace

My wife, Susan, was ill last spring with a serious stomach flu that took us to the emergency room. Tending her brought me closer to the paradox of true care: that giving our all is what matters though we can't take another's suffering from them. Yet this awkward tending means everything. On the eighth day, after fixing her pillow and rubbing her head, we heard a bird we didn't recognize, and that sweet short warble brought us back into life.

We enter the sanctity of our being in the simplest moments — while playing with animals and watching birds fly, or standing in the dark awash with the shimmer of the moon, or watching a loved one wake into their truth. These uncluttered openings are the bare bones of grace. We could name grace as the unnameable presence that lives under all we do or aspire to.

When stopped at the bedroom door while

stepping into the day, when the quiet warmth of our nest makes me realize how precious and irreplaceable the simplest things are, then what I'm given is more than enough and I am grateful. In this way, grace appears as a brief communion with the fragility of life. It changes how we move through the thousand tasks that lie before us.

The word *grace* comes from the Latin, meaning "thankful." Gratitude opens us to grace. Thankfulness lets in the energies of life that surround us. When humbled into the open, often against our will, our bones can rattle like wind chimes, making beautiful and haunting music, though it aches to do so. It takes a deeper kind of effort to live what is ours to live, while staying open to the mysterious forces that surround us. As the Buddhist teacher Ajahn Chah says:

Proper effort is not the effort to make something particular happen. It is the effort to be aware and awake each moment.

Grace is what wears down the face we show the world, until leaning into what we're given without a mask is the work of the soul. In time, we're destined to lose some of what is dear to us, which is only tragic if we forget that the dearness lives in us. Beyond our lifelong dance with loss, it's wondrous that we should litter the world with things we hold dear. This is one way that we make the world dear. And for all our shouting, we land in silence, and for all our barking about God and truth, we settle, if blessed, into living simply by just being true, the way a mountain is true.

A few years ago I was in Spain and went to visit Santa Maria de Montserrat, the legendary monastery set a thousand feet up the mountain. The pueblo-like cells and ornate basilica are wedged into the summit, carved in stone almost a thousand years ago. The sheer cliffs above the monastery are enormous, rising to a jagged crop of peaks overlooking all of Catalonia.

I wandered about the monastery, wondering, *How did they build so far up? Why did they stay?* They were neither far enough away from the living, nor any closer to Heaven. I took a tram even higher, where the first huts were built. There, I found telling cracks in the stone. They'd been slowly widened by hand into rough troughs that would steer and collect rainwater. The early monks lived off what the heavens provided through the cracks they worked so hard to widen.

Love works this way, slowly widening our ability to care so we can receive water from the heavens. The widening of our cracks is relentless work, but collecting water from the heavens is how we receive grace.

I was surprised to see wildflowers growing so high up in the cracks of these stones. Do they survive being so exposed because they're low to the ground, because they're grounded? Can we survive being so exposed by being as fierce and fragile as a mountain wildflower?

When grounded and bare, we can do small things with love and add light to the world. Given time, care turns into light, which helps all things grow. Care turning into light is the photosynthesis of grace. When we finally step toward another to clean her cut or soothe his mind, we break the illusion that we're different by living out our care, and light moves between us. Caring for anything lessens our loneliness.

Consider Trevor, a quiet man who was never comfortable with others, yet he felt lonely when by himself. One day, Trevor found a beagle, and since he wasn't a dog person, he didn't know what to do with her. So he took her to an animal rescue, only to learn that they would put her down if she weren't adopted in a month. He left her there and drove away, but halfway home turned around to retrieve her. He couldn't leave her to die and he couldn't keep her. So Trevor put an ad online: *Free beagle, kindness the only requirement.* Half a dozen people called and Trevor had them over for coffee, to meet and greet the little dog. He finally gave the beagle to Sally, a nurse with two young kids, because she had the sweetest smile when she petted the dog.

After finding the beagle a home, Trevor realized that he hadn't felt awkward while meeting these people. In fact, being involved with others in an act of kindness relieved him of his loneliness. What a simple and profound example of the photosynthesis of grace.

There's a rhythm to grace as we move through the years. In the first half of life, we're called to take things in. In the second half of life, we're called to empty out. Over time, we're shaped like an inlet, receiving and letting go as the tide of life softens us. Being emptied of everything but our care doesn't create certainty, but it lets us feel at peace with all that remains unknown.

Seeds to Water

☙ In your journal, describe a time when you were forced to drop the face you show the world. Describe the deeper face that showed itself. Which face do you meet the world with now and why?

☙ In conversation with a friend or loved one, describe a time when some form of giving relieved you of your loneliness. How do you think this works?

THE EFFORT TO
KEEP LOOKING

Henri Matisse was constantly working to put himself in a position to see the essence of things clearly and to render what he managed to see accurately. In 1912, Matisse visited Morocco to see first-hand the mysterious landscape he'd stumbled onto in the paintings of Eugène Delacroix. While there, he immersed himself in three new canvases prompted by the Villa Brooks estate near his hotel. He went home inspired. But as the months passed, he was afraid he'd missed the essence of the scene. So, a year later, he brought the second canvas, *Acanthus,* back to Morocco. He returned to the same spot and immersed himself again. Yet, after traveling all that way, he decided to make no change.

Matisse's effort to return in order to keep his rendering accurate, and his conclusion that there was no more to be done, speaks as much to the process of living as putting brush to canvas. For the effort to confirm what we've seen is never wasted, and staying true to our vision affirms our path. Whether we consider ourselves artists or not, we're all artisans shaped by our effort to live. The surety that comes from confirming the truth of our experience only deepens our journey through time. The word *respect* means "to look again." We respect our path, our way, and our sense of who we are when we look again to verify what we've seen and learned. Looking again is a worthwhile effort that often leads to the confirmation of grace.

In another decade and another part of the world, the poet e. e. cummings, after breakfast with his wife, Marion, entered his study to quietly work on a poem for several hours. When he emerged to have lunch, Marion asked, "How was your morning?" The poet answered, "Splendid." She continued, "What did you do?" Cummings offered, "Well, after breakfast, I took out a comma. And just now, as you called, I put it back in."

While the poet's focus could be seen as compulsive, I think of it as the effort to stay in relationship with whatever we're creating as it keeps creating us. What's useful here is not the mental press for some kind of perfection, but the heartful effort to see and hear what's calling from beneath the surface facts of the world.

In a global culture obsessed with what is new, it's important to reclaim the age-old truth that nothing is new. Our authentic relationship to everything we encounter makes *us* new. Our continual effort to remove everything in the way makes the glow inherent in all things knowable.

One of the braveries of effort is the commitment to *keep* looking, again and again, to *keep* returning to what moves us and intrigues us, like birders of mystery who return to sight shy truths that need to know that we're serious before they'll reveal their song.

Regardless of what Matisse and cummings produced from their devotion, what's most instructive is the immeasurable way *their seeing changed* for staying so engaged. This is the lesson for all of us. Sustained inquiry changes how we see and hear, and *that* changes how we experience life and the world.

In the 1800s, when whaling was a booming industry, the search for whales was chronicled in ship logs, journals of these long expeditions at sea. Many of the logs have detailed drawings of whale sightings and descriptions of whale behavior as the great mammals broke surface and returned to the deep.

We're always searching for the great things that live out of view, always hoping that truth and beauty and meaning will show themselves like great whales. We want to be nourished and reanimated by them. But sometimes, in our preoccupation, we grow misguided and long to hunt what matters, instead of relating to it. We become obsessed with killing what matters, as if slaying it will give us its energy. Of course, once pinned, the truth and beauty and meaning have gone elsewhere. So this never works.

In the realm of things that matter, we're compelled to sight the great things that swim in the deep, so we can learn from them how to live in the deep. All forms of art share this purpose. And all processes of art are essentially ship logs, in which we track the appearance of what matters, as it surprises us with its majestic breach into the ordinary moments of our day. We don't have to be great or talented to practice the effort of sighting truth and beauty and meaning. We simply have to give our heart's attention until, like Matisse and cummings, we keep looking, keep inquiring, keep returning to how life is trying to speak to us.

Seeds to Water

    ❧ In your journal, tell the story of a time when you didn't leave things alone and kept working on something beyond its point of completion. How did you know you had gone too far? What made you keep changing what you had worked on? What's the difference between overworking something and the effort to look again in order to verify the truth of what you've seen or experienced or created?

    ❧ In conversation with a friend or loved one, describe a time when you exerted a healthy effort to keep looking. What drew your attention? What kept you interested? What let you know you needed to look further? And what did your extended effort teach you?

IN DOSES WE CAN BEAR

Everyone in a body is chosen
for trouble and bliss.
— Naomi Shihab Nye

The Greek playwright Aeschylus said, "We suffer into knowledge." As if knowledge is the fruit that grows inside the hard case of living. And so we must help each other harvest meaning from our suffering in doses we can bear.

The word *dose* comes from the Greek *dosis,* meaning "gift," and refers to a small amount of medicine or healing. One way to endure the unexpected roughness of life is to nurse each other with small amounts of meaning, beauty, truth, and love. When we can help each other face the rigors of living with small doses of what matters, we participate in a complex yoga of the heart that lets us know our strength and lineage.

Michelangelo believed that the statue was

waiting complete in the uncut marble. The sculptor would carve away the excess to reveal the statue hidden in the stone. In the same way, we are shaped by life and experience, which reveals our living beauty. Sometimes, we're carved so harshly, we're damaged or even killed by the sheer force of life trying to release us. Most of the time, we're revealed slowly, given our lessons in doses we can bear, the way sap oozes from a maple tree in time to be collected.

During my days with cancer, I felt such fear from all directions, including the well-intended but negative scenarios of all the doctors preparing me for what to do when this would fall off or that would stop working. I needed small doses of what matters to make my way through all the fear. Regardless of what I tried, the only place I could retreat to was the moment at hand. Even when painful, that moment, paradoxically, had the calm certainty of already existing. No one could puncture it or take it away. And so, without any wisdom but out of desperation, I took refuge in each moment, one leading to the next.

To my grateful surprise, each moment was a dose I could bear. In each moment, built on the one before, there was a strength of eternal perspective that didn't eliminate what I had to go through, but which opened me through humility to a stream of life-force that began to carry me. What I thought was a refuge became a resource. This potent opening of time enabled me to slowly but solidly meet the onslaught of circumstance and pain that I needed to bear. The moment at hand was the dose I could bear that helped me through.

We all face this quandary: How can our heart adjust to being in the world without losing its sensitivity? Last week I had an eye exam and the doctor gave me drops to dilate my pupils so he could look through to the optic nerve. I realized that the eye itself is transparent, see-through, and that seeing is actually a mix of letting things in and out. My eyes were dilated for hours and I was unable to regulate what was coming in, and so simple things felt blinding and painful.

How we let things in and out determines how we suffer our way into knowledge. If we can hold things near, feel for what is true, set boundaries, and make integral decisions, we can regulate the flow of what comes and goes. This softens the jaggedness of what's broken and filters the abundance of life, so we can receive the profusion of blessings that life has to offer — in doses we can bear. If we can open and close in healthy doses, we will thrive.

Physically, our eyes adjust hundreds of times each day. They open and close quite naturally with imperceptible grace. When we can imitate this grace by regulating the flow of what comes and goes into our mind and heart, we can be led through the rough beauty that is the world without shutting down.

There's a torque to living that our soul is called to endure in order to reveal insight and meaning. To understand this, consider how the strenuous exercises of Kundalini yoga are designed to stimulate the pituitary gland, which can't be touched directly because it rests at the base of the brain. This all-important gland is out of reach, though we carry it with us everywhere. The strenuous exercises cause the pituitary gland to secrete hormones that heighten our perception and regulate our biology.

In just this way, the rigors of experience stimulate the center of our being, which can't be touched directly because it rests at the base of all our knowing, also out of reach, though we carry it with us everywhere. But somehow, the rigors of experience, when faced, cause our being to secrete aspects of aliveness that help heighten our perception and regulate our life in the world.

Still, in day-to-day living, we turn toward and from our fear, pain, doubt, and anxiety repeatedly. This turning to and away is how we grow. We move through difficulty by gathering in and reaching out from old ways to the new. This is how we heal. In the ancient Hindu Upanishads, it is said:

As a caterpillar, having come to the end of one blade of grass, draws itself together and reaches out for the next, so the Self, having come to the end of one life and shed all ignorance, gathers in its faculties and reaches out from the old body to the new.

While this Hindu saying speaks to how the soul moves from one life to the next, it also speaks to how our deepest nature moves from one identity or phase of learning to the next. And each time we draw ourselves together like a caterpillar, we often call out for a higher power or larger force to rescue us from our pain and trouble. During my cancer journey, I was forced into this conversation more than once, only to learn that part of our task in being human is to be worn of all our requests, until a deeper version of what we were born with meets the air.

I've found over time that to gather the courage to face what life brings me, I need a foundational belief that I will survive and evolve from the discomfort of psychological and emotional pain. This belief enables me to risk being shaped by what I face. In my darkest times, I've heard a voice say to me, softly and strongly, "Deny nothing and accept everything." Then, real choices start to appear.

Seeds to Water

  ❧ In your journal, begin to answer the timeless question, Where is God?

  ❧ In conversation with a friend or loved one, begin to describe one way life has carved away the excess in you and what has been revealed.

THE WORK OF
SELF-AWARENESS

> The only man I know who behaves sensi-
> bly is my tailor; he takes my measure-
> ments anew each time he sees me. The
> rest go on with their old measurements
> and expect me to fit them.
>
> — George Bernard Shaw

The feisty playwright pins it aptly: we must
take new measurements each time we see
each other. Each time we deny what is new,
we empower our habits and strengthen our
default settings. This is the work of self-
awareness: to be our own tailor and take
our measurements anew. Otherwise, we live
a reactive life and bounce off everything we
bump into, like a hapless silver ball in a
pinball machine.

This is why we need to develop a personal
practice of discerning things as they are, in
order to unfold our reflexes and undo our
patterns. All the traditions offer ways to be

still enough and quiet enough to loosen our patterns so we can receive the newness and freshness of whatever is before us.

Only through direct experience can we recalibrate what's authentic. Then, through the layers of worry that make life seem gray, we may chance to feel the wind through the elm and stutter, "My God — look at that tree." Then, after years of sleeping next to someone, we may wake a bit fragile, just watching our loved one breathe. And when they finally stir, we may utter, "My God — it's you."

As present as animals are, birds will keep pecking at anything if they think it still contains a seed. And dogs will always return to the same fence where they once found a bone. While we can learn from the presence of animals, it's the work of self-awareness that allows us to stop pecking and stop circling. Self-awareness lets us move through obstacles and hardship in order to become more essential.

There's an old Egyptian story of a father who rows his son along the Nile above Khartoum where the current is deep and swift. The father rows them into the middle of the current that takes them along. He tells his son, "Look into the water. Though you can't see yourself right now, you are there. Feel the mighty river carry us. This is the real work: to find the deeper current and let it take you. All else will follow."

Buddha said, "Live like a mighty river." A deep river has an unending flow that cleanses itself, though it's not going anywhere. A deep river is clear and reflective at the same time. A deep river is destined to join other water, and so all its effort is to join a larger sea. This also describes the fate of an awakened being. To flow without going anywhere, to stay clear and reflective, and to cleanse your self in order to join with other life — these are the aims of self-awareness.

The oldest rivers in the world are the Nile River in Egypt and the New River, which joins the Kanawha River to run through West Virginia, Virginia, and North Carolina. Given Buddha's instruction, we can hold these rivers as ancient sages. What would they say to us, if they could speak? Or is their very existence what they have to say? They keep cleansing themselves in a remaking of flow, right where they are, like the heart of all meditation and the depth of all love.

If we can endure the hardship of being broken open, we'll be worn to what matters, and the deeper current will take us. All else will follow. If we can paddle to where we know things run deep, we will feel the resources of life.

It's interesting that the word *sublime,* from the Latin, means "up to the threshold." Any depth that breaks our sense of what's familiar is indeed sublime. Just as the mud that blocks a river's flow is finally worn through by the relentless tide, we're cleansed of our stubbornness by the relentless tide of experience. When our stubbornness is defeated, we're deeply renewed by the greater stream of life. The great work of self-awareness is to bring us up to the next threshold.

Just as a drop of iodine will color an entire glass of water, one drop of insight will change who we are and how we see the world. More than finishing the things we set out to do or measuring the things we accomplish, our aims and goals and dreams are occasions through which to squeeze that one drop from our experience that will change everything. We're asked to work in the world with care and commitment, never knowing when that drop of insight will arrive. The work of self-awareness and our effort to be the work animates our place in the world.

Inevitably, the journey of self-awareness

takes time. As Sister Joan Chittister says, "To live is to be born slowly." And so, the work of self-awareness depends on our commitment to keep trying.

Last summer, I was sitting by a lake after a great storm. The water was still and everything was heavy with water from the sky. Then the sun filled the late afternoon and everything seemed possible again. There was a hollow pipe at the edge of the dock. The sun made it glisten. I found myself watching a drop of water slowly forming at the end of the pipe. It took a long time to form. Then it began to hang from the pipe without falling. The sun made a gem of it. By now, I couldn't leave until it dropped. After a while, the lighted bead of water became so full, it let go of the pipe and dropped into the lake.

This is the life each of us is destined for: to form after a storm in the dark, and to become so full of light that we let go in order to join a greater sense of life. The work of self-awareness is to be this thorough, this humble, and this clear. When we fight this unfolding, we add to the pain of life. When we accept this as our journey, we start to know an ancient form of joy.

Seeds to Water

❧ In your journal, describe a time when you were expected to fit old measurements. How did you respond to this situation? How did the fixed view of you affect the relationship? What can you do to update how people see you?

❧ Sit by a river with a friend or loved one. Watch the river for a while together in silence. Share what you have seen and heard. What is the river modeling for you? Discuss the threshold you are each approaching and what the river is modeling that can help.

Going Off the Deep End

When our beloved dog Mira died, there were those who walked with us, honoring the truth of where we were, no matter what had brought us there. These were the compassionate. And there were those who felt our grief from a distance, though they were puzzled at the depth of our loss, given that she was only a dog. These were the sympathetic. But there were those who thought our heartbreak too wide and deep, and they grew impatient when we didn't repair in what they thought was a reasonable length of time. For them, the depth of our heartbreak and the rawness of our feelings brought them to the edge of their comfort zone. Their fear of walking in this rawness with us made them minimize the nature of our loss. They thought we were too sensitive. They thought we'd gone off the deep end.

It doesn't matter what splinter the Universe gives us to stop us in our tracks. It doesn't matter if those around us, near or far, think that our pain or fear or sadness is out of proportion to what punctured our world. It really doesn't matter what triggers us into the depth of life, only that we swim there. And it's no one's place to judge or say that what unhinges us doesn't make sense or that our heartbreak is too much or that our grief is lasting too long.

There are infinite ways we can trip into what matters. Life simply and harshly demands that we dive into the depth of what we're given, meeting life, not avoiding it. All that matters is that we finally stand on the ground of things in the heart of the Mystery. There's no point in questioning the legitimacy of whatever breaks us open or the capacity of those who are broken open to meet what is opened. All that matters is that we walk through that opening. And love demands that we sweetly and bravely go there together.

The truth is that we are here *precisely* to go off the deep end — the way a diver opens up completely before entering the water — so we can be baptized in the Mystery of Life and renewed by the aliveness that only meeting life in its depth can offer. The test of love and friendship is the degree to which we can go there together, without judging or pushing each other; not letting each other drown in the deep or rescuing each other from the baptism of soul that waits there.

Love demands a soft patience, when a friend doesn't get that second interview and it crushes them. Or when your partner can't recover from the harsh criticism of a stranger that cuts too deep. Or your aunt gets depressed when she breaks her favorite mug. From outside the experience, a part of us wants to say, "It was only a job. It was only words. It was only a mug."

For sure, we can make things bigger than they are. But how we face and absorb the rearrangement that rises out of loss is a very personal journey that can't be compared to anyone else. Our work, alone and together, is not to minimize the pain or loss we feel, but to investigate what these sharp incidents are opening in us. It's not helpful to tell ourselves or each other to *get over it,* but rather to encourage and help each other to *get under it.*

Seeds to Water

    ❧ In your journal, look closely into the field of feeling that was stirred by a recent experience that stopped you, hurt you, and opened you more deeply than the incident seemed to warrant. Describe what you see there and your history with such feelings.

In conversation with a friend or loved one, describe the incident and what it has opened in you without reading what you have written. Ask for your friend or loved one to share their own story of being opened into an unexpected depth of feeling.

THE GIFTS OF EFFORT

For all the ways we're battered about — between wonder and tragedy, between striving and giving up, between feeling suffocated and then abandoned — how do we know where to put our effort: into will or surrender, into skillful means or a deepening of faith, or into some balance of them all?

The Japanese monk Gensei says, "The point in life is to know what's enough. With the happiness held in one-inch-square [of] heart, you can fill the whole space between Heaven and Earth." Gensei is saying that love is everywhere. If the things we love and the people we reach for and the dreams we work toward break or transform along the way, love what they turn into. Love what they are opened to. Don't hold out for the perfect dream when the wholehearted life is sprouting before your eyes.

This is one of the most difficult challenges

in life: to know what's enough. How do we know what's fulfilling if we're constantly reaching for something else? How do we put down the ideal in order to inhabit where we are?

As shells are lifted by the deep and swept along, we're borrowed by the ocean of time. We're asked to open ourselves to the drift and turbulence, letting the tide of life carry us until we settle on the bottom, smoothed and chipped in unexpected ways. We find our way like old fish who both master and are mastered by the unseen currents. In time, we become small masters of the deep as we are mastered by the deep. Along the way, we become students of effort.

But how do we discern what's enough? On the surface, effort seems fairly straight-forward. Try hard. If you meet resistance, try harder. Never give up. Until getting what you work for is enough. But like most things that matter, it isn't that simple. Often, the imposition of our will can turn resilience into stubbornness and then we chase our willful tail, because we're certain some-thing's missing.

This doesn't mean that we shouldn't exert our will, more that we need to be careful about where we put our effort. I have a dear friend who was one of the early pioneers of

Outward Bound, a program designed to offer experiences in the wilderness as initiations in self-sufficiency and introspection.
One day he showed me what it takes to start
a fire by rubbing two sticks. I was amazed
at how strenuous this is. It took ten or
fifteen minutes of constant effort. By the
end, his hands were sore and he was sweat-
ing. Finally, through his constant vigilance
and blowing on the heated place where the
two sticks rubbed, a spark finally took. An
equal vigilance is necessary to stay authentic
and rub against the days until we can spark
what is essential. Though it's easy to get
caught in the rub and not the spark.

In order to stay in touch with our spark,
we have to exercise a vigilance not to elevate
our painful moments into dark philosophies
to live by. We have to resist inflating our
darkness and pain, and instead understand
these passages as inevitable moods of the
human journey. When in pain or despair,
it's easy to squint and see nothing, and then
to accept that nothing as the premise of the
world.

One way to recover from the weight of
pain and darkness is to return to doing
small things with love, rubbing our care
against the needs we meet, like those two
sticks, until our kinship with each other

sparks. Whenever dark and hurting, there's always the chance to pour our bruised care into whatever small thing is before us. More often than not, that engagement will introduce us to our next teacher.

Sometimes, while being battered, I miss my next teacher because I cling to my own high standards like a raft, which often makes matters worse. Often we guard ourselves against the risk of being vulnerable by creating very high standards. We think, *I'm going to hold out for this type of friend and this type of partner and only work in this type of situation, because I have integrity, because I have standards, because I have values.* We can misuse ethics, standards, and values to encircle ourselves with unbreachable walls. Then, alone in the tower of our high ethics, we lament, "I'm holding out for the right person. I'm holding out for the right dream to come true. I'm working toward the right situation. I'm not going to settle."

Holding out for a taste of perfection insulates us from being touched by life. The point in life is to know what's enough, and then love it. When we do, that honest fulfillment can bridge Heaven and Earth. When putting down my dream of tomorrow, I can see what's before me, as if for the first time, and wonder, *Can I listen, and hold, and help one small thing today? Where will that tender and fierce effort lead me? What will such listening and holding teach me now?*

With the assurance of day following night, the gifts of effort are steadfast. They lead us between will and surrender toward our discovery of what's enough. They bring us closer to what matters through a vigilance of presence that sparks our days. Working our heart keeps us grounded in the gritty miracle of now. When holding nothing back, all our attempts to get out of here land us here. Who would have imagined?

Seeds to Water

👋 Sit outside or sit by a window. Now close your eyes and breathe slowly. Reflect on a point of pain or darkness you are struggling with. As you breathe with your eyes closed, remember that the sun is still shining whether you see it or not. Breathe steadily and feel the light of day on your closed lids. Inhale slowly and feel this inhalation as a form of holding yourself. As you exhale, open your eyes and let the light warm your point of pain or darkness. Repeat this meditation three times in your day.

ADMITTING WHO WE ARE

To participate in the experiment of inhabiting Heaven on Earth, we're invited to practice *admitting who we are*. *Admit* means to confess or acknowledge what is true about who we are, as in admitting to a crime or fault. Inwardly, though, *admit* is more comprehensive. It means to accept the flawed and gifted wholeness of who we are. Only through such acceptance can we access all our capacities. Only when a painter accepts that he is filled with all the colors can he access them to paint with. Likewise, only when a person accepts that they are filled with all the human moods can they access the colors of their humanity with which to paint their life.

The other definition of *admit* is to let in, to cross a threshold, to allow someone or some thing to enter. So once *accepting* who we are, we need *to let in* who we are. And one can lead to the other. When feeling shattered by the harshness of life, when feeling lost or cut off, just inhale deeply and slowly. This is a physical way to begin accepting who you are and letting in who you are. In practice, admitting who you are is the first step to saying yes to life.

Another practice we're led to is the effort to *compose our selves.* When agitated, through pain or fear or worry, when broken into pieces, we need to find a way to put ourselves back together. In a culture afraid of feelings, the instruction to calm down is often used to muffle what we're going through. But to *quiet* what we're feeling is not the same thing as to *settle* what we're feeling. It's the difference between putting a pillow over someone's head when they're crying and letting a churned-up lake settle, so you can see what's on the bottom.

Compose means "to form a whole by ordering or arranging the parts," as in composing music, where the arrangement of the parts creates a whole that releases its harmony. But in order to form a whole of our various parts that will release our music, we need to calm and settle our thoughts and feelings, and thereby calm and settle our features — those distinct attributes by which we know who we are.

To compose your self means to commit to

the effort to calm your agitation, enough to see and feel the wholeness of your being that is always under your agitation, the way the bottom of a lake is always under the agitation of its waves. The mystery is that while we're broken at times on the surface, we're always whole somewhere in the depth of our being.

Consider how a lake is always both still and moving at the same time, often still in the deep and moving on the surface. We are no different. So the goal is not to eliminate the surface movement or agitation that is part of the weather of life, but to learn the art of composing our selves: calming the surface, so we can see through and reconnect to the depth of our being.

To compose your self, then, is the practice of calming the surface, the part of you that meets the days, so you can arrange your parts back into their wholeness.

To refind our wholeness requires that we admit who we are, that we accept the totality of our humanness, so we have all the colors to paint with. To inhabit our wholeness requires that we let in who we are, so that nothing keeps the flow of life from mixing with the flow of our being.

When we can accept our humanness, we can taste our true nature. When we can calm and arrange all our scattered parts, we're blessed to be both rare and common. When all our effort evaporates into grace, we are the clear, lighted bottom that reflects the living Universe. When everything is as lighted from within as the sun lights the world from without, Heaven shows its face on Earth — through us.

Seeds to Water

❧ In your journal, tell the story of a time when you experienced Heaven on Earth. Describe the qualities of that experience and what led you to it. Were you alone or with others?

❧ In conversation with a friend or loved one, admit who you are by describing something you're proud of and something you wish you were better at. Then discuss the larger person you are that carries both your gifts and your flaws.

JUST A GLIMPSE

Be on the look for moments
that open to the deeper world.
They are everywhere but subtle.

On a sunny day on a visit to Seattle, I woke
heavy-hearted, as the clouds in my head
made me feel cold. Susan said, "Let's go for
a walk." We ambled down University Street
toward the harbor. Crossing Third Ave, she
spotted the top of an enormous Ferris wheel
poking above the buildings blocks away and
exclaimed, "C'mon! Let's find it!"

So we made our way to the pier. It took
thirty minutes. And there was the Great
Wheel, seven or eight stories high, painted
white. We eagerly bought tickets and waited
on line. The prospect of being lifted off the
earth into the open made me feel lighter.
Once the ride began, we were swaying in a
glass gondola, rising above the harbor. To
the left, we could see docked tankers, the

sun wavering off their slick hulls. At the top, I looked to the right and there, bright waves of light were flooding into the glass windows of a boathouse. This wasn't just a reflection but a threshold, a bright, compelling seam to the numinous world that informs everything.

From above the harbor, the sun reflecting off the water on the boathouse windows revealed a world of emanation that lies just below all that is physical. Swaying atop the Ferris wheel, I felt those windows open into a sea of shimmer. For me, this wasn't an illusion or an alternate world to escape to, but a glimpse of the ineffable depth that lines the daily world we all move through.

It seems to me that the Impressionist painters, like Monet, Van Gogh, and Pissarro, tried to paint such openings wherever light let them glimpse the deeper world. They captured the shimmer of being in their magnificent attempts to paint light. Monet's paintings of the Rouen Cathedral shimmer like these boathouse windows seen from the top of the Ferris wheel. As do Van Gogh's wheat fields and cypress trees. As do Pissarro's sunlit meadows.

This moment in Seattle was the culmination of different efforts that helped me see into the depth of things that day. First was the effort to outlast my heavy-heartedness and find my way, with Susan's help, into the open. Then the effort to wait for the edges of things to line up: the Great Wheel had to rise above the day, the clouds needed to part, the sun needed to shine through, the waters needed to calm, the time of day needed to slow. And then, I had to be in the right position to see all the way through, the way you need to bend and close one eye to look through a hole in a fence.

The deeper world is always there, know-able and reachable. It is we who by turns miss it and stumble into it. Even when all these efforts aligned, and I was able to glimpse the deeper world through the patch of diamond-glitter reflecting in the rickety old windows of the boathouse on Pier 57 in Seattle — even then, I could have dismissed it. My tired mind could have explained away the Mystery of Life by saying, *Oh, it's only a reflection.* When life aligns and we get to see through, we have to lean in and *accept* what we see, so we *can* be touched by the myste-rious.

When these moments align, we enter the deeper world. When we don't dismiss them, we bathe in the richness of existence, which opens our eyes to history and our heart to the indestructible feel of life. Being patient enough to align and pursue our efforts of awareness, we can enter the shimmer of life that waits inside ordinary time. This is a baptism of meaning that only authentic and patient presence can open.

Seeds to Water

❧ In your journal, describe a moment when a seam of the deeper world showed itself. How did it present itself? What did you have to do to receive it? Did you acknowledge it or dismiss it? How do such connections affect you?

❧ In conversation with someone you are close with, tell the story of a moment that has stayed with you though you can't quite make sense of it. After sharing, ask your listener what they think. Take turns sharing like this. Afterward, go for a silent walk together, ready to find such a moment together.

In a Greater Arc

Being on the Ferris wheel in Seattle, being lifted slowly above the city on the harbor's edge, was heartening. It made me wonder, *What on Earth compelled someone to imagine and build such an enormous, complicated, and ingenious machine that has no practical purpose?* Creating a Ferris wheel is like building a bridge into a circle that can move.

That day in Seattle compelled me to learn how this Great Wheel came to be. It was designed and built in 1893 by George Washington Gale Ferris Jr., an American engineer and bridge builder who died three years later at the age of thirty-seven of typhoid fever. Like a brief comet of innovation, he built the first Ferris wheel for the Chicago World's Columbian Exposition, responding to a challenge to construct an innovative structure that would rival the Eiffel Tower, which had been unveiled a few years before. The Great Wheel stood at a height of 264 feet, cradling thirty-six cars, each holding sixty people, able to accommodate a total of 2,160 people at a time as it rotated on a 71-ton axle.

That day in Seattle, I knew nothing of George Washington Ferris. That day, as we swayed in our glass gondola looking out on Puget Sound, I marveled with fresh eyes and wondered, *Just what does such a Great Wheel bridge?* The view from up high was soft and encompassing. From there, things seemed more possible. When cresting from the highest point of the ride, I realized that the transforming purpose of a Ferris wheel is to bridge us from ground consciousness to sky consciousness and back. All that engineering vision and massive effort were harnessed to build a circular steel bridge that will bring us back to where we started, the same but different, expanded but grounded.

Like great love and great suffering, the Great Wheel enlarges our consciousness and pulls us from our daily view, expands it, and returns us to our lives on the ground. And we are left to bring the larger perspective we've seen to bear on how we live. We return with the chance to have sky consciousness inform our life on the ground.

This movement from our entanglements

to a larger perspective is a good definition of what it means to be awakened. We seldom see the larger rhythms we're a part of when stepping on the ground. Perhaps love, the life of perception, and the gift of encouragement are Ferris wheels of relationship that enlarge our possibility and return us to our lives. In the same way, the mystery of transformation lifts us out of the thicket of our days, only to place us back in our lives, the same but different.

In authentic relationships, we move as if on a Ferris wheel. We come together from our troubled journeys to look from above for a while. Through honest care, we lift each other briefly. Once we've lifted each other and seen from beyond our particular story, once we've shared what really matters, then we have to re-enter our very personal paths with what we've seen from above. In truth, to be a teacher, a friend, a kind stranger, or a loving guide is to be a bridge for others, helping each other rise above our entanglements, so we can re-enter them with a larger understanding.

Whatever Ferris's motivation, the Great Wheel named for his effort mirrors the Wheel of Life and opens us to the physics of awakening. For on the ground, we remain convinced that we're thrown back and forth between dark and light, and failure and success. But once aloft and able to see from the view of all life, it becomes clear that we move in a greater arc from being closed to being opened, from feeling limited to feeling possible, and from being partial to being whole.

Often, our struggle on the ground feels like a tense journey between having things in our grasp and not. But the soul's unfolding is more a gathering of meaning over time until, through the movement of the Wheel of Life, we're able to rise out of our troubles, only to re-enter them shaped and refined more strongly for the journey.

As the afternoon glistened, our ride was over and we stepped more firmly on the ground and walked back into our lives. And everything, from the breath of children waiting their turn to the sound of the harbor lapping on the pier, everything seemed more vital.

Seeds to Water

❦ In your journal, tell the story of someone who's been a bridge for you. Describe how your view of things was lifted up and heartened, and how this enabled you to return to your life with new eyes.

In conversation with a friend or loved one, tell the story of a time when you were a bridge for someone else, how that came about, and how being a bridge affected you.

THE EFFORTS THAT
NEVER GO AWAY

Many temples in India have one large step at the threshold, twenty-four inches or higher. By design, this step is made large so that effort is required to climb over it in order to enter the sacred space. Once over the large step, you will often find a statue of a snake on one side of the temple door and a dragon on the other. The statues represent aversion and attachment.

Symbolically, the temples are constructed this way as a reminder that we have to climb over our obstacles, putting aside what we fear and what we cling to, in order to enter the sacred space that is everywhere. When we can do this, however briefly, the temple is the world.

So what large step looms before you? What obstacle is asking you to climb over it any way you can? What is it that you currently fear and currently cling to that you must put aside in order to enter the temple that is the world?

These are efforts that never go away: the effort to climb over our obstacles, the effort to put aside what we fear, and the effort to put aside what we cling to, so we can enter the sanctity of life that is everywhere.

Every day, we move from being blocked by the grit of life to being cleared by the force of experience. It seems our job is not to get dirty or stay clean, but to endure the abrasions of living in order to become essential.

The word *effort* comes from the Latin meaning "to extract or express," and that word is tied to another Latin word *fortis,* which means "strong." So effort of the deepest nature is the act of extracting or expressing strength. The Dutch word for *effort* is *inspanning.* So effort also implies the work of spanning or bridging distances.

We're always struggling between putting aside what we fear and cling to and extracting or expressing our strength. This cycle between entanglement and inner freedom is unending and appears most readily in the web of our relationships: to ourselves, each other, the world, and the unknown. On the one hand, what we avoid will only reappear, more intensely. And when we pretend our pain is caused by everyone else, and insist our plight has nothing to do with us, we are under the spell of aversion. On the other hand, the dragon of attachment is as dangerous as the snake of aversion. For when we cling, we lose confidence that we can meet life directly.

But regardless of these entanglements, effort can lead to grace. Over time, the rhythm of good work is like steadily rowing across a deep lake, needing to slip our oars in carefully so as not to disturb the deep, in order to see as far down as possible. Though we keep our appointments, we're not really rowing anywhere. Going here and there lets us keep crossing the deep steadily and carefully. The goal of inner work is to keep experiencing the deep.

Whether painting, writing, singing, woodworking, gardening, loving, or listening — giving our all is how we briefly join with all of life. We're most alive and fully present to all time through the effort we give ourselves to. When we inhabit such a moment, we're renewed. Regardless of how we find it, each experience of *at-one-ment* enriches our life.

The dance of effort requires constant attention. Forrest Smith, an engineer who grew up in Canada, recalls playing the following game by himself as a boy. He'd find a loose bicycle wheel, balance it, and give it a slow, steady push, sending it on its way. Then he'd run alongside, giving the wheel a spin with a stick every time the rim would start to wobble, trying to keep the wheel rolling as long as he could without guiding it. Too fast and the wheel would veer and bounce away. Too slow and the wheel would wobble and fall.

The tension between being and doing is like this game. Giving our all without being willful demands just the right amount of effort to keep the wheel of our life rolling by itself. Sometimes we try too hard and spin ourself out of control. Sometimes we don't do enough. Then we wobble like the untended wheel and fall. But here we are, always needing to exert both the effort to be and do: to stand alongside ourself as our life slowly turns — this is the effort of being; and to offer our self a timely push, only when needed, to keep our life going — this is the effort of doing.

Still, no matter how much we know, no one is exempt from the beautiful tumble through the thousand moods. We burst alive, then slip and fall. We dart through the hole in the clouds after a ray of light, only to get caught in the storm.

Like you, I wake up hopeful and sometimes go to sleep sad. After a sad day in a long week, I wandered into a dark part of a museum and found myself before a Buddha from the Tang dynasty. Thirteen hundred years old, his body was worn, his hands completely gone. Yet he kept reaching through the storms of illusion. The Buddha bowed slightly to make visible the empty center of his eyes. All the joys and quandaries of being alive were concentrated there. When I look into the pain of those who suffer, I see the same empty center. When I look into the eyes of wandering children, I want to drop the wounds I've carried for years, so the cuts might open into flowers.

Though his hands were gone, the eyeless Buddha held all that matters. Like the burn survivors I met in Sacramento who somehow go on without limbs or skin, without everyone else's dream of beauty.

The Tang craftsmen formed this Buddha out of mud and clay. Then covered him with hemp cloth. Then lacquered him — that is, painted him with the sap of the lac tree — and patted him dry with a fine powder of bone and shell. Then the clay core was removed.

This is how it goes, no matter our plans. Like burn survivors or lovers stripped of everything but our want to love, we're relieved of our sediment until we taste more than we can say. This seems to be the harsh secret of time: the more our bodies and minds are carved out, the more brightly we shine. These, too, are efforts that never go away: to empty ourselves of all that doesn't matter, to keep reaching through the storms of illusion, and to keep tasting more than we can say.

After a sad day in a long week, I came upon a Buddha thirteen hundred years old. He had no eyes and no hands, and yet the truth and love of the Universe seemed to glow where his eyes and hands once were. To be a human being is to be worn like this till truth and love glow from our person, till what matters pours through every opening.

Seeds to Water

 ❧ In your journal, describe a time when you were worn open and what poured out of you beneath the pain of being opened.

 ❧ In conversation with a friend or loved one, describe one thing you are averting or clinging to. If averting, what are you afraid might happen if you face this one thing? If clinging, what are you afraid might happen if you put this one thing

aside? Discuss what you think resides
beneath your fear.

FREEING OUR COMPASSION

What if we were born to have our hearts opened as widely as possible? What if transmuting our grieving hearts into hearts that are wide-open with compassion is the work we took human form to accomplish?
— Henk Brandt

We often relate to another's pain by comparing it to our own. We often minimize or dismiss another's heartfelt journey because it doesn't fit what we already know. Then we start to judge them: they're too sensitive, too passionate, too quiet, too loud, too cold, too reserved, too out there, too in there, and on and on.

Yet true compassion doesn't depend on what we know or where we've been but on utter authenticity. I was listening to a song I hadn't heard before, "Save the Best for Last," sung by the great jazz balladeer Ethel Ennis with the piano of Tommy Flanagan.

The song speaks to a lifelong intimacy between two people who've never been lovers, though they confide in each other constantly. Once older and worn down by other loves, they finally see each other as their destination. Their authenticity, in both voice and piano, brought me to the inside of this experience, as if I'd been through it myself. I felt the ache and truth of it and found myself lending my own history of heartache like paints to the canvas the song provided.

This small experience helped me realize that I can open my heart to whatever I meet in others, offering my compassion all the more freely and deeply when my heart isn't tethered to my own history. My history enables my capacity to feel, but how freely I can feel for others doesn't have to be limited by my history.

When we insist that we can only open our heart to those who travel the same path, we play a tight and narrow game of seek and confirm, of touching other life only to validate our own existence. Soon, from the dark comfort of our homes, we sit before our televisions and observe the struggles of others while not listening to their pain, because we've become numb to the human drama. Or we recognize the struggle and pain as too close to our own, and look away.

The poet Anne Sexton was painfully honest in the details of her life and her struggle with depression, despair, and thoughts of suicide. In many ways, her landmark book *Live or Die* was a raw and public cry for help, which won the Pulitzer Prize in 1967. But no one reached out to help her. Instead, she was admired from a distance. She continued to struggle and chronicle her difficulties in her work, as her reputation and fame as a poet grew.

On October 4, 1974, Anne Sexton had lunch with her friend, the poet Maxine Kumin, to revise galleys for Sexton's manuscript of *The Awful Rowing Toward God.* On returning home, Sexton put on her mother's old fur coat, removed all her rings, poured herself a glass of vodka, locked herself in the garage, and started the engine of her car, committing suicide by carbon monoxide poisoning.

Forty years later, we as a society continue to yell "Bravo!" while ignoring the pain people are in. Yet each of us is challenged not to ignore those in pain but to help them, even when they are eloquent about their suffering. When we can stop hiding what we feel and stop fearing the power of what others feel, we can transform our pain. When

441

we dare to trust that we are more together than alone, we can free our compassion.

So if someone in your life is depressed like Anne Sexton and the depth of their pain is keeping them hidden, keep reaching, even though they can't reach back. Hold them in your heart as if they're drowning, because they are. They're sinking in the undertow of their pain. And as they sink, things grow darker and they fear they won't be able to reach the surface. Keep reaching for them, though you feel alone and shut out and even hurt by their lack of response. To someone struggling to come up for air, the sight of loved ones reaching and stirring the thick tide between them and life is a comfort. If they can't cry out, remember they need every breath for air.

We don't have to be alike to feel our kinship. If we can feel each other's heart without judgment, the rest will take care of itself. No matter the tension we feel from conflict, we can enlarge our hearts beyond right and wrong, beyond he said, she said, beyond bad choices and good choices, even beyond our own fear of adversity.

When I stop pushing you away, I can remember that of all the times we could have been born into, we were born into this time together. Of all the places on Earth we could have arrived, we arrived in this place together. And of all the misshapen histories that could have brought each of us to today, we have found each other. Once everything is out of the way, my only thought is to speak to you softly and directly. These are the human faces of courage that no one can do without: holding nothing back and putting what is broken back together.

Seeds to Water

🌺 In your journal, describe a pain you've witnessed that you don't understand. Would understanding this pain deepen your compassion? What's preventing you from asking this person about their pain?

🌺 In conversation with a friend or loved one, tell about a time when you felt compassion for someone, though you didn't have a personal connection to them. What opened you to feel this person so deeply and how did this experience change you?

THE MOMENT THAT SAVES US

Often when I teach, profound moments present themselves. This one affirms the wisdom of the soul as it surfaces between people who can't hold back their care. I was in Charleston, South Carolina, at the Sophia Institute, a spiritual oasis, leading a workshop on the practice of being human. I began by acknowledging that no one knows how to do this. We each must find our way. All we can do is keep each other company and compare notes. This is why we gather.

The first night I was approached by a gentle woman, Donna, who had lost her son. She was in the throes of a terrible grief. Her soul was just behind her eyes, which could barely hold back tears.

Donna gave me a photocopied passage from my book *Seven Thousand Ways to Listen* and told me that this was what brought her, what compelled her to attend. It's a passage about staying in the fire together, though we're unable to name or prevent how the fire shapes us. It's something I wrote for my wife, Susan, a few years ago. I honestly can't remember what triggered this writing. But it was clear that night that it was returned to me by this kind woman so I could give it to Susan again now during what was a difficult time. That night, before bed, I e-mailed it to her as she slept.

The sweet souls in this group were so present and open-hearted that we went deep quickly. On Saturday afternoon, I invited folks to pair up for an exercise in deep listening. This was their invitation: Tell the story of one thing you know to be true and share your history of keeping that truth in your awareness.

I was watching the faces of these wonderful people open and relax as they leaned into each other, when DJ and her son Jack came to me. They stood before me a bit quizzical. DJ began, "I think we're at an impasse. I told Jack I hold many things to be true, but he said he doesn't think anything is true. So we don't have anything to say to each other."

I moved closer and said, "I'm not inviting you to speak to each other, but to *listen* to each other. Perhaps you could try asking Jack to describe what nothing being true looks like. What does nothing being true feel like? How did he come to see things this way?"

They looked at each other with some awkwardness and smiled. I gently encouraged them to re-enter their stalled conversation. From afar, I watched what unfolded. Though I couldn't hear what they were saying, I sensed a great teaching moment was opening and so I asked for their permission to bring it to the larger group. They kindly agreed.

As I shared their story, I marveled out loud that they had come to this workshop together. I've struggled over a lifetime to cultivate a relationship with my mother, and so I honored how they were on the journey together, facing each other, even though they didn't seem to agree on much.

Then we explored their impasse further, because it's really everyone's impasse. I was moved to say, "If we met someone from a different part of the world, say from Asia, we wouldn't declare, 'I don't believe in Asia,' but we'd readily inquire, 'What is Asia like? What's the geography there? How is the climate? What's it like to live there?' "

And so in DJ's case, I invited her to inquire of her son Jack, "What is the land where nothing is true like? What's the geography there? How is the climate? What's it like to live where nothing is true?" I could see young Jack sit up taller and smile. I could sense that he felt that even his view, which on the surface seemed to undermine my question, was welcome. For all things contain truth, even the feeling that nothing is true, and so young Jack's view *added* to the question. All this leads us to learn about places and things other than us. This is how we grow.

We think that listening means readying ourselves to speak, when if I truly listen to you, I will be moved by you, changed by you, and won't know what I will say until I'm moved. Yet we rely on this overpreparation, as if it will protect us. Too often, we refuse anything that is different from us or different from what we think or feel. Why? Because sometimes we feel so insubstantial, so insecure and without foundation, that we fear that anything different, if let in, will erase our identity.

Underneath this tension is an important choice in how we meet the world. When we fear that anything different will threaten our foundation, we push life away and live as if difference is an impasse. But sooner or later, life teaches us, through great love and suffering, that the diversity of the world is there to complete us, and then we can inquire into all that is not us with curiosity and wonder. This is how we begin to discover Wholeness. This is how we begin to be informed by other life.

The next day we spoke about the inescapable journey to turn sorrow into peace, not to get rid of sorrow or to minimize it, but to be transformed so that peace can rise from our sorrow the way warmth rises from the trouble of fire.

Madeleine spoke about her children as her masterpieces. They were both ready to leave home, and she felt torn between the sorrow of their leaving and the joy of their becoming who they are. And she felt uncertain about who she would be now.

This cracked Donna, who had lost her son, and will never see him grow. She burst into tears and rawly left the room. Two others went to be with her. We were all aware of what had just happened. It was tender, and just as the moment between DJ and her son Jack needed to be spoken of, the moment of Donna's grief needed to be held quietly as we waited for her to return.

It was clear that no one could take away the loss of Donna's son, any more than anyone could prevent Madeleine from feeling the empty joy of watching her grown children make their way in the world. I was grateful that we as a group had arrived in this collective humility where compassion was the currency between us.

Donna returned and we took a break, during which I saw young Jack make his way with some urgency to Donna's side. He towered over her and enveloped her with a tender hug. I could see Donna's tearful face on the young man's shoulder, thankful while imagining she was in her own son's arms one more time.

After a while, I found Donna and held her as she cried some more, then thanked her for her courage in not hiding the break in her heart. I told her that my wife, Susan, was treading the same rough sea, and how the page she photocopied was a gift to me. Madeleine came to our side and I backed away to give them space. The two mothers embraced and I could feel the conversation of that embrace: children dying, children living, no one hiding what they felt, everyone helping each other through.

As we closed the weekend, no one wanted to break the silence we had climbed to, for the view from there was both personal and eternal. But of course we had to climb back into our lives and out into the day and further into the world.

We all began to shuffle about and say good-bye. I thanked DJ and her son Jack for being so present and allowing us to share in their private moment. As they began to leave, I took Jack aside and asked, "Can I offer you something?" He said yes and I said softly, "It was beautiful how you reached out to Donna." Then I put my hand on his heart, "And whatever made you reach out to Donna — *that* is true." His shoulders relaxed and he opened a deep smile.

After everyone left, I lingered a bit to feel their presence in the empty room, to feel it mix with all the other conversations that have taken place there. I can't ask for more than this: to have fellow pilgrims open their lives, being honest and gentle about what they're going through, holding nothing back, and to have them reach and help each other along the way.

This is why I teach: to be surprised, again and again, when the young seeker from the land where nothing is true comes out of nowhere to hold and comfort the mother who has lost her son. And in doing so, they reveal the one moment that *is* true that continues to save us.

Seeds to Water

❧ In your journal, define for yourself what the moment that saves us looks like, and tell the story of such a moment that you've experienced. If you don't believe such a moment exists, describe what solid ground looks like for you when you're in the sea of trouble.

❧ In conversation with a friend or loved one, explore an area of difference — of opinion, belief, or experience. Don't debate the area of difference. Rather, invite your friend or loved one to describe what they know as if it were a country you've never been to. Ask them to share the story of how they've come to visit or live there.

Radiant and Broken

We're all in the same boat — radiant and broken . . .

> — Sy Safransky

Show me a tree that doesn't have a nick or a broken branch. Or a road that doesn't have a crack or a hole. Or a home whose foundation hasn't shifted in a storm. Then show me a heart that hasn't been broken by pain or love. Or a mind that hasn't been knotted by the tensions of life. To be alive is to be radiant and broken. Living with an open heart is the art of meeting our brokenness with our radiance.

It's a reflex to close when we break, but the radiance that emanates from what's been broken is what restores us. Understandably, we live in the midst of this strain: not wanting to be broken further and needing to let what's living within us come out, once a way is revealed. For our deepest nature shows itself in the darkest times, the way stars are more visible at night.

Sooner or later, everyone is presented with an experience that will jar them to their core. At that time, we're faced with the choice to say yes or no to life. There is no judgment or value attached to how we arrive at yes. The path to yes might unfold through a thousand nos. Or descend like lightning in one cataclysmic yes. What matters is our willingness to enter and taste of Life's Wholeness without reservation. What is opened in us is always more important than what has opened us.

So when you feel you have no more to give, keep your heart open just a while longer, because this is when the deepest gift we have is about to show itself. This is the foundation of a paradox that can't be explained: as we're humbled over time to honor our very real limitations, the light we carry is ever more exposed through those limitations. Just when we're at the end of what we know, the soul's lips are ready to meet the world. While the container we are can wear down and weaken, the Spirit we carry is indestructible. Just as we're feeling frail, we're asked to trust in the inexhaustible resource that is the heart.

Recently, I had a problem with my sight.

Susan and I were watching a movie, when the image split into overlapping halves. It lasted about thirty minutes. And there I was, in the heat of my conversation with being here and not being here. I tried not to panic, but when Googling "vision changes," I discovered that what had happened could be a symptom of a stroke. So much for not panicking. Then the trauma around my cancer from so many years ago gripped me, as if holding me under water.

It took two weeks to discover that I had experienced an ocular migraine. In those long, tense weeks, I tried on having a stroke, tried on not being able to speak, and feared not being able to remember all the things I remember. I rehearsed my death. I realize now that my father's death has heightened my fear of my own mortality. All these years after almost dying from cancer, I find that I'm not afraid of death, but I am afraid of dying.

My dear friend George visits his ninety-seven-year-old mother every day. She's led a full life and is accepting that the end is imminent. She has told George that she's ready to die. But in the day-to-day bumps and turns, as her body creaks and cramps, her aliveness reflex says, *What's happening? I want to live.* Her dilation of acceptance and constriction of fear is a poignant example of the conversation with being here and not being here that we each have to face. George's mother is beautifully radiant and broken.

We all experience the dilation of acceptance and the constriction of fear. When the tangle of the daily has us forget how precious life is, we tend to keep what matters from what needs to be done. Somewhere in the press of our day, in the press of a conflict that we won't let go of, in the press of a fear that makes us forget the deeper order of things — suddenly there's this shift and we make what matters a reward for getting to the end of trouble. But trouble never ends. It comes and goes like clouds. This is why what matters needs to come first. It needs to be our constant companion. For what matters is necessary in order to endure the weather of life. Even when we forget what matters, the foundation of life waits like a faithful friend to be found in the very trouble we move through.

Every day, we're asked to bring what matters along, and to slow down as we move through trouble. So I ask you to slow down now, to pause, to let what matters reappear. I ask you to identify two radiant voices in your own lineage who have taught you about what matters: one from the past and one still living. Make a cup of coffee or tea and sit with these voices. Listen for what they have to say.

When I'm broken, I often look for something filled with beauty to lift me from my pain, only to stumble into the irreducible thing we carry that allows me to see the beauty in everything, including my pain. I often look for some foundation of truth to stop all my confusion, only to rest after all my search in the beat of my heart that removes everything in the way. What a relief. Under all the useless facts speeding us through all that matters, what can't be broken down is what's beautiful, and what's left once everything is moved out of the way is what's true. Isn't this what time does to us? If we love long enough, we meet here in the irreducible beauty of what's true. If we don't give up or give in, we become in time beautiful and true.

Inevitably, we all lose something along the way. We each are hurt and we each do the hurting. When we can accept this fundamental truth, we're grounded in humility and compassion. If we fight this truth or deny it, our pain and isolation only grow. So what can anyone offer but a nod and a bow to what lives in the silence under all that we feel, which we're very close to when pried open by life.

It takes belief in the unfolding of life to let what's radiant show through the tender parts of what's broken. It's the radiance of life that lines our self-worth, not in a grandiose way, but with a fundamental worth. Rumi speaks to this radiance when he says:

A pearl goes up for auction.
No one has enough,
so the pearl buys itself.

It's the pearl we carry within that gives us the courage to recover what is true in our nature. This is just as brave as running into a burning building to save a child. Though this quiet, interior courage won't make the news, it's just as necessary to run into the burning confusions of our mind to save our own life.

Seeds to Water

 In your journal, describe a time when you discovered you were stronger than you thought you were. What led you to surface and own this strength?

&~ In conversation with a friend or loved one, describe a time when you felt both broken and radiant. Discuss your experience of both and what this experience has taught you.

TO BE OF USE

One thinks of the smallness of human
   hands,
of how soon they weary and of how little
   time is
granted to their activity.
> — Rainer Maria Rilke

The soul itself does nothing if you do
   nothing;
but if you light a fire, it chops wood;
if you make a boat, it becomes the ocean.
> — Robert Bly

Be a lamp, or a lifeboat, or a ladder.
> — Rumi

At the outset of this journey, I offered this
image and this thought: As a master carver
whittles aged and weathered wood into a
sturdy tool, effort and grace shape us in
time into a beautifully wrought instrument

ready for use. So our first step toward understanding grace is to summon the fortitude and openness not to resist being turned into an instrument by life.

Now, I ask you to consider the ways you've been carved by effort and grace. What kind of tool are you becoming? The more we're opened, the more music comes through us. The more finely we're shaped by our experience, the more delicate the wisdom that sifts through us. We have no choice in this. It happens the way erosion happens, the way trees grow toward the light and lean toward the wind.

I know in my heart that what shapes me is unseeable and unspeakable. It just passes through me, the way a flame uses up its wick. Our efforts are consumed, the way wood sparks as it feeds a fire. This is not sad but as it should be. The goal of a life is to have nothing essential left by the time it leaves its body. And the knowable point of love is always the hand that helps another up.

Walt Whitman became a volunteer medic in the Civil War. Leslie Jamison sets the scene in her introduction to Whitman's lifelong diary, *Specimen Days:*

Whitman initially journeyed to the battle-fields of the Civil War for personal reasons. After seeing a name he feared was his brother George listed among wartime casualties, in December 1862, he headed to Fredericksburg, where he discovered George had only suffered minor facial lacerations. But this was just the beginning. Whitman started visiting soldiers in hospitals — tens of thousands, all told — and doing what he could: writing letters to families, dressing wounds, bringing treats — rice pudding or blackberry syrup. He once distributed ice cream to all eighteen wards of Carver Hospital.

We're all born with a depth of heart that only unchecked love and care can open. We become of utmost use when we act on this opening of heart. Once we act, we start to live a life that is tender and resilient. Acting on that openness of heart, Whitman dropped everything and volunteered, caring for soldiers on both sides. Acting on that unchecked love made Mother Teresa stay in India to care for the poor. Acting on that depth of heart made Nelson Mandela say, "We will make a university of our suffering." The chance and challenge to be of use beyond all our plans is what made Albert

Schweitzer leave his tenured professorship in Vienna to become a doctor and open a hospital in Africa.

The ways we're called to be of use aren't always as dramatic as these examples. I cite them not for us to emulate but to mirror our own possibility. The call to be of use might appear simply and quietly as the impulse to help a stranger who's fallen in a parking lot. Or our need one day to stop e-mailing someone who's going through cancer, but to make our way across town to bring them dinner. Or to stop the car and help the stray turtle to the other side of the road. To be of use always begins with the smallest of steps and an open hand. Acting on our urge to be of use brings our kindness forward. Such humble engagement in the world helps us thrive.

Being well used without giving ourselves away enables our own resilience.

After the war, Whitman suffered a paralyzing stroke, which he recovered from to a great degree, because of his awakened capacity to stay tender and resilient. In this, he exemplifies a second gift that comes from acting on our care: that the reward for being of use to others is that in time we become useful to ourselves.

Jen went to Kenya as a photographer to

document genital mutilation. While there, she discovered that people in rural villages don't own mirrors, so most villagers have never seen themselves. While Jen went to gather evidence of a barbaric custom, once there she found herself taking pictures of the children and showing them their image. More than anything, this opened their little hearts. Beyond their giddy surprise, this small act of bearing witness to their very existence became magically empowering. Jen had traveled eight thousand miles to verify abuse and wound up enabling children to see themselves. She spent days being a mirror of their possibility. The little ones would stare into her camera, not sure what they were looking at, and their souls would bubble up and come out. This unexpected form of bearing witness humbled Jen and introduced her to a deeper view of her own heart.

The heart's job is to mirror each other with such love that our souls come out. And listening with our heart is being such a mirror. Ultimately, to love someone is to travel with them to their interior, so our love can be a mirror of all they have yet to see in themselves. The first step in being a global citizen is to honor everyone we meet by mirroring their possibility. In this way, we can be of lasting use.

To be of use is more than problem-solving; it shares the same purpose as art, no matter its form: to marry what is with what can be, to forge dream into reality and circumstance back into dream. Hephaestus was the Greek god of craft on Earth, half-human, half-Divine. In this, he's an apt personification of our hope to be of use while here.

Born lame, Hephaestus was cast from heaven by his mother, Hera. She considered him deformed. Seeking to come home, he was rejected again by his father, Zeus, after a quarrel. Yet Aphrodite loved him despite his human flaws. Unwelcome in Olympus, Hephaestus made Earth his home and became the Divine blacksmith and patron of craftsmen living here on Earth. He is the god of tools to be used in the world.

Hephaestus is closer to us than the rest of the gods. For we all arrive imperfectly, lame in some sense, though we carry the Divine within us. And try as we do to leave this earthly realm, our work is here, hammering the human and the Divine in the fire of our days, creating tools for the living. It's our imperfections and lameness that bring out our kindness. It's our suffering and confusion that make us want to be of use to each other.

I'm part of a men's group that has met for nine years. We've become very close, a small tribe of brothers. In the beginning, we gathered monthly to listen to each other's journey. But quickly, we became more than a witness to each other's lives; we were *in* each other's lives. The turn became obvious one evening after Don, our eldest, had gone through some back pain, which had restricted him to bed for a while. We all had called and checked in. But once better, he challenged us with his vulnerability, asking why none of us came over or offered to help. We were humbled and stunned. We love each other and we didn't act. We apologized, and from that day forward, our men's group has dissolved into a brotherhood that knows no schedule. In asking us why we didn't show up, Don was tender and resilient. This enabled us to be of use to one another. Now we tend each other's lameness and coax what is Divine out of our shadows.

Showing up in this way led to this poem:

Let's be honest
which doesn't mean
being harsh, but gentle.

Let's be clear
which doesn't mean

465

being dispassionate, but
holding each other up
in the face of what is true.

Let's be enduring
which doesn't mean
being important or famous,
but staying useful like a wheel
worn by rain after years of
carrying each other's burdens.

Let's be in awe
which doesn't mean
anything but the courage
to gape, like fish, at the surface
breaking around our mouths.

There is no greater grace than to have who
we are be of use. When able to be this real
and giving, we become elegant, which
means we presence truth without anger. We
become loyal, which means we offer an
unwavering kindness, reliable as sun after
rain. Belief has nothing to do with shouting, but with receiving, the way sand be-
lieves in surf. And strength is how we help
others stay alive without losing our true
nature, not caring how we're bent into the
next shape.

Seeds to Water

    🙠 These are the last questions in this book. In your journal, tell the story of a moment when you had the privilege of mirroring another's soul. What did you see there?

    🙠 In conversation with a friend or loved one, describe the ways you are becoming more kind and useful over time. How is this unfolding changing you?

STAYING TENDER AND RESILIENT

We know the dance, we still have half a
    chance,
to break these chains and flow
like light into a rainbow.
> — Michael Franks

I am grateful to live in a trust that now
deeply shapes my life.
> — Don Marek

Remember when you were young,
no experience was required.
> — Henry Miller

In writing a book, I dive into a depth that
calls and bring up what I can. On my way
back to the surface, I always drop most of
what I carry because things from the deep
want to stay in the deep. In the end, I return
with the few substantial things I manage to
hold on to, which don't look quite as shiny

once they dry. But it's from these shards that I weave the pages that you read.

The things I've found and shaped in this book affirm the need to experience all of what it is to be human. This means not hiding in our want to be happy, or retreating into a dream that puts off living until tomorrow, or inflating the refuge of being with another or being left alone. It means working and giving our all until our effort brings us fully alive.

We each have the capacity to expand our mind, to follow our heart, and to embrace the unknown. In this regard, there's one more story I'm compelled to tell about the Aboriginal god of the sky who had two sons and a daughter. Each contained a seed that he'd watered since they were born. When they came of age, he brought them together, asking each, "Do you want to know of the seed that grows inside you?" The first son said, "I think it is my mind, for my mind grows over everything." The god of the sky replied, "It is so. Do you want your mind to grow over everything?" And the first son said, "Yes. It is how I will have power over the Earth."

The second son stepped up and said, "I think the seed in me is my heart, for I feel everything." The god of the sky replied, "It is so. Do you want your heart to feel everything?" And the second son said, "Yes. It is how I will know the power in everything."

Then his daughter stepped up and said, "I don't want to know. I just want to live." To this, the god of the sky said, "You are the bravest of my children and you will grow greater than me."

He sent all three to populate the world. And so, each of us has a seed of mind, a seed of heart, and a seed of the unknown, all of which we must water, if we are to know this life.

Some of us meet the world with our mind as we try to climb our way through life. Some of us meet the world with our heart as we try to find where we belong. And some of us just want to live. Yet the god in each of us wants to grow and braid them all, so we can be useful and keep the world going.

What seed are you watering inside yourself? And how do you face the world and its sluiceway of challenges? We can never eliminate all the things that bother us in life, but only stay in right relationship to them. Both the light of the soul and the depth of the world are true. Our daily challenge is to be the crucible in which the light of the soul and the depth of the world mix.

When unable to see past our mind, we become literal and miss the depth speaking in everything. When lost in our fear, we harden and impose what is familiar on everything. But when able to put everything down and just live, we loosen our assumptions and the days begin to shimmer.

The clearest way to recover our aliveness is to *lean into life,* which means that, regardless of the nicks and cuts that experience gives us, we stay committed to moving toward what is true. To lean in means that while we have compassion for the times we need to look away or feel we can't go on, we stay committed to working with what we're given. I mentioned earlier that the word *respect* means "to look again." And so, to lean in means to pick ourselves up and look again: at life, each other, and ourselves, over and over, until we reanimate our care.

We can learn about leaning into life by watching how birds fly. When birds outstretch their wings, notice what happens. They lead with their chest and their heart. If they don't, their wings can't open fully and they won't be able to fly. So while the world of no presses us to keep our wings tucked, the instinct to lead with our heart can't be suppressed. We even dream about this birthright until we find the courage to open our heart. This is the instinctual response to the world of no: not to refute it or debate it or resist it, but to lead with our heart so we can spread our wings and fly.

It takes courage to stop resisting where life wants to take us. This is where the greatest learning takes place. To follow where life takes us, we need to own our missteps because admitting our flaws cleanses the heart. No one can do this all the time. But those who can put down what is false, no matter how dear, are my heroes.

In our vulnerability lies our strength. In the bottom of our brokenness lies our kindness. In the center of our grief lies our truest compassion. These are simple truths that are hard to accept. Yet, run from them as we do, life in the aftermath of its intensity and storm returns us to these truths. When we can stay tender though we're broken, we're larger, stronger, and more loving for the breaking. When we can lean in and resist manipulating others, we're opened to resources beyond our own. When we can lead with our heart, like a bird about to fly, we can lift ourselves from the tangle of our trouble.

Arriving at this simplicity, there is nothing to do but glow. And so, our work — no matter where life takes us — is to let the light of the soul and the depth of the world bring down the walls of fear.

However you want to frame it, love and suffering are the hammer and chisel by which the Living Universe sculpts us. Expression, story, and relationship are the ways we release meaning from being so sculpted.

So here we are, not very far from where we began, just deeper and more tender for this long conversation. I hope I've been good company and that we've uncovered one or two lanterns along the edge of what you know, by which you might better see your way. In the days to come, I hope you softly trip into an unexpected moment of bareness, where the glow of your heart will touch everything it meets, and you can't help but remember how dear it is to be alive.

In time, I hope you can listen to your pain and what it's saying to you. Listening to my own pain makes my heart ache the way a tree splits. And in the split, I realize that an entire life — a century if blessed — is a blink in the eye of the Many-Named God who gifts us love and suffering, so that in the split and ache that stuns us, we might know the full length of time: in the curl of a wave, in the flap of a wing, in the first breath of a child no one expected, in the last breath of someone who saved us from ourselves, in the dissolution of the clouds that mute our wonder. In that stunning pause of heart, life flies out in the open. When listening this deeply, I have no way to convey how beautifully ordinary we are. I just know, when bearing witness this tenderly, that everything matters.

How we endure the stunning pause in our heart is what allows us to grow. If you've been moved to pause by what we've uncovered, it may be disorienting or even disconcerting, as familiar ways of carrying who-you-are in the world might be falling away. Though what is next might be unclear.

Kierkegaard said, "Anxiety is the dizziness of freedom." More than our daily sense of worry and fear, I think he means the inner anxiety that comes when old identities give way and new identities have yet to form.

This is when inner courage is needed to withstand the free fall between what's no longer helpful and what's coming into view. This in-between fall into who we are becoming is part of the journey from our head to our heart. No one can bypass it.

During times of deep change, we're forced to kneel before the silent god of patience;

listening — not for direction, but for what feels real and true. Until presence leads to presence. This is how we come to listen to our soul.

I know from my own evolution that most of what the heart knows enters us like lightning, and is already true somewhere inside, while the rest of us struggles to catch up. I've also learned that we're never drawn into a change we're not ready for, though the change may be difficult.

Under the weight of living, I'm thankful for how gifted we are to have hearts that feel. Thankful for the chance to be tender and thorough and possible one more time. And whenever we dare or are forced to lift each other up or ease each other down, we have the glorious chance to find what we've lost in our common story. When we can truly behold each other, we slowly become each other. We become love itself. It's through love's eyes that we can see that it's sweetly enough to have come this far.

The American poet John Hall Wheelock proclaimed:

To have lived
Even once only, once and no more
Will have been — oh how truly — worth
    it . . .

So however uncertain tomorrow might seem, I encourage you to withstand the dizziness of freedom and to trust the wisdom that waits in your heart, which knows what it needs to be alive and to stay alive.

No matter what seems unbearable, the well of feeling in the center of our being will never let us down, just as the fire in the center of the Earth will never go out. As you leave our long conversation and walk back into the sweep of your flowering life, I can only assure you that nothing will keep you from being worn to your beauty, that all will be real, and that everything you touch will gift you something.

GRATITUDES

Retrieving this book has made me a better person. I'm not sure how this works except that immersing ourselves in whatever feels alive strips away what no longer works and refines what is left. So I'm grateful for the fire of aliveness that never stops drawing me to it. And grateful to the small tribe of loved ones who encourage me to keep at it and who care for me when I get burned for getting too close to the flame.

I'm grateful to my dear agent, Jennifer Rudolph Walsh, for her deep belief and wise guidance, as well as Eve Attermann, Raffaella De Angelis, and the rest of the WME team for their unfailing support. And to my gifted editor, Leslie Meredith, who always looks for what words can become and not just where they fall short. And to my publisher, Judith Curr, for her belief that books still deepen us and bridge us. And to Brooke Warner for the gift of good work and friendship. And to my publicist, Eileen Duhne, for representing me so wholeheartedly.

Gratitude to my dear friends. Without them the days would be hollow. Especially George, Don, Paul, Skip, TC, David, Kurt, Pam, Patti, Karen, Paula, Ellen, Linda, Michelle, Rich, Carolyn, Henk, Sandra, Elesa, and Sally. And to my brother Howard for never letting go of those he loves. And to the creative force that was my father. And to Oprah Winfrey for bringing so many to the well of their goodness.

And to Paul Bowler for all we've helped each other through. And to Robert Mason for our lifelong walk around the Universe. And to my dear wife, Susan, for seeing who I am, flaws as well, and loving me all the more.

NOTES

Epigraphs and poems without attribution are by the author.

"When all I wanted was to sing": Rainer Maria Rilke, from *The Complete French Poems of Rainer Maria Rilke,* translated by A. Poulin. Minneapolis, MN: Graywolf Press, 1979.

"The highest reward": John Ruskin (1819–1900), the art critic and watercolorist.

"Before practicing the art of immortality": Lu Yen, more commonly known as Ancestor Lu, in *Vitality, Energy, Spirit,* translated by Thomas Cleary. Boston: Shambhala, 1991, p. 103.

Shaped by Life

I was diagnosed with a rare form of lymphoma: Please see my book *Inside the Miracle: Enduring Suffering, Approaching Wholeness* (Sounds True, 2015), which explores my

479

cancer journey deeply. The book gathers twenty-eight years of my writing and teaching about suffering, healing, and wholeness.

The rest are details: For a deeper exploration of this theme, please see the chapter "The Art of Facing Things" in my book *Finding Inner Courage* (2011).

to keep what is true in view: For a deeper exploration of this theme, please see the chapter "Keeping What Is True Before Us" in my book *Seven Thousand Ways to Listen* (2012).

Getting Closer to Life

"You shall no longer": Walt Whitman, from "Song of Myself," #2, in *The Portable Walt Whitman,* edited by Mark Van Doren. New York: Viking, 1945, p. 71.

So brave your way on: This paragraph also appears as the poem "The Dive" in my forthcoming book, *The Way Under the Way.*

The Soul's Work

In the Sufi tradition, muhasiba: From "Sufi Practice and Contemporary Psychoanalysis" by Michele Rousseau, in *Sufi, A Journal of Sufism.* London: Khaniquahi Minatullahi Publications, Issue 88, Winter 2015, p. 42.

Legacy
Legacy: This story first appears as a poem in my forthcoming book *Compass Work: The Father Poems.*

Getting Closer to Life
he exhausted himself and fell asleep in the saddle: The poem referred to is "Sleeping on Horseback" by Po Chü-I, from *One Hundred Seventy Chinese Poems,* translated by Arthur Waley. New York: Knopf, Inc., 1919.

Making Our Way
on US 1 in late October of 1998: An initial account of "Bird-Rock" first appeared in "The Kinship of Gratitude," in my book *The Exquisite Risk.* New York: Harmony Books, 2005, p. 187.

Love Your Window
Love Your Window: I first explored this theme in the poem "Love Your Window" in my book *Inside the Miracle: Enduring Suffering, Approaching Wholeness.* Sounds True, 2015, p. 230.

The Secret Kingdom Is Everywhere
"Once you see directly": Shidō Munan (1603–1676), from *The Roaring Stream,* edited by Nelson Foster and Jack Shoemaker. New York: Ecco Press, 1996, p. 293.

Knocked Off Our Horse
"Remember that everyone": H. Jackson Brown Jr., from *The Sun.* Chapel Hill, NC, Issue 362, February 2006, p. 48.

The Three Dreams
I found a way to love him: I have written extensively about my journey with my father. Please see the chapters "To Immerse Ourselves" and "What More Could I Ask For?" in *The Endless Practice,* and my forthcoming book *Compass Work: The Father Poems.*

Taking Off the Armor
"Love takes off the masks": James Baldwin, from *The Sun.* Chapel Hill, NC, Issue 454, October 2013, p. 48.

The Path Is Wider Than We Think
In her profound book, Heart . . . *imprints on it:* Paraphrased from *Heart* by Gail God-

win. New York: William Morrow, 2001, p. 35.

What Talent Do I Have?

the effort to learn . . . a transformative question that we somehow awaken into together: An earlier version of this passage first appeared in the anthology *Teaching with Fire: Poetry That Sustains the Courage to Teach,* edited by Megan Scribner and Sam Intrator. San Francisco: Jossey-Bass Publishers, 2003, p. 142.

I Awake

I was reading a heartfelt poem by Ryōkan: "Reading the Record of Eihei Dōgen" by Ryōkan. A version can be found in *The Roaring Stream: A Zen Reader,* edited by Nelson Foster and Jack Shoemaker. New York: Ecco Press, 1996, p. 348.

"Instead of playing scales": From *Django: The Life and Music of a Gypsy Legend* by Michael Dregni. New York: Oxford University Press, 2004.

Drawn to What We Need to Learn

"Weep and then, smile": From *The Illuminated Rumi,* translated by Coleman Barks, illustrated by Michael Greene. New York:

Broadway Books, 1997, p. 121.

Regret
"Everything that slows us down": May Sarton, from *The Sun.* Chapel Hill, NC, Issue 464, August 2014, p. 48.

The Journey Before You
The hummingbird sucking . . . "not to be feared": Parts of this paragraph are from a stanza in my poem "Coming of Age," which first appeared in my book *Inside the Miracle* (Sounds True, 2015), p. 196.

Loving What You Do

"Will you ever bring a better gift": William Stafford, from "You Reading This, Be Ready" in *The Way It Is: New & Selected Poems* by William Stafford. St. Paul, MN: Graywolf Press, 1998, p. 45.

The Story Behind the Story
New Criticism: This was a formalist movement in literary theory that dominated American literary criticism in the middle decades of the twentieth century. Still foundational among writers and scholars, the movement derived its name from John Crowe Ransom's 1941 book *The New Crit-*

icism and was supported by the work of the English scholar I. A. Richards, whose books *Practical Criticism* and *The Meaning of Meaning* offered an empirical scientific approach to literature.

Finding Inner Courage: For the full exploration of the transformation of Nietzsche, see the chapter "What Is Necessary" in my book *Finding Inner Courage* (2011), pp. 267–72. For the exploration of Petrarch's story in the same book, see the chapter "Judgment or Compassion," p. 232.

"It is more important": From "On His Own Ignorance and That of Many Others" by Petrarch, quoted in *What Is Ancient Philosophy?* by Pierre Hadot. Cambridge, MA: Harvard University Press, 2002, p. xiii. Francesco Petrarch (1304–1374) was an Italian scholar, poet, and early humanist.

two small deer: The earliest deer fossil dates from twenty-three million years ago in Europe. The early Old English word for "deer" (*deor*) originally referred to any wild animal.

Rodin['s] legendary sculpture: Details about Rodin's journey in creating his sculpture of Balzac come from http://en.wikipedia .org/wiki/Monument_to_Balzac and *Rodin* by Judith Cladel. New York: Harcourt,

Brace and Co., 1937. In the summer of 1902, the poet Rainer Maria Rilke went with great admiration to Paris and became Rodin's secretary for almost two years. From this time, Rilke wrote and published two remarkable essays about Rodin, exploring the nature of art and the power of creativity. Together, these essays stand as a profound inner profile, a rare chance to see a great sculptor through the eyes of a great poet. *Auguste Rodin* by Rainer Maria Rilke (New York: Dover Publications, 2006) survives as a compelling tour de force, a canteen found in the desert.

What It Means to Be Awake

What It Means to Be Awake: Deep thanks to my dear friend Tami Simon, the founder of Sounds True, whose heartfelt questions led me to this chapter. I love our friendship and where our conversations go. It's like going on a walk into the forest of spirit; stopping along the way to watch some native bird move in and out of a tree we've never seen.

Heart and Path

"Any path is only a path": From *Journey to Ixtlan: The Lessons of Don Juan* by Carlos Castaneda. New York: Washington Square

Press, 1991.

"In many ways": From *The Heart of a Pilgrim* by Henk Brandt, 2014, in manuscript, p. 197.

The Power of Holding

at a workshop at the Cleveland Clinic: Rich Frankel and Tom Inui are pioneers in Relationship-Centered Care, a movement in medicine that holds the web of our connections as central to any healing that might come. At the Cleveland Clinic, Rich and Tom were inviting doctors to talk about a patient that has changed how they practice. After a long silence, a rheumatologist shared this story.

Swimming Through Pain and Sorrow

"You will earn": León Felipe, from the remarkable anthology *Roots and Wings: Poetry from Spain, 1900–1975,* edited by the great translator Hardie St. Martin. New York: Harper & Row, 1976, p. 93. The raw and gentle León Felipe (1884–1968) was a pharmacist turned actor who became a poet in the tradition of Whitman. He left Spain in 1923 to become a professor at Columbia University, then Cornell, before spending the rest of his life teaching and writing in Mexico.

The earliest form of stethoscope: I learned this from the wonderful Seattle physician-poet Peter Pereira. Please see his book *What's Written on the Body.*

Our Authority of Being
"I do not trouble my spirit": Walt Whitman, from "Song of Myself," in *The Portable Walt Whitman,* edited Mark Van Doren. New York: Viking, 1945.

The Great Threshold
In the Middle Ages: I learned this from Gail Godwin's profound book *Heart,* p. 15.

Understanding Success
Understanding Success: This chapter first appeared in an earlier version as a feature article "The Success of the Soul" in *Integral Yoga Magazine,* Winter 2014.
"I can no more count": Sue Caulfield, a fellow artist and friend.

Walking Together
Walking Together: This chapter traces the evolution of a poem and the lessons that it holds. I first gave voice to this as a track on my Sounds True box set, *Reduced to Joy: The Journey from Our Head to Our Heart* (2014). That live recording led me

to take notes from my talk, which I then shaped into this chapter.

Loving What You Do

Kurtis Lamkin: A gifted poet-musician, a praise-singer who has mastered the West African kora, a twenty-one-string lute-like instrument, as well as the jinjin. Kurt is a dear friend whose work was featured in Bill Moyers's documentary *Fooling with Words*. Kurt's latest CD is *Big Fun*.

vocation is that which calls us into who we truly are: See Parker Palmer's very personal book, *Let Your Life Speak*.

A Song for Pilgrims

"Like a bird with broken wing": George Seferis, from *George Seferis: Collected Poems,* translated by Edmund Keeley and Philip Sherrard. Princeton, NJ: Princeton University Press, 1967.

E daí: I explore the practice of *E daí* more thoroughly in the chapter "Going Back into the Fire" in my book *Seven Thousand Ways to Listen* (2012), pp. 117–19.

"The Slow Arm of All That Matters": This first appeared in my book *Inside the Miracle: Enduring Suffering, Approaching Wholeness*. Sounds True, 2015, p. 239.

Finding What Can Last

"Before the inexplicable mystery": Agapi Stassinopoulos, from *Unbinding the Heart.* New York: Hay House, 2012, p. 188.

Fire in the Temple
I entered this poem: This poem is called "Fire in the Temple" and it also appears in my forthcoming book of poems, *The Way Under the Way,* p. 61.
"A deeper enlightenment came": From *The Art of Zen* by Stephen Addiss. New York: Harry N. Abrams, Inc., 1989, p. 85.
two of Sokuhi's seminal ink drawings: From *The Art of Zen* by Stephen Addiss, p. 84.

The Sacred Grove
"Walking is the great adventure": Gary Snyder, from *The Practice of the Wild* (Counterpoint Press, 1990), cited in *The Sun.* Chapel Hill, NC, Issue 464, August 2014, p. 27.
"A thousand miles, the same mood": Yunmen, from *The Roaring Stream: A New Zen Reader,* edited by Nelson Foster and Jack Shoemaker. New York: Ecco Press, 1996, p. 142.
"Learn your theories well but": Carl Jung, from *The Sun.* Chapel Hill, NC, Issue

439, July 2012, p. 48.

Making Honey
"We are bees of the Invisible": Rainer Maria Rilke, *Duino Elegies,* translated by Edward Snow. Berkeley, CA: North Point Press, p. 70, in the notes.

Reading the Cracks
And so, a lost culture: I am indebted to the incredible research of Peter Hessler for his work in *National Geographic:* "The New Story of China's Ancient Past," July 2003, pp. 56–81, and "Driving the Great Wall," January 2003, pp. 2–33. *"We cannot imagine God":* From *Looking Back: Memoirs,* Lou Andreas-Salomé, translated by Ernst Pfeiffer. New York: Marlowe & Co., 1991.
The Jungian analyst Robert Johnson: Please see Robert Johnson's books, *He: Understanding Masculine Psychology; She: Understanding Feminine Psychology;* and *Owning Your Own Shadow.*

Finding What Can Last
"Dialogue is a matter of understanding": Raimon Panikkar (1918–2010) was born in Barcelona, the son of a Spanish Catholic mother and a Hindu father. He was a lighted being who believed and practiced

the common heart at the center of all spiritual traditions. He was an ordained and practicing Catholic priest, Hindu priest, and Buddhist monk, as well as a professor of philosophy, chemistry, and theology. The author of many books, his 1989 Gifford Lectures were published in English under the title *The Rhythm of Being*. I heard him speak and felt his presence at the 2004 World Parliament of Religions held in Barcelona.

At the Center of Every Feeling

"Adrift": This poem first appeared in my book *Inside the Miracle* (Sounds True, 2015), p. 217.

Unbearable and Unbreakable

". . . because the mind": From the poem "The Mind Turns Back" in *Songs of Sophia* by Henk Brandt. Henk is a dear friend who is a poet, philosopher, and therapist. Please see, as well, his memoir *The Heart of a Pilgrim*.

I jumped in to save her without a thought: Please see my poem about this experience, "So Much Is Carried," in my book of poems *Reduced to Joy*.

"In its inviolable wholeness": From *Looking Back: Memoirs* by Lou Andreas-Salomé,

translated by Ernst Pfeiffer. New York: Marlowe & Co., 1991, epigraph.

Being Kind and Useful

"It's not our job": L. R. Knost, from *The Sun.* Chapel Hill, NC, Issue 482, February 2016, p. 48.

Cultivating Wonder
"Don't misuse your mind": The Blue Cliff Record, translated by Thomas & J. C. Cleary. Boston: Shambhala, 2005, p. 20.

The Effort to Keep Looking
Henri Matisse [1869–1954] was constantly working: These details are from a very thoughtful exhibit, "Matisse: In Search of Painting," which I saw at the Metropolitan Museum of Art, New York, March 8, 2013.

In Doses We Can Bear
"Everyone in a body": Naomi Shihab Nye is an extraordinary poet and a dear friend, from her poem "Hello, Palestine" in *Transfer.* Rochester, NY: Boa Editions, 2011, p. 63.
"We suffer into knowledge": In Greek "Pathei mathos" from the Greek playwright Aeschylus, in his play *Agamemnon.*

"As a caterpillar": From "The Brihadaran-yaka Upanishad," in *The Upanishads*, translated by Eknath Easwaran. Tomales, CA: Nilgiri Press, 1987, p. 29.

The Work of Self-Awareness
"The only man I know": George Bernard Shaw, cited in *The Sun*. Chapel Hill, NC, Issue 355, July 2005, p. 48.

The Gifts of Effort
to know what's enough: For an in-depth exploration of our struggle to know what's enough, please see Wayne Muller's pro-foundly helpful book, *A Life of Having, Doing, and Being Enough.*

Admitting Who We Are
Admitting Who We Are: I first explored this notion in my book *The Exquisite Risk* (2005), p. 146.

Freeing Our Compassion
"What if we were born to have our hearts": From *The Heart of a Pilgrim* by Henk Brandt, p. 220.
On October 4, 1974 . . . carbon monoxide poisoning: The details of Anne Sexton's suicide in this paragraph are from Herbert Hendin's article "The Suicide of Anne

Sexton" in *Suicide and Life-Threatening Behavior,* Issue 23, Fall 1993, pp. 257–62.

Radiant and Broken
"We're all in the same boat": From Sy Safransky, "A Thousand Elephants," in *The Sun.* Chapel Hill, NC, Issue 373, January 2007, p. 47.
"A pearl goes up for auction": Rumi, translated by Coleman Barks with A. J. Arberry, in *The Enlightened Heart,* edited by Stephen Mitchell. New York: Harper & Row, 1989, p. 52.

To Be of Use
"One thinks of the smallness": From *Auguste Rodin* by Rainer Maria Rilke. New York: Dover Publications, 2006, p. 1.
"The soul itself does nothing": Robert Bly, *Iron John: A Book About Men.* Boston: Addison-Wesley, 1990.
"Be a lamp": Rumi, from *The Sun.* Chapel Hill, NC, Issue 467, November 2014, p. 48.
Specimen Days: This is the remarkable lifelong diary of the great American poet Walt Whitman, which chronicles his years as a volunteer medic in the Civil War as well as his life as a naturalist and living witness of a maturing if troubled America.

More than a literary curiosity, this is a testament to self-exploration, service, and community. In 1882, the *Boston Sunday Herald* printed this review: "Had *Leaves of Grass* never been written this book alone would be enough to establish the author's fame as a great poet." Please see the outstanding edition *Specimen Days and Collect* by Walt Whitman, introduction by Leslie Jamison. Brooklyn and London: Melville House Publishing, 1991.

"Carver Hospital": From *Specimen Days and Collect* by Walt Whitman, p. x.

Staying Tender and Resilient
"We know the dance": Michael Franks, from "Antonio's Song," on the album *Sleeping Gypsy,* Rhino, Warner Brothers Records, 1977.

PERMISSIONS

497

An initial account of "Bird-Rock" in the chapter "Making Our Way" first appeared in "The Kinship of Gratitude," in my book *The Exquisite Risk.* New York: Harmony Books, 2005, p. 187.

The passage about learning in "What Talent Do I Have?" first appeared in an earlier version as a feature article "The Success of the

Soul" in *Integral Yoga Magazine,* Winter Issue, 2014.

The chapter "The Effort to Learn" first appeared in the anthology *Teaching with Fire:
Poetry That Sustains the Courage to Teach,*
edited by Megan Scribner and Sam Intrator. San Francisco: Jossey-Bass Publishers,
2003.

My poems "The Slow Arm of All That Matters" and "Adrift" as well as a stanza from
my poem "Coming of Age" first appeared
in my book *Inside the Miracle: Enduring Suffering, Approaching Wholeness.* Sounds True
Publishing, 2015, pp. 239, 212, 223, courtesy of Sounds True, Inc.

ABOUT THE AUTHOR

Mark Nepo moved and inspired readers and seekers all over the world with his #1 *New York Times* bestseller *The Book of Awakening*. Beloved as a poet, teacher, and storyteller, Mark has been called "one of the finest spiritual guides of our time," "a consummate storyteller," and "an eloquent spiritual teacher." His work is widely accessible and used by many and his books have been translated into more than twenty languages. A bestselling author, he has published seventeen books and recorded twelve audio projects. In 2015, he was given a Life Achievement Award by AgeNation. And in 2016, he was named by *Watkins: Mind Body Spirit* as one of the 100 Most Spiritually Influential Living People.

Recent work includes *Inside the Miracle* (Sounds True), selected by *Spirituality & Health* magazine as one of the Best Ten

Books of 2015; *The Endless Practice* (Atria), cited by *Spirituality & Practice* as one of the Best Spiritual Books of 2014; his book of poems *Reduced to Joy* (Viva Editions), cited by *Spirituality & Practice* as one of the Best Spiritual Books of 2013; a six-CD box set of teaching conversations based on the poems in *Reduced to Joy* (Sounds True, 2014); and *Seven Thousand Ways to Listen* (Atria), which won the 2012 Books for a Better Life Award.

Mark was part of Oprah Winfrey's "The Life You Want" tour in 2014 and has appeared several times with Oprah on her *Super Soul Sunday* program on OWN TV. He has also been interviewed by Robin Roberts on *Good Morning America*. *The Exquisite Risk* was cited by *Spirituality & Practice* as one of the Best Spiritual Books of 2005, calling it "one of the best books we've ever read on what it takes to live an authentic life."

Mark devotes his writing and teaching to the journey of inner transformation and the life of relationship. He continues to offer readings, lectures, and retreats. Please visit Mark at: MarkNepo.com, Threeintentions.com, and info@wmeimgspeakers.com.